HISTORY OF THE TURKISH JEWS AND SEPHARDIM

Memories of a Past Golden Age

Elli Kohen

University Press of America,® Inc.
Lanham · Boulder · New York · Toronto · Plymouth, UK

Copyright © 2007 by
University Press of America,® Inc.
4501 Forbes Boulevard
Suite 200
Lanham, Maryland 20706
UPA Acquisitions Department (301) 459-3366

Estover Road
Plymouth PL6 7PY
United Kingdom

Library of Congress Control Number: 2006937061
ISBN-13: 978-0-7618-3600-1 (clothbound : alk. paper)
ISBN-10: 0-7618-3600-4 (clothbound : alk. paper)
ISBN-13: 978-0-7618-3601-8 (paperback : alk. paper)
ISBN-10: 0-7618-3601-2 (paperback : alk. paper)

™ The paper used in this publication meets the minimum
requirements of American National Standard for Information
Sciences—Permanence of Paper for Printed Library Materials,
ANSI Z39.48—1984

Dedication

This book is dedicated to my beloved Turkish nation and to the memory of the Sublime Sultan Bayezid II.

Table Of Contents

Acknowledgements

The Author acknowledges the masterly advice of historian Dr. Albert de Vidas, editor of the Sephardi Quarterly Erensia Sefardi, in restructuring the book. The author is greatly thankful to Emeritus Professor Joseph G. Hirschberg for his invaluable help in copy editing the book. The author greatly appreciates the help Mr. Scott Colmery, for his assistance in formatting the book, beyond the call of duty.

INTRODUCTION

The history of the Turkish Jews spans more than more than five centuries if one starts counting from 1492, but the encounters at the Jewish-Ottoman interface certainly started two centuries earlier during the rule of Orkhan son of Osman. Recently on the occasion of the Quincentennial of Sephardi life in Turkey a number of scholarly books have appeared. Yet there is still a need which remains largely unfulfilled: a LIVING history of the Turkish Jews, with all its vibrancy, folklore, ethos, moments of triumph and also its pathos. Part of its echoes have emerged in the nostalgic book of Leon Sciaky (Farewell to Salonica), the Nobel-prize winning work of the Bulgarian Sephardi author Canetti, and also in the seven-volume History of the Jews of Salonica by Joseph Nehama; certainly also in the numerous volumes in French and Turkish of Abraham Galante.

The present book has attempted to combine the patience of a chronicler with the folksy humor of the storyteller, endeavoring to recreate the atmosphere of the times, but also with a concern for the cultural history of the Sephardic Jews, its continuity and maybe its future role as a catalyst for a broader cultural synthesis. This book also aims to be a book of love for All the cultures which have come to coexist on the shores of the Bosphorus or in the metropolis of Salonica, whether Sephardic, Karaite, Byzantine, Ottoman or neo-Turkish. A small novel which was awarded in 1964 the French literary prize, Le Prix des Deux Magots, **La Rose de Büyükada** (the major island of the Archipelago of the Princes in the Sea of Marmora), published in Paris by the Greek author Clement Lepidis (Kleanthis Tchelebides) exemplifies this kind of multicultural and nostalgic affectionate feeling, that of a Greek for the Turkey of his ancestors. Affectionate feeling, however, does not mean blindness, and the book does not intend to overlook the shortcomings of the various players in the historical drama, whatever their nationality or allegiance.

There is in the present book historiography combined with history. Some pages could have been written by the chronicler of the Sultan or the archivist of the Grand Rabbi. In other pages, past rulers of the Turkish Republic might have been surprised to find themselvers the subjects of an existencialist analysis in the Sartrian style, or included in a tenuous chain of continuity going back to the fallen messianic dreamer Sabbatai Sevi.

The book has also a thesis: that of a very hard to realize but not altogether impossible cultural synthesis at the interface of the various elements coexisting near the shores of the Bosphorus. A recent statement by Samuel P. Huntington, Director of the M. Olin Institute for Strategic Studies at Harvard University (Foreign Affairs) presents the hypothesis that World politics are entering a new phase in which the great divisions among humankind and the dominant source of conflict will be cultural. The clash of civilizations will dominate world politics. If cultural differences are to become the major source of conflict, some good may come out of the converse, a multicultural synthesis for which the shores of the Bosphorus, and the cosmopolitan nature of life at this station, seem a natural breeding ground.

The nurturing of such a synthesis offers an interesting challenge. While it would not be a panacea for the malaise of Western culture, it could still offer, through the wealth and resiliency of its many cultures, a certain remedy and possible soothing to the malaise. It is at least an exciting venture to look forward, to a time in which the Sephardis would serve as a catalyst together with the Turks and other elements of their cosmopolitan environment.

The hard question maybe, is the Sephardic Jew fitted at all for the kind of role postulated? The image built by the Turkish Jew since the advent of the Turkish Republic stands without euphemism as a rather "timorous" one. Recent visitors to Turkey express the feeling that while the Jews are integrated in Turkish life as full citizens, still they often look over their shoulders when questioned by foreigners about their life. Maybe it is not that they are not fully candid, but they may be somewhat cautious in their words. However Jewish poets, writers, journalists, historians who are more daring, more forthright, have started to project themselves; they can expect a similar openness from their Turkish counterparts. Inaugurated at the time of the Sultans, the Lyceum of Galatasaray (now University) symbolizes the openness of Turkey to the possibility of symbiotic culture delving on a multiplicity of sources.

This brings into play the myth of "the survival of the fittest" which has not always brought to us the best of the possible worlds, by encouraging unbridled competition. Of course there is much going for a dominant culture, with the new opportunities for a wave of "Turkism" spreading from the Black Sea, to the lakes of Baykal and Balkash and even beyond through the Turkish trail till Vladivostock. Panturkism has been tried and failed when Enver Pasha perished under the bullets of the Soviets in Central Asia. There is however a possible chance for a cooperative commonwealth of Turkic nations, based on mutual tolerance and some kind of looser links, cultural rather than imperialistic or ultranationalistic.

Rather than a dominant culture, a symbiotic culture drawing also on its more gentle participants can unleash a wave of creativity. As expresesed in the poems of a new generation of young Turkish Jews, there is a certain dynamism at work. Like Jimmy Carter said "Why not the best?"; why not expect after the Sephardi Quincentennial a Turkish Sephardi revival, like the phoenix renascent from its ashes. A Turkish culture open to the yet largely untapped riches of Sephardi culture, capable of recuperating the **élan vital** of the Sephardi Golden Age, tolerant and affectionate enough not to ignore the treasures of Byzantine civilization, in a coexistence of the equals, can bring about a new age of Renaissance at the shores of the Bosphorus, and hopefully to all the Turkish realms far away...What of a Turkish world standing again at the gates of Europe, this time not with armies of Janissaries but with its gift of a culture blended from the souls of all those that cohabit in its realm? Could it be the beginning of the long-sought cultural bridge between the Occident and the Orient envisioned by Chateaubriand, Lamartine, Richard Burton, Pierre Loti and many other of the Orientalist dreamers?

CHAPTER 1

THE FIRST OTTOMANS

Ertughrul (1188-1265), the father of Osman, the founder of the Ottoman dynasty, earned his credentials to a fiefdom (a *Beylik* in Turkish) by his respect for the perennial maxim of his clan: "Go always on the side of the weaker." As the clan of nearly 400 moved west in Anatolia, Ertughrul's forces encountered a battlefield where the forces of the Seljuk Sultan Alaeddin Keykubat I, engaged in combat with the Turcomans, were on the verge of defeat if it were not for the daring intervention of Ertughrul (1). As a reward, Osman's father received an Emirate located in the northeast corner of the Anatoliasn peninsula. Permeated by the spirit of *Djihad* (Holy War) against the Unbelievers, the Ottomans became the *Gazi* (Victorious Warriors) committed to extend the rule of Islam over the remaining territories of decadent Byzantium (2). Within three hundred years from these small beginnings, the Ottoman dynasty which included a number of gifted and long-reigning monarchs would expand into a gigantic empire ruling from the confines of Persia in the east to the borders of Morocco, the Adriatic Sea and the gates of Vienna in the west, Crimea in the north and the coast of Erythrea and Somaliland in the south.

Basking in the euphoria of their national War of Independence and their victory over the Greeks, the promoters of the *Turkism* movement sought to explain the Ottoman success by a return of Anatolia to its pre-Byzantine and prehellenistic Hittite roots. According to the Turkish myth, the Hittites were *bona fide* "Turks"!. The tiny Ottoman state was the catalyst of a titanic rebirth! it meant the reawakening of the Hittite *Turk* gloriously returning as the Ottoman Turk.

Of course in their enthusiasm, and in their rewriting of Anatolian and Turkish history, the Turkists were overlooking the fact that the Hittites themselves did not represent an homogenous ethnic group. We still have residues of six different Hittite dialects which belong to the Indo-European and the Semitic group of languages.

When the Turkish warriors appeared on the scene, the existing Byzantine urban and rural structure was near collapse through the misrule of *tekfurs* (local Byzantine princes) and the discontent of an overtaxed population submitted to perpetual abuse. The Turkish historians Mehmet Fuat Köprülü and Ömer Lutfi Barkan emphasize the beneficial effects of Turkish pacification of these areas which had been suffering from interminable wars and sanguinary conflicts. Such a view is not shared by Bulgarian scholars. Angelov writes that the Turkish conquest had as its result the mass destruction of entire cities, the massacre, deportation, and enslavement of thousands, the general and enduring decline of all productive forces. The Turks, had neither a superior culture nor the necessary organizational talents, he claimed.

The actual truth may be complex. Even Emir Murad I, the third Ottoman ruler, who was praised as mild-mannered, emphasized that "countries of infidels must constantly be devastated." However after the battle was won, Murad I instructed his commander that the governors to be appointed should be righteous persons and that the *rayas* (non-Moslem subjects) should be kept in good condition. Absolute ruthlessness during the campaign was to be followed by a just regime. According to what was taught in history classes in Turkish schools, when Turkish soldiers would enter an orchard to supply themselves with fruits, if the local owners could not be found, they would hang money on the trees for payment, such was their integrity.

Ottoman rulers were gifted enough to build a powerful military and bureaucratic structure; they also acquired a modicum of culture and were surrounded by competent, enlightened advisers. When the fourth Ottoman ruler, Bayezid I, secured in 1394, the title of *Sultan of the Rum* from the shadow Caliph of Cairo, the Ottomans became in effect the successors of the defunct Seljuk Sultanate of Rum for centuries to come.

The first Jewish-Turkish encounter came when Osman's son Orkhan (1324-68) extended his rule to Bursa, at the foot of the *Uludagh*. After the conquest by Orkhan, many Jews who had fled were allowed to reestablish their community in accordance with the *Shari'a* (Islamic rule), subject as *Dhimmis* (second class people) to a poll tax and other special imposts, but otherwise enjoying full religious freedom and much communal autonomy. The Jewish street which was in the center of the city included a synagogue built after the return of the Jews. Under Orkhan, the city became a great center of commerce and industry, with participation by Jews and other ethnic groups. The Ottomans erected new Muslim hospitals to serve the whole population. The most valued credential for admission was the poverty of the admitted...

The enigma of the *Chiones* (possibly Crypto-Jews) represents an aspect of Judaizing tendencies in the early Ottoman days. It centers around the dispute of Gregory Palamas, Archbishop of Thessalonika, with the *Chiones* (3) which took place around 1354.

There is no evidence that Orkhan's son Murad I was in any way influenced in favor of Jews by his wife Mara (7). Since few of the Jews lived in villages they suffered relatively little from the raids scorching the countryside to soften the Byzantine adversary before the final assaults by regular Turkish armies on fortified cities. Murad I's reign ended tragically when, after his victory at Kosovo he was assassinated by a Serbian, Milos Obillo (Kabilovich). There is no indication that Murad's son Bayezit I (1389-1402), nicknamed *Yildirim* (the Thunderbolt), showed any preference for the Jews. He destroyed the French chivalry and the other Crusaders at the battle of Nicopolis, and with his coronation as *Sultan of Rum* nothing in the world seemed to be able to stop the Thunderbolt. But then came a storm over Asia Minor: the clash of two giants: the Thunderbolt against Tamerlane. Bayazit met his match when he confronted Tamerlane at the battle of Angora in 1402. He ended up abjectly, a captive in the hands of Tamerlane, allegedly meeting an inglorious death in a Mongolian prison. Tamerlane himself did not survive for long and his gigantic empire crumbled like a castle of cards.

Ottoman restoration came only in the aftermath of a terrible internecine war between Bayazit's sons, which kept for a while in its throes the whole of Anatolia and Ottoman possessions in Rumelia. In the end Mehmet I assumed the Sultanate.

Byzantium ravaged by war, internal strifes and revolutions, still presented itself as a safe haven for the Jews persecuted in Western Europe and especially the Iberian peninsula, from where came the first immigration waves. Byzantines and Turks engaged in a life and death struggle agreed on one point: they were both willing to welcome the Jews. During the black plague (8), from 1348 to 1359, previously prosperous Jewish communities In Fribourg, Spire, Strasbourg. Worms, Frankfurt and Mainz were being exterminated. The survivors were finding, by small groups, their way in the Balkans and Thessalonika. As the terrible persecutions of 1391 created havoc from Gibraltar to the Pyrenees, the first contingent of Spanish Jews was on its way, They appeared in Thessalonika, with among them the Nahmias family, originally from Mallorca; this family held the recipe for the preparation of a famous spirit (*eau-de-vie*). In 1492, when a new contingent of their compatriots arrived in Thessalonica, the Mallorcan, Jews remembering their roots, were to found the synagogue of Mallorca. In 1394 during the reign of Bayazit I, a few French Jews came to ask the hospitality of their brothers in Salonica. They were victims of the French king Philip IV le Bel. Under Charles VI, in 1394, the French Jews were expelled once and for all; from then on, each time the French crown would annex a new province, the Jews would be systematically expelled.

The first assault on Salonica was launched in 1388 under the rule of Murad I. The Turks did not occupy the city but garrisoned a military post in the citadel. They also initiated their notorious practice of *devshirme*, whereby Thessalonikian Greek Orthodox *éphèbes* (young men) were forcefully kidnapped from their families and raised as Moslem warriors (devshirme) to swell the ranks of the fearsome *Yeniçeri* (New Soldiers, *i.e.* Janissaries). Jews, as a protected nation, were exempt from *devshirme*. In March 1438, the Osmanli Turks, under Murad II, were engaged in the final assault against Salonica (38). When the Turks entered Salonica, the great metropolis and port had only 7,000 remaining inhabitants; the crows and errant dogs were the masters of the city. Sultan Murad II took action to repopulate Salonica; to accelerate the economic life of the conquered city Jews were encouraged to settle there. Jews who had left in the years of strife hastened to return and even issued calls for their correligionists in neighboring regions to come there. The Turks, trusting the loyalty of the Jews conferred them privileges and prerogatives which were not granted another community.

By superior order a group of Jews from Bursa were resettled in Adrianople. The city was to become a metropolis of Judaism with a flourishing rabbinical university attracting students from the most remote territories and islands.

The conqueror of Salonica, Murad II (1421-1451) was quite favorable to the Jews, with a famed physician Ishak Pasha Galeon (30) in his service, and also the contingent of *Gureba* created by his command. One of the Gurebas was to distinguish himself for bravery. Still as all the non-Moslems, *i.e.* the so-called *raya* (the herd), the Jews had to pay the **haraç** (the head-tax, or poll-tax) (30). the *haraç* was levied at different levels according to wealth; the rich paid 40 drems, the middle class 20 drems, the poor 10 drems. Exempted from the *haraç* were in each Jewish community, the Grand-Rabbi and his staff, the professors, the officiants, the sacrificator (*shohet*), the communal administrator and those who had rendered notable service to the State, as certified by a *firman* (Sultan's decree).

CHAPTER 2

COMMUNISM BEFORE MARX: A SYNCRETIC REBELLION IN ASIA MINOR

During the reign of Manuel II in Byzantium and Mehmet I over the renascent Ottoman Sultanate, an ecumenical fervor of Muslim- Judeo-Christian cooperation swept over Asia Minor, inspired by the Dervish creed. The three main perepetrators were:

--The *Kazasker* (military governor) Bedreddin from Simavna under the Pretender Musa.

--A "demented fanatic" named Bürklüdje Mustafa "who immediately proclaimed himself *baba* (father) and religious leader, called by his followers *Dede Sultan*".

--A "Jewish?" disciple, Torlak-Hu-Kemal, also called Kemali-Hubebbin.

The *Kazasker* Bedreddin, ex-tutor of the son of the Mamluk Caliph in Cairo, was also the author of masterly works in theology. He had continued to receive a pension from the not so vindictive Sultan Mehmet I's treasury until he raised the standard of rebellion. Escaping exile, he became the proponent of a new sect in order to realize his greedy aims. He found an associate Bürlükdje Mustafa, self-named Dedeoghlu, native from the mountain of Stylarion in Karaburnu (facing the island of Samos), who would be his instrument for the propagation of his new creed (2). Torlak-hu-Kemal, went at the head of the dervishes. The creed was based on collective ownership of all property (except the women), equality of all and dedication to poverty. Hammer calls these rebels "deviates" who went on from place to place preaching: "I shall live in thy house; thou shall wear my clothes, hold my arms, drive in my carriages--as I shall do with yours." Bedreddin and his co-conspirators had a secret aim: "the foundation in Europe and Asia of their own government" and to gain the allegiance of the Greeks; their Dervishes proclaimed that those denying that the Christians pray to Allah are themselves unbelievers, and the Christians who came to join their ranks were welcome with actions of grace as if they were angels descending from the sky.

Delegates went to Samos, bare-headed and their feet wrapped in simple clothes, to recruit new believers among the local clergy. The legend spread that Dedeoglu could cross at night to Samos walking over the sea.

Mehmet I reacted swiftly, ordering troops under the son of the Servian king and Shishman, the governor of Saruhan, to quell the rebellion of the Dervishes. In the passes of the Stylarion mountain the Ottoman army was surrounded by six thousand religious fanatics and nearly totally destroyed. Inebriated by their victory, the rebels decreed a vestimental reform, as they all started to move around bare-headed, garbed in identical clothes made of a cheap kind of tissue. A second army dispatched by the Sultan met again a total defeat. Mehmet I sent a third army commanded by the twelve year old Crown Prince Murat, under the tutelage of the famed Ottoman commander Bayezid Pasha. The most decisive battle took place at the place in the Stylarion Mountain where Bürlükdje Mustapha had declared his capital ending in the total defeat of the Dervishes. Those who did not perish in battle were all taken in captivity to the city of Ayaslug (Selçuk). An attempt was made to bring Mustafa back to Islam. Tortured, he remained obstinate. He was put on a cross and in this condition moved all over the city on the top of a camel. Those who refused to abandon their new faith to return to the fold of traditional Islam, were slaughtered before the eyes of Dedeoglu. With screams of:

"Dede Sultan, came to our help..." they precipitated themselves on the drawn daggers, confirming by this supreme act their deep belief in their faith and their dying leader. The legend of Mustafa continued to live amidst the remnants of his followers. The tradition was maintained that he was still alive in the island of Samos, where he had retired to a retreat while waiting for a new life.

After the defeat of Mustafa, the main target of the Ottoman punitive expedition was the "Trotsky" of the rebellion, the organizer and commander of the Anatolian "Red Army," the enigmatic Torlak hu-Kemal himself...but it was only the remnant of an army weakened both physically and morally by the crushing defeat and death of the leader Dedeoglu. The three thousand dervishes of Torlak Kemal were vanquished at Magnesia. Torlak Kemal was hanged in the company of his most devoted *Mürid* (Followers).

A third faction of the sect was gathering in the Balkan mountains, where Bedreddin had a great following from the time he was *Kazasker*. A new offensive was carried out, as an army under the dual command of Bayezid and Murad crossed the straits of Marmora. Bedreddin was defeated and captured near the town of Serez. The *fetva* (edict by the highest religious authority in the Ottoman sultanate) for his condemnation as the leader of the sedition and for his hanging was issued by the theologian scholar Mevlana Said, a student of the famed Teftezani. The punishmnt was made to match the crime in order to stamp out the abhorred heresy.

A fascinating account of the same events is given by Alphonse de Lamartine, the French romantic and orientalist, a great lover of Turkey (3).

The historian Vryonis (4-5) elaborates on the religious syncretism in the Anatolian *Volksreligion* which almost resulted in a fusion or synthesis of the three monotheisic faiths at the time of the Dedeoglu and the Bedreddin uprisings.

There is also the point of view of Turkish authors who find a pervasive Jewish influence penetrating purportedly utopian, humanitarian and idealistic movements inspired by syncretism (6).

CHAPTER 3

MURAD II: THE AGONY OF BYZANTIUM. THE DAWN OF AN EMPIRE

Most important of all for Jewish history was the conquest of Thessalonika (Salonica) by the Turks (1). After a long and protracted war Murad II occupied Salonica which remained under Turkish rule until the Balkan war in 1912. The prolonged hostilities had led to a massive flight of residents from Salonica, its population declining from 40,000 to 7,000. After the final Turkish assault the city rapidly attracted an increasing Jewish population when it regained its important position as a major Aegean harbor. It was soon to become one of the few metropolises with a permanent Jewish majority and a great center of Jewish culture. This situation remained fundamentally unaltered until the Nazi occupation in 1941.

One of the greatest advantages of the expanding Ottoman regime for Jews was the uniformity of the legislation introduced. This replaced the enormous variety of laws and usages under which they had lived in the former Balkan countries, Venetian and Genoese colonies, and in the numerous feudal subdivisions of the Byzantine Empire. The evolving *millet* (ethnoreligious groups eligible for self-rule) system realized the long-sought Jewish dream of running internal affairs in full autonomy, except for the taxes to be paid to the Ottoman state.

After Murad II's victory at Varna (1444), all of Bulgaria, most of the Balkans and the bulk of the Byzantine possessions in the south, came under Turkish domination. Bulgaria alone included at least four Jewish communities: in its capital Tirnovo, Sofia, Vidin and Plevna. About Murad II we are told by Ducas: "his anger was never of long duration". The envoys of the vanquished party were received in a friendly fashion, their proposal was accepted and war was discontinued.

Franco (2) relates that, at his ascension to the throne, Murad II created a military corps of non-Moslems (*Gureba*) where Jews played a significant role. Later day Soncinos were engaged in less martial occupations, such as the printing press, and the publication of books in Hebrew, Ladino and Latin. Under Murad II there was a revival of Rabbanite and Karaite culture (3).

The glory of the Byzantine Jews of Salonica had been that of a tiny Hellenized community and its elite (4). The glory of the Ottoman Jews of Salonica would grow to become that of a huge cultural and spiritual center with tremendous impact throughout the Ottoman Empire and the rest of the Jewish world. Already during the reign of Murad II, the arriving Ashkenazi Jews marveled at the wonderful fate of their coreligionists living under the Osmanlis. Here in Salonica and the rest of Ottoman Turkey Jews were treated with equity and mansuetude, a felicity experienced perhaps only earlier under the rule of Charlemagne in the West, Harun-ur-Rashid in the East, and more specially under the Umeyyad Moors of Andalusia.

Towards the middle of the Fifteenth Century, two young scholars from Germany, Kalman and David ha-Cohen arrived in Turkey. In Adrianople they visited the rabbi Isaac Sarfati, recently arrived from Hungary. Sarfati was a man of doctoral prestige. Kalman and David suggested him to launch a circular letter addressed to the Jewish communities of Europe, inviting Jews wherever they were persecuted to abandon these accursed lands in exile and to come to Turkey (4). At the time the circular letter of Sarfati was issued, the Franciscan monk Jean de Capistrano (6) was roaming through the territories of Bavaria, Bohemia, Moravia, Silesia, Austria, Hungary and Poland, to inflame the masses against the heretics. The monk even though he spoke in Latin and could not be understood by his auditors, was through his impassionate tone, able to carry with him the fanaticized masses in an orgy of terror. Stigmatizing the Jews as unbelievers and practitioners of usury, Capistrano promoted pillages, mass expulsions and the cleansing of Jewish souls over the pyres.

Massive embarkment towards the Turkish destinations took place from Italian ports under the name *Geroush Italia* (Exodus from Italy). Many of the departing Jews were attracted to Salonica. The Ashkenazes arrived with their bizarre customs, long mantles, a special cuisine and a distinguishing bigotry. The tiny autochtonous Greek Jewish community was totally submerged by the new arrivals. In those times one could witness the spectacle of a Greek Jew speaking Yiddish and starting to forget his mother tongue.

CHAPTER 4

MEHMED II
THE NEW ROME: ISTANBUL

From different vantage points, Byzantium's last four historians--George Spharantzes, Laonikos Chalkokondyles, Michael Kristovoulos and Doukas have preseved the sound and fury of its death throes (1). Among these the opinions expressed by Doukas on the Jews, or the analogies he makes are typical of the Byzantine state of mind in these days of ultimate crisis. Doukas writes that when the Christians who had assembled in the Great Church (Santa Sophia) had listened to the Cardinal's (Cardinol Isidore, the legate from Rome, there to sanction the Union of Byzantium's Greek Orthodox Church with Rome's Catholic Church) words there were many who did not receive the offering of *antidoron* (bread of oblation which is blessed during the divine liturgy) because it represented together an abominable sacrifice celebrated in the unionist liturgy. The Great Church was deemed to be a refuge of demons and was deserted. The Constantinopolitans shunned it as though it were a synagogue of Jews. They looked upon the church as a pagan altar and the sacrifices as offered to Apollo..."

The last Emperor Constantine XI Dragoses (4) ignored Mehmed's request for surrender. It was not possible to take the city of the Romans and hand it over to the Turks. Were he to do this, along what road in what place or Christian city could they settle where the inhabitants would not spit upon the Romans and revile them and mortify them? Even the Turks and Jews would treat them with contempt?"

Did the Galatiote Jews, in violation of Jeremiah and Talmudic Tractates stab Byzantium in the back?

Starr (2) directly asks if the Jews took an active part in the defense of Constantinople. Most of the "Venetian Jews" in Constantinople were "residents of imperial territory" over whom the Emperor had graciously waived control, but they could not claim extra-territoriality. The Empire already was in mortal danger, when the last Emperor, Constantine XI, formally pledged himself to respect the rights of the Jewish wine exporters (3).

 Including the Genoese three separate Christian powers were established over the last remnants of the Empire (4). With three powers in control, the problem of Jewish allegiance was a complex one. The Byzantine Jews were placed under the historical accusation (5) of having betrayed their Byzantine motherland, which in the last century had spread over them its benevolent mantle of both imperial and ecclesiastical protection. If the Byzantine Jews had indeed betrayed their country, they were in flagrant violation of Prophet Jeremiah's injunction (*Jeremiah* 39:7) "Search for the good of the city in which I have made you to be brought, and pray the Eternal in its favor; because of its prosperity will depend yours." They also would have gravely violated the recommandations of their Talmudic doctors " *Dina de Malhuta dina* (The Law of the Kingdom is the Law)" and Tractate *Ketuboth*: "God has made Israel swear not to take a rebellious attitude against the country where it lives."

Most of the Byzantine Jews were supposed to be residing in Galata and its extension Pera (5).

The merchants of Genoa had established themselves in their own suburb of Galata between the Jewish quarter of Pera and the Byzantine Old City across the Golden Horn. During the siege of Constantinople, Genoese and Venetian ships were helping in the defense of Byzantium, but they also maintained relations with Mehmed. In 1451, two years before the capture of Constantinople, the Galatiotes signed a special treaty of alliance with Mehmed II, which had promised to the Genoese of Galata to recognize their rights and privileges, if they would abstain from helping the Emperor of Byzantium. As described by Sphrantzes, Mehmed attempted to gain entrance to the harbor (6, 7).

As a postcript to the Jewish role of abstention during Mehmed II's conquest of Constantinople, (in 1453), in the last year of Mehmed III's reign, the Jews of Istanbul asked for the fourth reconfirmation of a promise first made by Mehmed II (8) concerning "a commitment secretly taken not to provide help and assistance to the Emperor of Istanbul (Byzantium)." Before Mehmed III (1595-1603, the promise seems to have been reconfirmed in a *fetva* (opinion or decision rendered by the *sheikh-ül-islam*, the highest religious authority in the Ottoman Empire) issued under Süleyman I, Selim II and Murad III. Then since all the evidence had disappeared in a great fire, Mehmed III in good faith, upgraded the lost three *fetva* by the promulgation of a *firman* (imperial decree), reissued in 1695 (Mustafa II), 1744 (Mahmud I) and 1755 (Osman III).

During the first days of Byzantium's agony, the wealth of the Jewish quarter, considerable even in those terrible times, determined one of the points at which the Turks made a landing (9).

In a splendid gesture, Kapsali the last Rabbi of Byzantium was elevated to the exalted title of Grand Rabbi of the Turkish conquered Constantinople (10).

Two documents express the Jewish attitude towards the conquest of Constantinople (11):

With the fall of the Paleologues and the Sephardi wave submerging Romaniote Jewry there had been a missed chance for a Jewish-Byzantine cultural synthesis, and one can only get a glimpse of a possible unachieved Renaissance which might have been. If the Judeo-Byzantine cultural Golden Age never happened on a scale comparable to the Judeo-Moorish Golden Age in Andalusia, one could still hope for a cultural revival at the Judeo-Turco-Hellenic interface. This was felt on the Hellenic side, by George of Trebizond (12), the Byzantine émigré-intellectual born in Crete and settled in Italy who wrote to Mehmed II little before his conquest of Constantinopl.

At the conquest of Constantinople by the Ottomans in 1453, Mehmed II, had recognized the Greek Orthodox Patriarch Gennadios II Scholarios as the *Patrik* of the ex-Byzantine subjects, to be responsible for the personal and religious life of the non-Moslem communities now under Ottoman rule (12). Thus until the recognition of separate organizational statutes for Jews and Armenians, those who had been Byzantine subjects at the time of the conquest, were initially placed under the authority of Gennadios II (a function which before the conquest had been the domain of the Emperor of Byzantium).

When, three days after the chastisement which he inflicted on Constantinople, Mehmed II proclaimed that all the fugitive inhabitants might return and he was benevolent to the Jews. Yaqub Pasha, Mehmed's Jewish physician, who held the highest military rank, may have been involved in behind-the-scene negociations (12) leading to the establishment of a separate Jewish community. The Karaites also were recognized as a separate group.

Mehmed II permitted the Jews to settle freely in Constantinople, and other towns, allotted them special dwelling places, and allowed them to set up synagogues and schools. Soon after his capture of Constantinople he nominated a chief rabbi to preside over the Hebrew communities. This rabbi was a pious, learned, upright Israelite, named Moses Kapsali. Mehmed even summoned the chief rabbi to the divan, and singled him out for special distinction, giving him a seat next to the mufti.

Moses Kapsali also received from the Sultan a kind of political suzerainty over the Jewish communities in Turkey. He had to apportion the taxes imposed upon the Jews among communities and individuals; he was to superintend their collection and pay them into the sultan's exchequer. He was empowered to inflict punishment on his correligionists, and no rabbi could hold office without his sanction. In short, he was the chief and the official representative of a completely organized Jewish communal system.

An account of the appointment of Rabbi Moses is rendered by Elija Kapsali (13) which says that Sultan Mehmed loved the Jews very much, and many of them used to frequent the King's presence in the courtyard of his palatial garden. Among these were physicians of the king, his servants and those who prepared the food, but of all the most pious and humble was R. Moses Kapsali.

The settling of Jews was determined by the Ottoman practice of **sürgün** (forced or enforced resettlemen) (14). The **sürgün** policy exerted its influence on Jewish life in the Ottoman Empire over a period of two hundred years. According to Hacker "The reason for this may lie in...their perception in the eyes of the government as a positive colonizing element. Among major resettlements: the transfer of Jews from other areas of conquered Byzantine territory (1492) and from Egypt (1517) to Constantinople, from Salonica to Rhodes (1522), from Buda to the Balkan cities (1526).
The *sürgün* system had the following consequences:
1. The fate of the individual Jew as well as his legal status were determined as late as the Seventeenth Century on the basis of his origin as a **sürgün**. Sürgün Jews were bound to their new locations and were forced to pay a double share of taxes if they abandoned their place of residence. They also encountered numerous personal difficulties relating to marriage and other issues.
2. The majority of Byzantine Jews were rendered **sürgün** and transferred to Istanbul. When the Jews of Spain, Portugal and other lands arrived they could establish new communities throughout the Ottoman Empire with relatively minor tension or opposition, but not the *sürgün* Jews tied to their sites of resettlement.
3. Thus, paradoxically, the immigrants from the Iberian peninsula were allowed a freedom of movement which the *sürgün* did not have.
4. The system of *sürgün* led to the communal organization of *kehalim* with those from the same origin establishing residence around a synagogue accordingly named.

Istanbul had forty-two synagogues, and as many separate congregations, according to their native places, each of which anxious to retain its own customs, rites and liturgy. There were Castellan, Aragonese and Portuguese congregations, also Cordovan, Toledan, Barcelonian, Lisbon groups (*kahal*), besides German, Apulian, Messinian and Greek. The taxes payable to the state were trifling: a poll-tax on everyone subject to taxation (*haraç*). There was a kind of rabbinical tax levied on the congregation, according to different classes of property. Only the family of the palace physician Hamon was exempt from taxes.

A year before the conquest of Constantinople, Hekim Yakub (15), the Jewish physician of the Sultan was elevated to the highest military rank in the Turkish Army and glorified in a magnanimous *firman* (imperial decree) as a luminary no lesser than Hippocrates and Galenus.
According to Franco (15), author of *Histoire des Israélites de l' Empire Ottoman*, the Jewish physician Ishak Pasha, had received from Sultan Murad II, father of Mehmed the Conqueror the title of *Hekim Bashi* (Physician-in-Chief), with the comparisons to Galenus and Hippocrates. Ishak Pasha, the first Jew to have been

elevated to the exalted rank of *Pashalik*, was further granted a *firman* franchising himself, his family nd descendants from payment of any taxes to the sultanate revenues.

According to Abraham Galante (16) even higher honors beyond the *firman* of tax-exemption were bestowed upon the Jewish physician Hikim Yakub by Mehmed II. Hikim Yakub was not only elevated to the of *Pasha*, he also was made a vizier. There is no indication from Franco or Galante on what relationship Ishak Pasha might have had to Hikim Yakub. However, Franco adds that during the reign of Mehmed II, the physician Hekim Yakub was appointed *Defterdar* (Minister of Finance). Eight other Jewish physicians were elevated to the rank of *Pasha*. Yakub Pasha reportedly was the first physician to treat Addison's disease, a disorder of the adrenal cortex affecting renal sodium reabsorption, first described by Thomas Addison in 1855. Yakub Pasha inculcated in Mehmed II his special interest in medicine, and the sultan's library contained no less than fourteen celebrated works.

Yakub's biography continues, with a strange twist or even more a possible touch of the Borgias! It seems that the Jewish Pasha was approached by Venice {17) based on a decision by the Council of Ten, The Pasha in a fourteenth bizarre plot to eliminate Mehmed the Conqueror by poisoning. Maestro Iacopo of Gaete, by his Italian (alias name), having completed his medical studies in Italy had become a court physician at the Ottoman capital of Edirne (before the conquest of Constantinople). While successively serving under Murad II and Mehmed II, Maestro Iacopo, alias Yakub Pasha, alias Nisim Yakub, remained in contact with Venice, but had no scruples in feeding the **bailo** of Venice concocted information, such as a purported conversion of Mehmed II to Christianity. In 1465, Maestro Iacobo travelled to Dubrovnik in quest of medical books, namely Latin translations of Arabic works, as the Sultan's ailments became more incapacitating. It was in 1471 that Maestro Iacopo received the Venetian offer to put Mehmed out of the way by poison. The deal with the **Signoria** included 10,000 ducats outright, 20,000 ducats after execution of the plot, a security of 260,000 pieces of coined gold in the event of Venetian failure to pay within a month of Mehmed's death, intercession for recovery of confiscated property in Florence, Venetian citizenship for Iacopo and his descendants and exemption from all taxes. It is not known whether the Venetian intermediary Lando degli Albizzi ever reached Istanbul.

Was the Jewish Pasha a potential hired killer or was it all a ruse to serve the Sultan in a world which abounded in master plotters of the Borgia breed? The facts are that the Sultan survived the Venetian plot for ten years until his death on May 3, 1481, that Maestro Iacopo remained to the last in the Sultan's favor and was present near his deathbed, but that the Venetian intermediary somehow vanished. Mehmed II mysteriously died at the age of 52, it is said from a poisoning instigated by his son Bayezid (18).

There is also the Turkish point-of-view on Mehmed II's untimely death (19).

Among the taxes paid by the Jews to Mehmed II's Treasury, there was one called *Rav Akçesi* (impost of the rabbi), *i.e.* the amount to be paid for the right to have a grand-rabbi (20). The Sultan would issue a document called *berat* officializing the dignity of grand rabbi. In the absence of a "glorious" **berat**, the Jewish community could only have a **locum tenens** at the Grand Rabbinate. It seems that after 1528, even though the *rav akçesi* continued to be paid, upon the death of the Grand-Rabbi Mizrahi, there was no official Grand-Rabbi until 1836. However from the Jewish standpoint there was a *Rav Hagadol* acting as Grand-Rabbi.

Karaite renaissance.

The Karaites were undergoing a great religious-cultural renaissance (21). In the time of Mehmed II and his successor Bayezid II, headed by outstanding scholars such as Elijah b. Moses Bashyachi (1428-1498) and his pupil Kaleb B. Elijah Afendopulo (1464-1525). Basyachi and Afendopoulo are the two luminaries of Karaites under Turkish rule (33-36).

Elijah Basyachi (33) was the "last codifier" of Karaite law. There is correspondence (34) between Elijah Basyachi and the Karaite communities of Troki (Lithuania) and Luck (Volhynia).

From the Fourteenth Century to the second half of the Fifteenth a Karaite-Rabbanite rapprochement had become a political necessity and Bashyachi was broad-minded and enlightened enough to become a protagonist of such rapprochement.

Frankfurtian Jews, Apulian Jews, Romaniote Jews.

Towards 1478 (40) the first group of Frankfurtian Jews came to settle in Salonica. Their leader was Rabbi Simon Eskenazi, author of *Yalkut Simoni*, published in Salonica in two volumes (1521 and 1527). There were also Italianized German Jews who had been unable to settle in Italy, Apulian Jews, and a strange breed of Jews from Asia Minor and Alexandria who had lived for long generations in Italy but were still Greek-speaking. The original Romaniot Jews were struggling to maintain their culture, but they were submerged by the newcomers. From 1470 to 1500, they still had their luminaries, such as the prestigious astronomer Salomon ben Eliyahu, author of *Charbit Hazahav*, Solomon Capistrano, author of scientific works and Sabetay ben Talviel, mathematician and philosopher.

Yiddish, lingua franca in Salonica.

The streets of Salonica resounded for almost half a century, with Yiddish as the new *lingua franca*. The Ashkenaze elements were rigoristic and unexpectedly they found nothing wrong with polygamy, having failed to endorse the prohibition ruling of Rebi Gerson Meor ha-Gola (Light of the Exile 1960-1020). They also ignored another matrimonial ruling of Rabbi Gerson Meir, the requirement for the wife's consent in divorce. They were very ritualistic, rejecting any intervention in their religious affairs and casting of the *herem* (excommunication) at anyone having recourse to the courts of the State.

CHAPTER 5

BAYEZID II: THE GATES OF PARADISE

Sultan Bayezid II (1481-1512) has been described as a saintly man, but his biography leads to suspicion that he was not all that saintly after all... His way of ascending the throne may have included a touch of parricide (1). Bayezid was not content with the official titles of his father, "*Ever Victorious Khan, Sultan by the Grace of God, King and Emperor of both Continents of Asia and Europe*". To these titles he added "*and the Rest of the World*".

The next episode, a fratricidal war, came when Bayezid's younger brother Cem made a bid for the succession at the Ottoman throne, but was defeated by the Janissaries and forced into permanent exile. Cem, an unwilling guest of France's Charles VIII and the Borgia pope, ended poisoned, not before writing some of the most lyrical poetry contributed by an Ottoman prince.

The Janissaries demand Rabbi Kapsali's head.

The Janissaries engaged in the fight against Cem were restless (1) and they resented Grand Rabbi Kapsali's earlier reprimand of some Jewish youths for having taken part in their licentious bouts. The aroused Janissaries set siege for one night (2) around the courtyard leading to Kapsali's residence. A charitable Turkish woman came out shouting that the houses all around were inhabited by Moslems and not by *Yahudis*. Her words convinced the Janissaries to leave.

1492.

1492 is the year of the great Exodus for Spanish Jews escaping the Inquisition and forced conversion, Torquemada and the auto da fés. In Bayezid's, maybe apocryphal, words: " You call Ferdinand a wise king, he, who by expelling the Jews, has impoverished his country and enriched mine!" (2a).

Another consequence came in a form of the protest by the Palermo leaders, under Spanish rule. They protested against the Spanish decree of expulsion of Sicilian

Jews because their city would be deprived of skilled workers for the production of weapons and agricultural implements.

The greater part of the Jewish exiles found asylum in Turkey. Immigrant Jews enjoyed happy days there, because they were a Godsend to this comparatively new and not sufficiently populated State. The Sultan could depend on the fidelity and usefulness of the Jews. Hence they became, on the one hand the business people, and on the other, the citizen class of Turkey. They not only carried on the wholesale and retail commerce by land and sea, but also were the handcraftsmen and artisans. The *Marranos* (Jewish converts to Catholicism, Crypto-Jews, striving to return to their Jewish roots) especially who had fled from Spain and Portugal manufactured for the warlike Turks new armor and firearms, cannons and gunpowder, and taught the Turks how to use them. These weapons enabled the Turks to overwhelm the nations against whom they were involved in war.

What kind of person was Bayezid II, Benefactor of the Iberian Sephardim (?), would his other contemporaries have thought of him as a benefactor, considering his already mentioned megalomania, possible involvement in parricide, and also fratricide? There is more to tell of the acts of this complex historical figure.

The Turcomans of the region of Ermeni who had delivered Cem to Bayezid after insulting and plundering the unfortunate Prince, came to the Sultan, asking for their reward. They were promptly obliged! Bayezid ordered them to be crucified on the trees of the nearby forest. Addressing the peasants of the province, Bayezid said (3): "This is the salary of slaves who intermix themselves in the quarrels of the sultans. How could such vermin lift a hand against the sacred head of my brother?"

Bayezid had quite a memory when it came to remember a past outrage. In the campaign against Cem he had all the reasons to be thankful for the actions taken by his general Keduk Ahmed Pasha. However Bayezid was hiding an old grudge: in the course of an inspection Keduk Ahmed had severely reproached, the then Crown Prince, Bayezid, the lack of discipline in the unit under his command. Bayezid had then said: "You will repent of your insolence when I will be your master!"

"And me" answered the old warrior, "I swear hereby, by my father's head, that I will never carry my sabre for a master like you."

At the review of the troops in Scutari, after Bayezid's access to the throne, Keduk Ahmed appeared before Sultan at the head of the spahi cavalry, with his sabre hang on to the saddle of his horse. An apparently gracious Bayzezid II, relieved Keduk from his oath, asking the warrior to loyally serve him as he had served his father Mehmed II. Still the memory of the old offense was not erased, it kept lingering...

Then it happened! On one occasion, oblivious of religious commands, Bayezid had the wines of Cyprus and Shiraz poured out, and asked all those present to join in. Inebriated he spoke of himself as the Sultan of Peace, claiming that he would reduce the pride of his military chiefs to the modesty and obedience of slaves. Against his noblest instincts Keduk himself had indulged in wine and lost his inhibitions. He went into a diatribe, attacking sovereigns and viziers who cement their power with the blood of the soldiers. He made Bayezid suspect that the Janissaries could very well withdraw the throne which they had given him. A silence of terror followed. Bayezid's face was purple. At the conclusion of the banquet, it was customary, to bring a cloak of honor for every guest. The cloth that came for Keduk Ahmet was black, a sign of repudiation. Keduk understood, he got up...

"Stay!" thundered the Sultan. With a single gesture from Bayezid, his *Chiaoushs* (attendants from the Palace Guard) wrested away the general's clothes. The executioners had already prepared to strike his bare shoulders, when the *Kizlar Aghasi* (Chief Eunuch) threw himself at the feet of Bayezid, asking him to suspend the execution. The Sultan ordered Keduk Ahmed to be thrown instead into the dungeon of the Seraglio...But the aroused Janissaries poured into the streets, thirty thousands of them, torches and bare sabres in hand and their axes plunged into the gates of the Seraglio which were quickly opened.

Beyazid's attendants barely had time to remove Keduk from his jail cell. Keduk adressed the Janissaries:

"In the exuberance of a banquet, I have myself lacked in the respect that every Ottoman must have for his master; the Sultan has punished me...but I was deserving a chastisement and I am owing him my life. Go back in good order, ask forgiveness from your master for...having violated the approaches of the sacred Seraglio. Go back in peace to your barracks!"

The matter did not end there...Bayezid was waiting for the propitious moment to strike. To distance Keduk Pasha from his partisans, Bayezid devised the plan of a voyage to Bursa and, accompanied by his *Divan* (Council of Viziers) he left for that city. In his quality of vizier Keduk Pasha had to follow the **D**ivan. A few days after the Sultan had arrived in Bursa, the final act of the drama was played out. Keduk ended strangled in the Seraglio of Bursa.

Then, just before the wave of Sephardi immigrants, came a major change of character. After an attempted assassination, Bayezid was a different man. Until then the Sultan had been more inclined to debauchery than mysticism. The blow of a fanatic's dagger was interpreted by Bayezid as a celestial warning, because of his wickedness. He resolved to mend his ways. For the rest of his life he was to remain in a daze of dreamy melancholy and mystical thought.

As described by Lamartine:

"The prayer, the pious conversations with the sheiks, the poetry in which he excelled almost as much as brother Cem, became the only diversions from the important worries of the throne...He repudiated the shining colors, the golden embroiderings, the Persian bonnets, and the feathers which decorated the clothes and turbans of Mahomed II...The Ottomans did not call him anymore the Sultan, but the sheikh, the sufi, the philosopher, the saint."

Thus, Bayezid probably had already undergone his mystical conversion when the first Sephardi immigrants appeared in sight of the Bosphorus (4).

Abravanel had given the Messianic answer to the question of "Quo vadis, Israel?". When the waves of Sephardim reached destination, the exiles entering Turkey encountered the actual answer, and it was almost a garden of roses. The Iberian immigrants immediately formed a congregation of their own (10) according to their respective towns or districts of origin in the Iberian peninsula. In Salonica, they began with a congregation called *Gerush Sefarad* (the Expulsion from Spain). It was followed by the congregations of Castellan, Mallorcan, Catalan as well as Portuguese and Sicilian groups, each quite autonomous and cultivating its own ritual. In the presence of other Jews, such as the Romaniotes (ex-Byzantine Jews often called *Gregos*), Ashkenazes and Italians, many of the newcomers became polyglot. This circumstance made them particularly useful for the service as *drogmans* (semi-official interpreters), often serving as trusted agents for foreign diplomats and merchants in negotiations with local authorities and businessmen. In the course of time the Judeo-Spanish finally dialect resulted from the incorporation of loan words and occasional sentence structures not only from the Hebrew, but also from the Turkish, Slavic and Greek. Ladino (Judeo-Spanish) developed into a language in its right with its own literary wealth and cultural validity.

The community next in importance to Istanbul was Salonica. This settlement offered more leisure for peaceful occupation than the noisy capital of Turkey. The Jews of Spain, Sicily, Calabria, Apulia and Portugal came in many groups to fill the city. It was towards the end of the summer of 1492 (11) that the first group of Sephardis, reached the Thermaic Gulf, Salonica, the port where the Osmanlis ruled supreme. In the words of Nehama (11):

"...Crowded on the decks of the ships, they watched on their right the somber heights of the Great Cape, on their left the snowy summits of the Olympus... They...entered a bay looking like a lake of tranquillity. Their eyes then encountered a magnificent sight. Under the shining sun, and the pure blue sky appeared what was a 'beauty of a city'...It was a sight out of the paradise,

Finally the exiles touched the land. They were not asked any disembarkation tax. Obeying strict orders emanating from the capital, the Turkish officials welcomed them with a sweet affability and strove to their best to facilitate the installation of the new arrivals. Sultan Bayezid II, the Sufi, had generously opened to them the gates of his Empire and his commands were being reverently observed. Bayezid was the new and blessed Cyrus delivering the Jews from the Iberic Babylonia. The Grand Rabbi Moshe Kapsali (1420-1495), leader of the Jewish Nation, who resided in Constantinople and enjoyed the favor of the Imperial Court, had obtained from the Sultan a *firman* whereby the "penalty of death" was decreed against anyone who would dare to mistreat them (the Sephardi imigrants) or cause the slightest injury...

...The province of which Salonica is the capital, happened to be a true garden, watered by an abundant river and full of lakes, full of fish. The region was endowed with orchards, olive trees and exquisite grapes yielding an excellent wine. The port at the head of a gulf offered all kinds of security to ships engaged in maritime trade. Salonica was at the crossroad of maritime and terrestrial routes."

Ten congregations were formed in Salonica. Eventually they increased to thirty-six. Salonica became a town with a Jewish majority. The leading language of Salonica became Spanish.

The Jews that the immigrants found already in Salonica were largely Ashkenazis. The native Jews speaking Greek, the **Romeis** or Romaniots, the **Griegos**, were no more than a few hundred families. The Italiots, native of Northern countries latinized by a sojourn in Italy, were more numerous. There were also a few Mallorcan or Catalan families escaped from the 1391 persecution, and a small group of Provençal Jews still remembering their country. Most of the local Salonica Jews had Yiddish for their common language, but among themselves the **Griegos** spoke Greek and the Italians spoke Italian.

The new arrivals found a very advantageous situation with an aboundance of unoccupied houses. These were the property of the sons and grandsons of the veterans who had participated in the conquest of Salonica and had received real estate as gifts from the Sultan. The owners were eager to let the Jews enjoy these houses and shops for very modest rents.

The son of one of the last Spanish-Jewish ministers of finance, Judah Benveniste, settled in Salonica. From his paternal inheritance he had saved enough to possess a noble library. The Taytaceks, and Jacob Ibn-Chabib, were representatives of Talmudic learning. The physician Perachyah Cohen, his son Daniel, Aaron Afia (Affius), and Moses Almosnino, cultivated philosophy and astronomy.

Other important towns of Sephardic settlements were Adrianople, the former residence of Turkish sultans, and Nicopolis. More Sephardic settlements were in Amasia, Tria and Tokat. Smyrna, which later on had a large Jewish population, was then of little importance.

As stated in Baron (12): "these new arrivals...were pioneers in the art of printing." In Constantinople and Salonica Hebrew presses preceded in time any similar establishments in Greek and Slavic scripts. As to the printing of books in Turkish and Arabic it remained prohibited by the Ottoman state until the Eighteenth Century. In 1494 the brothers David and Samuel Nahmias published in Constantinople a Hebrew *incunabulum* (*i.e.* a book printed before 1501) *Arba Turim* (the Four Pillars) an edition of the well known codes of law.

The extension of the Ottoman dominion to Syro-Egyptian and North African territories under Bayezid's II son Selim I was to reinforce cultural ties between Balkan Jewries and the Jewish communities in those regions. The Ottoman Empire had grown beyond the rigid bonds of the *Sharia* (Religious Law) into a multinational state, with the Sultan committted to the prosperity of all the *millet* (ethnoreligious groups), plus a special motivation to be benevolent towards the Jews whose loyalty for manifold historical reasons appeared more dependable than that of the other groups. Thus, the Golden Age of Turkey was also to the Golden Age of the Jews.

At first the local Jews were quite hospitable to the newcomers. Many of them felt ,as later expressed by R. Moses Joseph di Trani, that they "ought not to interfere with any man arriving from the end of the earth if he wishes to engage in business and make profits, for the local people will profit together with him." Two Kapsalis, Elkana Kapsali of Canca (Venetian posssession in Greece) and the Grand Rabbi Moshe Kapsali of Constantinople, were the driving force in mobilizing funds to affranchise former captives and help the destitute. With the passage of time, however, the differences in appearance, habits, and outlook led to intercommunal friction. The Germans deprecated the Romaniots and Sephardim as lacking in rabbinic learning; the Mediterraneans looked at the Ashkenazim as uncultured and uncivilized in wordly matters.

The greatest point of conflict with the Ashkenazim were on the delicate matters of family purity, legitimacy of divorces, the old law of marriage ceremonies to be conducted in the presence of ten adult male Jews. Many tiny German communities could not assemble a quorum of ten adult men for every wedding. Rigid as he was, Kapsali probited the incoming Jews to wear scarves (*sudarim*) on their clothing on the Sabbath.

Among the new arrived Mallorcans, were the *Chuetas* (word not used by the historians of the time), disguised at Las Pelmas as pseudo-Christians, which neverthless have given Spain a profusion of monks, priests as well as foremost politicians and financiers. The members of the small Mallorcan community in Salonica were designated by the appellation *Baale Teshuva* Teshuva (the Repentants) in remembrance of their return to Judaism after long generations of Christian practice. The congregation of the repentant *Chuetas* was tightly organized and was to continue till the end of the Sixteenth Century as a separate entity with its own *dayan* (judge).

Other Spanish Jews had first sought haven in Portugal; with the worsening conditions there they left the Lusitan harbors and arrived in Salonica under the leadership of the venerable Isaac Abuav in late 1492 or early 1493. A most significant group of Jews arrived from Portugal to Salonica in 1497, including Abraham Caro, the father of Joseph Caro (author of *Shoulkhan Arouch*). The very numerous and illustrious family of Taitacek followed suit, and among others Salomon and his son Joseph the future glory of Salonica's high level teaching. Among the arrived also, a full roster of Salonica's glory: Jacob ben Habip and his son Halevy at the helm of the rabbinate, an important branch of the extremely rich family of benefactors the Ibn Yahya, including David ben Solomon Yahya and his son Jacob (or Tam), also Joseph ben Yahya, all erudite and magnificent scholars.

With the arrival of the Castillan community, many members of which were familiar of the royal court in Spain, Salonica was to acquire a new glamor and splendor as the focus of Jewish aristocracy.

The proud Aragonese, were conceited in the extreme, somber, taciturn, rigorously honest and meticulous, but somewhat prone to apathy and indolence. If the Aragonese represented the introvert type, the Catalans were extrovert, full of activity and exuberant in energy. It was told about them: "*Los catalanes de las piedras sacan panes* (the Catalans are able to extract breads from stones). The Spaniards used for them a laudatory saying: "*El aire de los Catalanes agudece* (The air of the Catalans renders perspicacious, increases mental acuity)."

There were also more primitive, less educated Galician Jews (*Gallegos*), patient and sober, but with rude manners, who settled in closely packed neighboring *cortijos*. Their dialect was a guttural and nasal "patois" close to Portuguese. They were poorly understood by Catalans and Aragonese, which led to the dictum:

Somos Gallegos non nos entendemos (We are galicians we cannot make ourselves understood".

The Sicilian Jews had been in that island possibly from Roman times and were arriving in Salonica to escape the far-reaching tentacles of the Inquisition.

A family of Spanish origin (12) represented by David Nahmias and his son Samuel, which had emigrated to Turkey, printed in Constantinople in 1503 under Bayezid II, a new edition of Rabbi S. Ascher's religious code called *Tourim*. This is the first book certified to have been printed in Turkey by a Sephardic Jew according to *Les Incunables Orientaux* by Schwab where it is listed under No. 96. After his father's death in 1511, Samuel continued till 1522. The press had on its staff a certain Astruc from Toulon.

David Ibn Yahya's *Lashon Talmudim* (Language of Erudition), a Hebrew grammar, followed by *Shekel Hadash* (New Coin), a compendium of poems by an anonymous author, was published in Constantinople in 1506.

In 1589 Moise Maimon's *Yad Hazakah* was published by Nahmias in Constantinople. It was an abbreviation of the Talmud with four commentaries, printed in two volumes, small format. In 1518, *Yossef Ben Gorion (Joseph Gorionides)*, published an abridged history of the Jews which appeared in Constantinople. A Hebrew translation of an alleged text by Philon entitled *Hanhagat haDever* [On the Regimen (Cure) of Plague] was published in Constantinople around 1518.

Bayezid's reign saw the rise of the Hamon dynasty of Court Physicians. The court services of the famous Hamons began with Joseph the Elder (13). The family seems to have arrived from Granada, where Joseph's father had functioned as court physician, under one of the last Muslim ruler. After moving to Turkish-controlled territory, Joseph Hamon entered into the service of the Ottoman court, functioning in the capacity of a physician next to Bayezid I and Selim I in Constantinople. A rumor, perhaps originating in the apocryphal stories about Mehmed II's Galenus, Hekim Yakub, attributed to the Elder Hamon a leading role in the poisoning of Bayezid II, masterminded by his son Selim. As a sequel, the story goes on to relate that Selim reserved to his co-conspirator the usual fate of regicides, death at hand of the executioner. It seems, however. more probable that Joseph Hamon continued to serve Selim for six more years. He accompanied the Sultan in his fulgurant campaign against the Mameluke Empire which was in the throes of death. Assuming that Hamon had indeed remained in the good graces of Selim, he did not survive the anti-Mameluke campaign. In the midst of the war, he seemingly died a natural death in Damascus in 1518. Had he earlier been a casualty of Selim's ire, a distinction not so hard to earn, it is unlikely that his son Moses would have succeeded him without any break of continuity. Another indication that Joseph the Elder had died while still in the Sultan's favor emanates from the obituary address delivered by R. Joseph b. Gerson at the Elder's death. This eulogy is mentioned in several sources (14). It emphasizes that Joseph Hamon the Elder had "stood in the breach to save the Jews from danger". As to the Turkish sources (15) they are silent on the alleged conspiratorial activities of doctor Joseph Hamon against his patron Sultan Bayezid II.

CHAPTER 6

SELIM I: CONQUEROR OF THE HOLY LAND, SYRIA AND EGYPT

Selim I the Grim (1512-1528) a no-nonsense ruler, with a predilection for keeping the executioner busy, was quite fond of his Jewish physicians and he also had a soft heart for scholars in general (1-4).

Under Sultan Selim I, son of Bayezid II, many Jewish scholars took pride in placing themselves in the service of this glorious but cruel ruler, who was to conquer Syria and Egypt. It is rather strange that Jewish physicians would feel themselves rather safe under an Oriental potentate, whose smallest whim would suffice to bring a call to the executioner. Even the defiant and enormously powerful Sultan Tomanbay of the Mamluke Empire in Cairo did not escape the ire of the mercurial sultan and rapidly met his death after the battle of Ridaniye which brought an end to Mamluk rule on the shores of the Nile (5).

Sultan Selim's mounted Jewish physician, who accompanied him on military campaigns, was Joseph Hamon born in Italy, from the famous family of Obadiah Bertinoro (2). According to another tradition Joseph the Elder, as he was called, seems to have arrived from Granada, where his father Isaac had functioned as a court physician of one of the last Muslim rulers. After settling in Constantinople, he functioned in a similar capacity at Bayezid's court. He accumulated a large fortune which he used to support Jewish scholars.

To Sultan Selim I's entourage belonged the Spanish-born erudite Salomon Almoli, who in addition to his Hippocratic talents also was a highly respected Hebrew grammarian, author of a Hebrew lexicon published up to the letter *nun*, under the title *Sharshot Gabluth*. Almoli also was a vigorous polemist and the text of a polemic in which he participated was published in 1517 under the title *Magen David*. The Turks of Salonica, from the most powerful to the most humble, had full confidence in their Jewish physicians. There is to be found in Salonica a mass of funeral inscriptions dating from the first generation after the Exodus where the title of Doctor is repeatedly encountered.

For a description of a *Hahambashi* (Chief-Rabbi) in the Ottoman Empire, one can refer to the successor of Kapsali who was rabbi Eli son of Abraham Mizrahi (1497-1535). He was a scholar both in Talmudic and profane sciences. He belonged to the liberal faction of the Rabbanites favoring the teaching of Oral Law to the Karaites. He was proficient in many sciences, teaching mathematics and astronomy. He was not particularly a favorite of his professor Kapsali, who had little tolerance for Eli's fraternization with the Karaites (3). As grand Rabbi he had to deal with immigrants from Pouilla (Italy) who having assembled in the synagogue of *Poulia*, had pronounced an act of excommunication against all those who would teach the Karaites, even if it was something as innocent as the Hebrew language. The resulting *herem* drew an annulment from Mizrahi.

Grand-Rabbi Mizrahi was the author of several *responsa* (answers to written questions asked the Grand-Rabbi by Jews all over the Diaspora). He had two major works of exegesis, one of interpretation on the Judeo-French scholar Rashi's commentaries on the Torah, the other a commentary on the *Mitzvot* (Good, Praiseworthy Actions) of the Torah, their ordinances and their sources as indicated in the two Talmuds or elsewhere. He also authored a treatise on "arithmetics and geometry". This work was translated into Latin, and had a second edition published under the name *Kofer hamesaper*. Mizrahi was the author of an illustrated work on astronomy, dealing with the shape of the earth and the stars. His commentary on the work of Ptolemy remained as a manuscript.

Rabbi Mizrahi carried the responsibility of maintaining the liaison between the Ottoman State and the Jewish community (3, 4). He later found it more convenient to discharge himself from this responsibility and to confer it upon a secular appointee, the *kehaya (kiahya)*, Liaison Officer, under the Ottoman State. The first such official went by the name of Saltiel. The Mizrahi-Saltiel team encountered a cabal of adversaries. In 1519 these succeeded in obtaining the dismissal and excommunication of Saltiel, which led to a vacuum in communal affairs and the necessary liaison with the governmental offices. Finally the Jewish community returned to its senses and a year later Saltiel was restored in his position. Eli Mizrahi outlived Selim I and died in 1526.

Sultan Selim I together with his conquest of Syria and Egypt, also was the conqueror of the Holy Land after his victory over the Mamluks at the battle of Mercidabik (5, 6). He entered Jerusalem in 1516. There is a folk story about the discovery of the Western Wall of the Second Temple of Jerusalem by Selim (7).

In the last decades of the Mamluk rule, the city had witnessed a decline from the 250 Jewish families encountered there by Meshullam de Volterra in 1481 to only 70 families reported seven years later by Obadiah Bertinoro who assumed leadership there. According to the latter, Jerusalem was for the most part a deserted (8). The situation greatly improved after Bertinoro took over and introduced numerous reforms. Authentic flourishing came after the Turkish conquest. Of even greater importance than their numbers was the larger geographic spread of the new arrivals and their formation of new communities in more compact localities.

In 1514, the second triumvirate of Jewish leaders was established in Salonica, as the first attempt to form an official federation of Jewish communities with a centralized authority (9). It was a gerontocracy. The triumvirate members were three venerable old men: Jacob ben Habip, Salomon ben Taitachek and Eleazar Ashemeoni, all three known for their impartiality and integrity. Jacob ben Habip had been a member of the first triumvirate. Salomon Taitached had arrived from Portugal in 1497, and was highly appreciated for his erudition; he was a master in science and logic. The prestige of his family was to grow further, with the accomplishments of his brothers and sons who were to reach the highest rabbinical summits. The third member of the triumvirate, Eliezer Ashkenazi who belonged to an ancient Ashkenazite family, long established in Barcelona, had been *Marbitz Tora* of the Catalonian synagogue. He was by popular voice given the title *Rav ha-Colel* (Chief of the whole collectivity of Salonica) without however any official consecration forthcoming to confirm such function.

The installation of the triumvirate took place with great ceremony in the first days of 1514. The three magistrates were invested with the task of administering public affairs. Officers of the sacred mission for the collectivity (*Ovede avodath behol ha-ir*), they were at head of the synagogues. Their high intervention was accepted without discusssion, when passions and special interests risked the disturbance of the good harmony of the communities.

The Salonica gerontocracy could not have continued for long. Intercommunal strife was on the rebound; fragmentation of the communities continued. Towards the end of Selim's reign, however, in 1520 a revival took place around the foundation of an admirable institution, the *Talmud Tora*. The institution was to rapidly become the most important creation of the Salonician Judaism, which would keep its spiritual beneficence radiate for long generations, exerting a happy influence in the areas of education, social welfare and philantropy. The *Talmud Tora* was simultaneously a popular school, a central synagogue and a common house for all the Jews living in Salonica, without any distinction of origin.

From the beginning the *Talmud Tora* was installed in a vast building at the center of the urban zone occupied by the Jews. One of its functions was to receive and educate the orphan and indigent children unable to pay the taxes demanded by private schools. A seminary was soon annexed which was to rapidly rank among the best in the Orient. It was also at the *Talmud Tora* that the great solemnities and public prayers were celebrated and performed. The members of the Jewish communities would assemble there for common deliberations, and also the sermons addressed to the whole Jewish population of Salonica would be pronounced there. The *ascamoth* (ordinances) accepted by all the synagogues and having force of law for all the Jewish residents of Salonica would be proclaimed at the *Talmud Tora* and registered there in the Book of Minutes of the institution. This superb institution which was to defy the centuries, would in effect procure glory and pride throughout centuries to come, not only to the city of Salonica, but to the Sephardim as a whole.

With particularism in the ascent, and federalism on the wane, the revival of unifying tendencies would come from the need to collectively face the evil of the *haradj* [tax to be paid by the *ghiaours* (the non-Moslems)]. The *ghiaours* could live as they pleased, but none was to act easygoing with the *haradj*. The system was voracious and insatiable. The *haradj* was a capitation tax, based on the number of contributors. The Ottoman fiscal agent would base himself on a summary census. The names of the contribuables were recorded in a special register, and the total to be paid by the religious community was figured as a lump sum to be settled every year. This total remained invariable for a long series of years, with absolute disregard of births and deaths. No abatement was allowed for the *non podientes* (those who can't pay) and the *minus habens* (those who own little). In general the total number of taxpayers was highly inflated. In time of war, further taxes were levied to amortize the military expenditures.

There was a full list of other taxes and *angaryas* (unpaid forced labor). There were imperial taxes, provincial taxes, urban taxes and communal taxes. Taxes also could devolve from the whims and pleasure of the Sultan, the fantasies of the Court Grandees, and the ingenuous rapacity of local functionaries. The *ghiaours* were supposed to pay for the maintenance of soldiers, horses, imperial courriers, lodging of the recruited draftees, guards of the Seraglio and courts, for exemption from military service (*bedel*). A Turkish-English dictionary defines *haradj* as "tax-paid by non-Moslems *in lieu* of military serrvice"; there were further taxes for the repair and reconstruction of city walls, fortifications, trenches, for public works and levelling, for the painting of Imperial palaces, for the prairies and falconries of the Sultan, for the commerce of wool and meats, for the furs of the Sultan, presents to Pashas and ambassadors. There were other taxes for inheritances, residency rights, buildings, distribution of drinking water, wines and spirits. Taxes could also be added or invented at any time, just on a whim. The story goes that a Jew had daringly told a Moslem that only the Jews would have a place in Paradise, while Turks would be camping under tents to guard the horses of the Jews. These words were reported to the Grand Vizier who did not lack in sense of humor. He laughingly said, since money is not in use in Paradise, it will be decreed that Jews should pay every year, in this world, the fee for guarding their horses in Paradise. From then on an impost on tents was established which all the Jews of the Empire had to pay.

There were also Jewish communal taxes to pay for: salaries of rabbis and Jewish functionaries; maintenance of synagogues, schools, seminaries and needy seminarians; subsidies to widows and orphans, to the poor, to the disabled, to travelers without resources passing through the city; medical and pharmaceutical relief of the sick; collections for the pious institutions of Jerusalem and Tiberias; back purchase of captives; free delivery of shrouds to indigents and burial expenses for such cases. There were also funds to be collected to face emergencies such as particularly deadly epidemics, money to buy the good will and protection of high functionaries against vexations.

The big direct tax to be collected by the Jewish comunity was called the *pesha*. It was destined to pay the *haradj* and divided by a common accord of the leaders among all the synagogues according to their respective abilities. Every synagogue (congregation) represented a fiscal district (fiscal circle) and was charged of taxes from its members. The congregation elected from within itself a "commission of taxation" called *hariha*. Individual quotas were fixed for three years. Taxpayers were divided in three categories: the wealthiest paid four ducats (two hundred aspers); the second category two ducats; the third twenty aspers. The poor were exempted. Every taxpayer was counted in the tax census and none could escape. In emergency situations additional contributions were required. There were also contributions perceived for circumcisions, weddings and funerals.

There were also indirect taxes (the *Gabella*) which increased the prices of consumer products. The products affected by the *gabella* calculated by oke (2.8 lb.) were meat, wine, spirits, cheese, unleavened bread, pascal sugar. To facilitate tax collection and avoid feuds, the constitution of corporations was encouraged for butchers and auxiliaries, *shohetim* (sacrificators), cheese traders, merchants of wine. Every synagogue assumed itself the fabrication of unleavened bread and imported the sugar destined to Passover needs, to distribute these products among the faithful with an increase of prices. Every food product which did not acquit the *gabella* of its category was labelled *taref* (impure and improper for consumption).
The communal treasury also had at its disposal resources from the rental of buildings donated as legacies or built as investments during periods of prosperity. Imposts and revenues were once a year put up for auction to the highest bidder for "tax farming". The auction time was strictly limited: a candle was lighted and the auction would be terminated when all the wax was consumed and the candle burnt. Widows were tax-exempt, rabbis were also, in consideration of the low financial means of those devoting themselves to scholarly studies. However, rabbis who happened to be personally wealthy would at times forfeit their exemption and pay their quota of the *pesha*.

Tax evaders trying to escape the *pesha* by hiding under the protection of a state official or a foreign consul were stricken by the **herem** (excommunication). Heads of household who did not regularize their situation were refused all religious assistance regarding weddings, circumcision, funerals. Those voluntarily leaving the city as a device to escape taxation were still liable, and their liability only stopped if they were forcibly removed from the city by the Turkish authorities. All the new immigrants were registered in the census books from the moment they disembarked and if they had the means their quota was immediately allocated.

One of the worst taxation period, extended from 1508 to 1515, first under Bayezid II, and then under Selim I. Bayezid II had to face a formidable league created by the Pope with participation of Venice and Hungary. Despite this situation, the collection of the war tax and surtax at first proceeded with nonchalance. The situation drastically changed when Selim I, nicknamed the Ferocious, came to power in 1512. An imperial *irade* (order from the Court) reached the *Cadi* (Moslem judge) of Salonica for the immediate entry of all the taxes in arrears, with as addendum the worst menaces to the Jews in case they would fail to immeditely pay up. The Jewish leaders asked each synagogue to determine the quota of its members. The tax collection was expedited to avoid triggering the ire of the Sultan. Salonica's taxation was particularly heavy and a number of taxpayers moved to Serres, Üsküb and other locations, which increased the burden of those remaining, as the city's population was fixed to a certain number in the *haradj* register and was unchangeable, regardless of evasions.

Some members of the Lisbon community had come to be informed by insiders about their allocation. They left the city before its promulgation. They returned later, claiming that the new war *pesha* could not apply to them since at the time of its proclamation in the midst of the community, they were actually residents of other localities.
The tax evaders had the support of Isaac Alatin, spiritual leader of the Lisbon synagogue. Alatin sought a *parere* (opinion) from Tam Yahia ben David, who happened to be in Salonica at the time. This master of *responsa* noted the guilt of tax evasion and lack of communal responsibility. Not only did he firmly pronounce himself against the tax evaders, but he also voiced the opinion, rare in rabbinical *responsa*, that the Jewish leaders could even make an appeal to the state authorities in order to enforce payment of dues by recalcitrants.

The scholar Don Samuel Meir Benveniste was to die in Salonica the same year as Selim I (1528). Highly cultivated, physician by profession, and a passionate bibliophile he had been able to carry to Salonica in his impressive train of luggage a significant part of his library in Spain, and he continued to enlarge his book collection untill his death. Most of his fortune was dedicated to the acquisition of rare and precious books. These scholars arriving in Salonica had in their possession a triple golden key to the gates of knowledge: Hebrew, Arabic, Latin. Surprisingly they ignored Greek, or had acquired only a rudimentary knowledge of this language in their passage through Italy. The said scholars maintained their freedom of judgment, exercising a sovereign right of commentary on ideas and acts. As Castellans they were free thinkers at heart.
In 1517, during the reign of Selim I, Levy ben Habip assumed the succession at the head of the Castillan *yeshiva*. He was a perfect talmudist, a prolific author of *responsa*, a mathematician and an astronomer. When after the edict of Alhambra, he was as a child residing in Portugal, he had been forcibly torn from the arms of his parents and baptized. He embarked out of Portugal in 1497 and immediately reentered the fold of Judaism. On the seventh year of his teaching at the *yeshiva* he

departed from Salonica and, together with his family, he took the road to Palestine by land. Upon arrival in Jerusalem, now incorporated in the Ottoman Empire as the Holy City of *Al Kudus Sherif*, he was appointed Chief Rabbi. He reorganized the Jewish Hierosylamite community, as an increasing number of Marranos started to converge there. A clear rationalist, he relentlessly fought against the deleterious influence of mysticism, the most striking manifestation of which was cabbalism. He forced the visionary Salomon Molho out of Jerusalem.

Despite the harshness of Selim I's character, his sense of fairness is cited by Galante who reports that to finance his campaign in Egypt, Selim, called the *Inflexible*, had borrowed money from a Jew (3, 4, 10). The lender died before any repayment of the loan could be arranged. *Yavuz* (the Stern) Sultan Selim was presented by his *Defterdar* (Finance Vizier, Finance Minister) a *müzekkere* (note) suggesting that since the lender had died there was no necessity to acquit the debt. After reading the note the Sultan added the comment: *"Merhuma rahmet, yetimlerine afiyet, bereket, gammaza la'net* (Misericord upon the deceased, health and happiness upon his orphans, abundance upon his estates, curse upon the cheater).
Selim I had a *Defterdar* named Abdul Selam, a Jew convert to Islam. Evliya Çelebi asserts that he was quite good in accounting.

The Jews had already started to hold a monopoly on the trade of alum. They also were at the forefront in the export of various drugs, Angora wool (*mohair*) and spices, oak leaves, carpets, cotton, corals. They equally were importers of camlet, porcelain, tin, canvas, construction woods, nails and dyes.

Then there were also the pitfalls of silk trade! This trade largely under Jewish control threatened to get Jews in serious trouble with the "Inflexible" Sultan:
"When Zembelli Mufti [the *Sheik-ül-Islam* (the highest Muslim Authority under the Sultan, but with powers to depose even the Sultan if it is proven that he transgressed the Religious Law or Canon Law--the *Sheriat*--the Minister responsible for all matters concerning the *Sheriat*, the religious schools and coming next to the Grand Vizier in precedence)], *alias* Zembilli Mevlana Alaeddin Ali Cemali was coming back from Edirne (Adrianopolis) he encountered 400 persons bound with ropes. Having asked for what reason these individuals were being subjected to such harsh treatment, he was answered: "They are *Bezirgian*" (persian word for merchants). In Turkey the word was used as synonymous to "Jewish merchant" and to just Jew, the Greek merchant being designated by the word *çorbaci* (one who makes the soup). The Jewish *bezirgian* Zembilli Çembilli had seen were under accusation of having carried on silk trade with the Persian Enemy, at a time Persia was under the rule of Selim I's mortal enemy Shah Ismail. Upon hearing these words the *Sheikh-ül-Islam* returned to Edirne and told the Sultan: "They have tied (with ropes) a certain number of men. If you want to kill them, this is contrary to the will of God." The Sultan angrily answered: "Mevlana (Our Lord), isn't it permissible to kill one third of the world, to assure the tranquillity of

the rest of the world? The *Sheikh-ül-Islam* retorted: "This is true only if one is dealing with a matter capable of creating a perturbation in the world; however such is not the case in this question." Thereupon the Sultan shouted: "Can one imagine a greater perturbation than going against my orders?. Without losing his composure, the unwavering *Sheik-ül-Islam* answered: "These people have not acted against the will of the Sultan; you have appointed *emin* (superintendants), which does signify by deduction that you have authorized the trade of this article." The Sultan continued: "I have already told you that you have no right to intervene in the affairs of the Sultanate." The Grand Mufti (*i.e. Sheikh-ül-Islam*) pushed his point: "This is a business which concerns the Heaven; it is my duty to interfere" and he left without bowing to the Sultan. Selim I remained thoughtful after hearing the way the Mufti had responded and the audience was stunned, petrified. After some thought Selim ordered a reprieve of the condemned, and furthermore he heaped favor upon favor on the Mufti.

In fact, there was indeed an ordinance of the Sultan forbidding silk trade with Persia, but the Sultan had preferred to listen to the compassionate plea of the Sheik-ül-Islam.

CHAPTER 7

SÜLEYNAN I: SHELOMO HAMELEH

The reign of Süleyman the Magnificent (1528-1566) marked the apogee of Ottoman power. He was called by the Jews *Shelomo HaMeleh.* When he ascended the throne, Eli Mizrahi was still Grand Rabbi of Constantinople. Süleyman is described by Turkish historians as *Kanuni* (Lawgiver). The achievements of the then consolidated Ottoman Empire in legislation were matched by the glory of Turkish architecture, literature and jurisprudence. Süleyman also is known as the great conqueror of Hungary, the terror of the Austrian Empire under Charles Quintus, and the great friend of the chivalrous king of France François Premier (Francis the First).

With the end of the shadow Mamluk Caliphate of Cairo, and the assumption by the Ottoman Sultans of the titles of Caliph and *Khadim al-Haramim* (Protector of the Holy Places), these rulers gained the opportunity for interference outside their own borders. In 1534-1535 Süleyman I annexed Iraq. Iraqi Jews welcomed the Turkish troops entering Baghdad (1). The territories of Syria, the Holy Land, Egypt and Mesopotamia were to remain under Ottoman rule until World War I (except for temporary occupation of Baghdad by Persia, but the Ottomans always came back). In terms of Judaism, the opportunities for cultural communication and synthesis between the ex-Iberian, Balkanic, Romaniote and Eastern Jewries were enormous.

At the time of Hungary's conquest by Suleyman, the saga of the Hungarian Jews comes from confusing and complementary reports, with another accusation of " a stab in the back". According to Aladar Ballagi and other chroniclers, it appears that the Buda Jewish quarter at first fiercely resisted the Turkish onslaught. During the siege Jews are told to have lost 3,500 fighters. Occupying the Jewish quarter by storm, the Turks allegedly "gave the Jews the choice of either departing with them or remaining in Buda...they (the Jews) unanimously decided to stay in Buda. This reply angered the Turk and he ordered that the Jews be divided into three groups: Adult men from thirty or forty on; young men twenty to thirty; all women and children. Each group had to choose where they wanted to live. When the Turk heard that they all decided to remain in Buda, he ordered the slaying of all older Jews, while the young men of twenty to thirty, as well as all the women and children were carried off with him."

It is unknown whether the Jewish prisoners of Buda were sold into slavery, or what is more likely, were handed over to the existing Jewish communities for resettlement and rehabilitation. In some cases Ottoman Jewry had to ransom these "slaves". Most of them quickly rejoined their correligionists in the Balkan or other Ottoman possessions. As to the many Jews who had left Buda before its occupation, the Hungarian Queen Mary (widow of the last king Louis II) issued the following decree: "Those Jews, who, had fled from the city are not to be allowed to return; their houses become property of the state." Jews who had remained behind should be exiled, but they were to be permitted to dispose of their homes."

Despite of all the confusion in the divergent reports by historians and chroniclers, it has been convincingly alleged that the many Jews who had remained in Buda had betrayed their native country and opened the gates of the city to the Turks (2).

The *firman* confirming the prerogatives of the Hungarian Jews was promulgated in year 1201 of the Hegira (1865), that is several years after the constitutional reform of the *Tanzimat* (3).

Among the new Ottoman realms, a region where the Jews did not fare as well was Baghdad. For them Baghdad under Suleyman was not the Babylonia of Talmudic times or even the Baghdad of the Abbasid caliphs. From the time of the Mongol invasion (1253) the Jewish community in Babylonia had fallen into obscurity. In 1578-98 the Jewish population of the entire province of Baghdad counted 683 families in a general population of 68,636 households. In the other Ottoman dominions Jewish life generally prospered. An interesting corollary of Ottoman power was that the ruling circles, so secure they felt in their ability to control their dominions that they believed it was much better to allow the non-Moslem communities a certain degree of autonomy. it became apparent to these enlightened rulers, that total Islamization of the religious minorities would dry up their spontaneous dynamism and creativity, reducing a very important source of Imperial revenue and strength.

Within the Ottoman Empire under Suleyman I, there came to be two Sephardi Metropoles, Constantinople and Salonica...but from these two Salonica was a *Malkhout* (Kingdom). Constantinople's Jewish settlements, which in 1478 had already grown to 10,000 souls, continued to increase to reach 18,000 souls before the death of Grand Rabbi Elijah Mizrahi in 1524. The mere fact that some members of their family had already settled in Constantinople or Salonica, or other Turkish cities, facilitated the initial adjustments of newcomers from Portugal, Spain, Navarre and Italy. Constantinople's Jewish population exceeded 30,000 by the middle of the century. Salonica too had become "a city whose majority is Jewish" according to R. Samuel de Medina, one of the outstanding leaders in the second half of the Sixteenth Century (4).

The streets of Salonica knew considerable animation with happy sounds coming from the multiple boutiques and workshops where ironsmiths, caldron makers, polishers, carpenters, strap-makers, shoemakers, dyers, tailors, goldsmiths, fabric weavers, rope makers, mill workers, bakers and oil makers kept busily working. The construction yards resounded with the Aragonese and the Sevillan airs of joyful workers, painters and master masons experts in the art of obtaining the best out of their materials. In the countryside a feverish activity was going on with vine growers, vegetable growers and gardeners lovingly working in the terrains and fields on which they had rented farming rights from the Turkish owners. Others more technologically oriented were busy at the copper and lead refineries or engaged in fabricating *vitriol* (a sulfate of any of various metals such as copper, iron or zinc). There even were gold hunters prospecting the mineral-rich zones of the Chalcedonian peninsula.

Where the new Salonicians excelled, was in the art of weaving and dying tissues. They manufactured fabrics of all kinds, drapes and carpets and silk tissues. They were the inheritors of the famed Jewish fabric waivers and dyers of Barcelona, Toledo and Segovia. Women and children also were engaged in these tasks which continued at night under the light of candles. Starting from a rough drape, they accomplished marvels by a succession of brushing, drying, dyeing, and applying mordant to fix the dye by combining with it to form an insoluble compound. With thousands of concerns they ended up in obtaining a perfect presentation.

In the interior of their quarters there was quite another kind of animation at the stalls of the grocers and wine merchants. Couriers went from shop to shop trying to bring together various sellers and buyers who did not know each other. The right of weighing was a professional *hazaka* (privilege) exercised by one family only, the Venezia, who had derived it as monopoly from the time the Republic of Saint-Marc (Venice) was ruler in Salonica (1423-1430) and would keep it for five centuries.

Modern commercial methods were applied by the Apulians who came in 1502 and the Marranos of Portugal who had started to come in 1506. At that time the Jews were the only international merchants in Salonica, because of their knowledge in geography, finance and administration. Traveling from country to country, they studied the products needed in each region and maintained a correspondence with their coreligionists everywhere. They also were audacious speculators, crossing all the seas, giving life to fairs, establishing contacts between Orient and Occident, Europe and India. On the world markets the Jews became indispensable and acted as arbiters of the major exchange products, such as sugar, coffee and spices. The Jewish economic cosmopolitanism was facilitated by the presence of trusted relatives and friends in different countries.

The exiles from Iberia had brought with them the notion of credit and the science of international exchange. They were able to freely cross boundaries; they kept valuable informers everywhere, in the ports, at the fairs, on the markets, even in the smallest localities. They had everywhere guides, indicators, representatives, commissioners rightfully called consuls. The Jewish traders had also inventingly developed a system of international insurance guaranteeing against the vicissitudes and misfortunes of transportation by sea. The rabbinical works of the time, written in Salonica, are full of the most complex contracts and ingenious acts, in use among the traders of the epoch.

The Jews moved through the Macedonian highways and back country roads, at the risk of their lives, dressed as Moslems, bearing a large belt of red wool garnished with yatagans, speaking Turkish, with a haughty tone to gain respect and keep away the malefactors. Penetrating into the remotest villages they offered coffee, sugar, pepper, indigo, fabrics and scores of other goods imported from all over the world. They proposed credit to cultivators, obtaining as security the products of harvest stored in the granaries as well as the products of the next harvest. They bought cattle, fowls, tobacco, feathers, and furs. From the beginning they participated in the fairs; the fair calendar was adjusted according to Jewish practices with no fairs on Sabbaths or Jewish festivals. Traveling to Europe Jewish merchants would often disguise themselves as Moslems, covering their head with a heavy turban and wearing a broad caftan, to better escape the spies of *La Santa Hermandad* (the Holy Brotherhood, the Holy Office of the Inquisition). The trade with Italy was opened to them and opulent Jewish bankers were in command of the Adriatic where their counters covered the whole of the Italian peninsula.

In 1535 a grave menace was floating over the Jewish community of Salonica and other Jewish communities in the Empire, when a number of Greek debtors brought a complaint to the Sublime Porte against Jewish leaders in Constantinople, Nicopolis and Salonica, with the accusation of exorbitant usury. The complaint was to Sultan Süleyman in person. The monarch ordered, without any inquiry, draconian measures against all the Jews in his domains engaged in the commerce of money. It took very difficult approaches to the authorities and considerable financial sacrifices to obtain a review of the matter in a spirit of justice. The total abrogation of the measure resulted.

Jews lived in the same neighborhoods and *cortijos* (houses around a shared courtyard) with the Greeks and Turks, and they befriended each other. From the exterior, not to arouse jealousy of excess opulence, Jewish houses had a rather austere aspect. They were surrounded by courtyards separated from the street by high and thick walls destined to protect residents and goods. In the upper floors, there were a few windows, generally quite small and narrow, solidly barred and barely allowing some light to penetrate. The doors were massive, wooden or made of iron, and fortified by thick crossbars. Nothing that happened inside could be accessible to the outside. There would be a total change of scene, however, once the outside door was crossed; one entering would discover bright air patios open to the sky, marble pools crowned by delightful sparkling water jets, the whole adorned by rose shrubs, honeysuckles, in the midst of a profusion of fruit trees and fig trees, jujube trees.

On all propitious occasions, Hanuka, the half-festivals of Passover, Souccoth, weddings and circumcisions, the banquet tables would be festively loaded with salted and pickled fish in vinegar and spices, delicious Sephardic dishes and sweets, fresh fruits, dried, grilled and salted fruits, nuts, hazelnuts, almonds, *vardariot* wines with a strong grab on the tongue. The meals completed, people proceeded to the final benediction. Then rose the hymns and *pizmonim* of the poets, the local airs. Married people executed exuberant Aragonian and Andalusian dances, slow harmonious, grave and gracious Turkish dances mimicking the scenes of a chaste love.

On Sabbath day a certain immobility was expected; a traditional custom required that no one cross the *erub*, the limit of the urban zone, strictly marked by a rope or a wire. The *Tisha be Ab*, the commemoration of the Temple's fall was the occasion for other rituals. Squatting in open air in the courtyards or terraces, the faithful would chant with muted voices the lamentations of Jeremiah, intoning then, elegiac poems relating the dolorous martyrdom of Israel, a work of Juda Halevy, the greatest of the post-biblical poets who lived in the first half of the Twelfth Century. Among the intellectuals who immigrated to Salonica the doctors dominated. A special place must be assigned to Solomon Lebeth Halevy who bore the title of *maestro*, implicitly meaning that he had followed a regular university curriculum.

During the siege of Sultan Süleyman, in 1525, the Castillan Yeshiva continued under Joseph Taitacek. Born in Castille (1490) and living in Portugal from 1492 to 1497, he was the most distinguished pupil of the scholar Joseph ben Habip. The codifier Joseph Caro with whom he entertained a friendly correspondence, and who had met him during a brief sojourn in Salonica, enjoyed calling Joseph Taitecek "the torch of Israel and the crown of the Jews." These titles may have an esoteric meaning, as Taitacek was not only a rationalist, he delved into the mysticism of the Kabbalah. All of the Salonician cabbalists of the generation to follow derived from Joseph Taitacek in terms of the doctrine he professed.

In the summer of 1525, the social disintregration of Salonica, originally provoked by the heavy taxation during the wars of Bayezid II and Selim I, had further progressed due to relentless tax evasion. The interdiction of movements of the faithful from one synagogue to the other, primarily for purposes of tax manipulation was in the spirit of the old *ascama* proclaimed on the initiative of Eleazar Ashemeoni during the reign of Selim I, at the Catalan synagogue.

The *ascama* was more forcefully and universally renewed on Saturday July 1525 (Tamouz 17, 5205), in front of all the notables and a huge crowd gathered in plenary assembly in the vast hall of the Talmud Tora. From then on no Jew in Salonica, could in isolation or in group, get his name erased from the roll of taxpayers wherever he decided to go. Everyone was to obligatorily be counted on his own synagogue without any possibility of change.

In 1526 the famed visionary Solon Molho, spent some time in Salonica, assiduously attending the Yeshiva to acquire deeper knowledge of the Holy Scriptures (5). The Kabbalah had already been cultivated by Salonician thinkers. One could gain access to it, after having gone through the regular cycle of juridical and scientific studies, which in one way pre-immunized the mind against Messianic delusions, the fantasies of divination and the thaumaturgy (the performance of miracles).

The Reubeni (Pseudo-Messiah who pretended to come out of Ethiopia) episode illustrates the kind of naive but wish-fulfilling Messianic expectations which had, in the spirit of the times, gained control of Jewish masses, from the least educated to the most scholarly trained (5).

Under Suleyman I, a Sephardi giant was Abraham Lebeth Hazan, a native of Girone in Catalonia, who had arrived in Salonica with the first influx of exiles, and he ended there his days in 1535 (7). A person of firm and open character, he combined an extended knowledge to a magnificent practical language giving him a considerable edge over his contemporaries. The charming poem entitled *Ahot Ketana* "The Little Sister", still sung in the synagogue on the eve of Rosh Hashana with the air of a gracious melody borrowed from the popular repertory of Agean lands, is attributed to him. *Ahot Ketana* with its bitter allusions to the recent exile, is expressive of the sufferings experienced by the wanderers:

"Let pasture your ewes which the lion has dispersed;
Release your anger on those who say: 'Destroy!'
And who have annihilated the branch planted to your right,
All the nations which have plundered our riches and despoiled us,
They have quenched their thirst on our goods and have torn our heart,
And despite all of this we have not gone astray from your paths."

From the nine stanzas which form the poem, the first eight give in acrostic the name of tha author.

In Salonica during Süleyman I's reign), the *Soferim*, calligraphists and copiers kept quite busy, reproducing on beautiful parchment of Jewish production, the Pentateuch, the Megiloth, the rituals as well as the works of contemporary and ancient authors ordered from them by the rich bibliophiles desirous to enrich their libraries. Soon the printing press apppeared. As early as 1458, a family of printers native of Spire, had settled in a small locality of Lombardy, near Cremona, in the small town of Soncino from which it borrows its name. The Soncinos formed a glorious dynasty of printers, spreading over the rest of Italy and Turkey and providing in books of all of Judaism.

In Constantinople, the exiles from Spain introduced the printing press as early as 1494, while the first Turkish typographic workshops, of which a Polish Jew was the engraver, would not start functioning before 1727 under Ahmed III.

In Salonica, the first presses were brought about 1512, by a fugitive from Portugal, Juda Guedalia, who arrived there with all his family. In the bagage of Guedalia, who had been a pupil of the master printer Eliezer Toledano, were present, preciously packed, his master's printing materials, solid presses and a superb collection of square Hebrew characters. When he came to Salonica, Guedalia already was a man of advanced age, all broken by the emotions of his flight and the plight of his painful Odissey. Don Abraham Benveniste, son of the philanthropist Juan Senor, helped him mount the press, probably assuming the costs of the first

editions. Soon Guedalia was at the head of an excellent team of young workers
joined by a Soncino, Moshe. One after the other, numerous books started to come
out of the printing house. It is to the Guedalia Press that was bestowed the honor to
have thrice given the light of day, in 1521, 1526 and 1527, to *Yalkout Shimoni*
(Shimon's Collected Works) of Shimon Ashkenzi of Frankfurt, a vast collection of
Aggadic legends,

The Jewish Commonwealth in Salonica was not a perfect democracy. In 1529, the
Rabbinical Council of Salonica instituted a censorship commission of six members
(censors) which had the task of examining every manuscript before it went to press.
None could under the penalty of excommunication, not only print, but even buy or
read a work which had not received prior approval by the censors. The *imprimatur*
was given or denied depending upon whether the censors thought the text was in
conformity or not with orthodoxy.

In their new land it was Spanish Marrano *contra* Portuguese Marrano. Profound
differences separated them. On one side were bourgeois accustomed to riches for
many generations, authentic aristocrats proud of their noble lineage, cultivated,
able to face any attack: on the other side there was a population of indigents,
humble, scared, with no recourse to the storm. One should not confuse the native
and impoverished Portugues Marranos, with the exuberant and wealthy Spanish
Marranos who had passed through Portugal, before going into exile from the
Iberian peninsula.

In Salonica the Spanish always the upper hand. The Spanish Marranos' language
and mores were common currency for elegance. The Spanish Marranos provided
the Jewish colony with an elite of notables (*quebirim*), leaders, rulers and scholars.
They constituted the true social framework of the high classes. Compared to them
the Portuguese Marranos and the *Gallegos* formed a deprived class of paupers with
no ressources, culture or elegance. They lived in the shadow of the Spanish
Marranos' wealth and palatial residences. They formed a class of servants, small
merchants and lowly humble people. Their Portuguese itself was a cause of
derision, as a sort of vulgar jargon used to address servants and peddlers. For
Castillans, Aragonese and Catalans, the names *Portuguese* or *Gallego* used to
imply a sort of pejorative undertone.

A new kind of religious mimetism developed among a certain class of Marranos.
Wandering against all odds, between the two worlds of Occident and Orient, there
were individuals who with dazzling speed would change from Jew in Salonica or
Venice, to freely moving Christian in Bordeaux or Barcelona. Catholics,
recognized by all as such in Lisbon, were known to have been active participants of
the synagogue administration in Salonica, and to have worn the red hat in the
Ghetto of Venice. There were priests fulfilling their parochial duties as
accomplished Catholics in Iberia, who once in Salonica or Adrianople would be
found wrapped in the levite of the rabbi, legislate on mosaic jurisdiction.

A most important underground of proselytiam was that mysteriously run at the
faculty of medicine of the University of Salamanca. There, scholarly and daring
Marranos, were well hidden mixed with the scholarly population at the risk of their

lives. They dispensed to the crypto-Jewish youth the essential knowledge of the Mosaism. Thus, it so happpened that the great breeding center of physicians in Salamanca, was despite the ever vigilant surveillance of the Inquisition, the occult focus of Hebrew science. The traffic of Marranos worked in two ways. While a number of Marranos had returned to Spain to exert their open and occult missions, a number of those who had returned to Spain by nostalgia to reside and even prosper there, were seized by a new nostalgia in their old age, that of ending their days near a synagogue, in the realm of the pious sanctuary affiliated with the mosaic faith. In those days these reciprocal relapses from Catholicism into Judaism, from judaism into catholicism and then again into judaism seemed quite normal.

There were many Salonicians with Marrano ancestry! The Almida, the Angel, the Arnaldo, the Baena, the Benveniste, the Bueno, the Caro, the Castro, the Crespin, the Diaz, the Ergas, the Ferrera, the Fernandez, the Franco, the Henriquez, the Pieto, the Saporta, the Silva, the Sulema descendants, most of them with ancestors having practiced Christianity for a long time. The "repentants" who ostensibly returned to the Jewish side, were at times the targets of popular oprobium. In the rabbinical office and in the synagogue the insult "Goy, son of Goy" was occasionally heard as well as in the *cortijos* and market place in the course of heated discussions, and quarrels between neighbors.

The rising tide of the Iberian element ended up submerging everything else. However, still for a very long time, Romaniots conserved Greek for the study of the Bible and for the debates in their tiny seminary. There also was a curious practice: *i.e.* the high value that the Romaniots attached to the *Siblonoth* (pre-matrimonial presents). Among them it was sufficient for a young girl to accept a present from a non-married man to be already considered bethroted or married to this man. The gift sent and accepted would take even the significance of a marriage contract; then to untie the union thus formed, all the divorce proceedings, with their complex ceremonial and the difficulties they raised became obligatory. This practice bore for the Romaniots, in their contacts with the Jews from other rites, the usual risk of becomimg entangled in hilarious and vaudeville-like misunderstandings and quiproquos. Supposed a man from another rite and not well versed in the ritual of the **Siblonoth** would send a present, without thinking much of it, to a Romaniot girl or woman eligible for marriage; there was an entire plot for the beginning of an opera-comique.

In the course of his trans-danubian conquests Süleyman I authorized the settling of the Jews from Austria, Hungary and Transylvania within his Empire, going as far as placing "galleons" at their disposal. Süleyman ordered the repartition of the Jews between the main places of his Balkanic possessions, mainly in Constantinople and Salonica. Most of these Jews were of Rhenanian origin.

When the poet Samuel Usque came to Salonica in the period 1545 to 1552, he was carried away by joy at what he saw. He was really marvelled at the progress which had been accomplished. The privileged situation occupied by his correligionists made him deliriously enthusiastic. Salonica was formed in "the little Jerusalem."

He ecstatically said: 'In the vast sea which bathes the Ottoman land, God has elevated the scepter of his mercifulness, and he has made to be engulfed the river of your misfortune, O Jacob!...Salonica is solidly sited on the foundation of the faith. The Jews of Europe and other lands who are persecuted and banished should come to seek refuge under its shadow and they were received with cordiality, as if this city was our respectable mother Jerusalem itself.

From Samuel Usque's poem:

"Salonica is a mother of Judaism,
Built on the deep foundation of the Lord,
Full of excellent plants and fruitful trees.
Such as are found nowhere else on earth.
Their fruit is glorious,
Because it is watered by an abundance of benevolence.
The greatest portion of the persecuted
And banished sons from Europe
And other parts of the world have met therein,
And have been received with loving welcome,
As if it were our venerable mother, Jerusalem. "

"*Ir vaem be-Israel* (a maternal city in Israel), thus, Salonica appears to the eyes of Samuel Usque, this ardent apostle who had made it his mission to bring to his brothers, the Marranos throughout the Diaspora, the "winged words" of poetic prose, to instill in them comfort, courage and hope.

The Karaites under Süleyman.

Within the Byzantine regions incorporated by conquest in the Ottoman Empire, there was another Greek-speaking element, jealously guarding its character of originality without allowing itself to be affected or even dented by the Sephardic onslaught. This was the tiny Karaite sect living in Salonica (8). Its presence had been recorded, at the beginning of the Sixteenth Century, by the preacher David Messer Leon who had loaned his services to the Calabrese synagogue of Salonica towards 1512. Extremely conservative, repudiating with a fierce energy all the rites of the Talmud and confining themselves to the Biblical text which they traditionally interpreted, the Karaites of Salonica, like the rest of their congeneres, wherever they may been found, absolutely isolated themselves, avoiding any contact with the Rabbanite Jews. Around themselves they inspired in the Rabbanites no better feeling than horror and repulsion, and the latter were not far from treating them as miscreants and pagans, and for holding them as accursed. The Karaites could not ignore the deep antipathy surrounding them. They felt uneasy faced with the rising tide of bigotry, not unlike that which had so much traumatized their Rabbanite Sephardic persecutors in Spain. *Mutatis mutandi*, the Rabbanite victims of the Iberian fanatics had well moved on the very path of becoming the Rabbanite Sephardic tormentors of the Romaniot Karaites. Reneging on the poetic words of Samuel Usque, Salonica "the maternal city" was well on the verge of becoming the "*marâtre* (bad mother, unloving stepmother) city" of its Karaites. Most Karaites decided to leave Salonica and to start a new ghetto in the Golden Horn locality of Hasköy in Constantinople.

There was not much love either in the Sephardi-Ashkenazi relations (9). In Süleyman I's time the Ashkenazis (*Tudescos Germans*, in the words of the Sephardim) were primarily mocked for their excessive use of garlic in amounts to put off a whole legion of vampires. To make matters worse they also over-indulged in onions! The local dictum among the Sephardim was: "*Nia ajo dulce ni tudesco bueno* (There is neither sweet garlic nor good *tudesco*)." Conventionally an Ashkenazi German had little hindrance in repudiating his first wife and taking a second one); he only was bound to return to his first wife the dowry plus an indemnity. Sephardi girls avoided like the plague to contract marriage with an Ashkenazi. It was a great communal taboo.

The gravest dissimilarities existed in alimentary practices, which made it quite impossible for members of the two rites to fraternize. The Sephardim recognize that a slaughtered animal is proper for consumption, if, among other things, the lung, after *nefika* (filling with air) does not reveal any fissure. They consider negligible and inoffensive pulmonary lesions which are already scarred. For Ashkenazes, the slightest lung lesion they can discern makes the animal improper for consumption. The Ashkenazes are quite lax on matters concerning the fat content of the meat. This makes it impossible for members of the two rites to sit around the same table. Jacob ben Habib himself would have preferred the Sephardim to accept, on the basis of precedence, the practices established among the earlier settlers, *i.e.* the Ashkenaze, Romaniot and Italiot Jews; however, Jacob ben Habib had to abide by the opinion of other scholars.

In 1573, under the reign of Süleyman I's successor Selim II, an Ashkenaze Jew addressed himself to a Salonician doctor begging him for enlightenment on the rules of Rebi Gerson relative to polygamy, adding that in the northern regions there were no more scholars versed in the matters of jurisprudence and religion. Towards the end of the sixteenth century the bulk of the Ashkenaze community was ready for a true "rapprochement" with the Sephardim. In Salonica, all the faithful universally adopted the clauses of the Spanish *Ketuba* relative to divorce and succession, also the alimentary rules of Castille on matters of ritual slaughter. The Ashkenazis, however, were insistant on what was their *forte*, their exclusivism, in what concerns the synagogue rites. In fact the communities in Salonica all shared special veneration for the antique Ashkenaze synagogue and it is from these very premises that the most important ascamoth were promulgated. The Ashkenazes continued to maintain their ancient ritual characterized by the extreme length of its services.

In the melting pot, which ended up by unifying within the Sephardic majority most of the heterogenous elements of the community, each group had brought its own characterristics and virtues: the Ashkenazis had added their spirit of continuity, tenacity, perseverance, habits of discipline and hierarchy; the Sephardim their mediterranean qualities of clarity, common sense, logical sequencing and juridical taste. The Tower of Babel that Salonica was had turned into a happy amalgam.

The cultural amalgam did not, however, result in a fusion of all communities and synagogues which continued their autonomy (10). One of the illustrious leaders and scholars of Salonica's commmunity, Samuel Moise Medina del Campo (11) fought with all his strength in favor of synagogal independence which was always under attack. Salonica was stepping on the independence privileges of Patras, Constantinople was overstepping on Safed and Safed on Salonica.

In one instance, Medina gave a blunt talk on the Safed rabbis intervening in Salonica affairs. Safed, at that time, was taking the initiative to establish its supremacy over the whole Diaspora by the dispensation of the *semiha* (rabbinical ordination). Salonica was resisting the attempt to fall under the suzerainty of Safed. Medina became the authorized spokesman for the salonician Rabbinate in a conflict at the Catalan synagogue of Salonica. The *Marbitz* at the synagogue had taken on his own authority the decision to confide to his son the function of "predicator". His faithful took an oath that, as long as the *Marbitz* is alive, they would not listen to any sermon given by another person than the *Marbitz* himself. Safed ruled against the recalcitrant members of the Catalan synagogue. "Lamentations and misfortune upon Salonica which is to receive such a sentence", cried out Medina. He added: "The great city of science and glory is dishonored by the people of Safed who have no regard for our scholars...O you, rabbis of Safed...have you so forgotten our synagogues and our seminaries? Have you forgotten...We are sufficiently expert in juridical matters to straighten out our own differences."

The Turkish authorities contributed a supplement of prestige to the rabbinical dignity (12, 13). They granted it an official recognition. When it was necessary for the rabbi to travel, he and his following were allowed to ride a horse, to dress like Moslems, to bear arms, and even to have themselves escorted by a squad of soldiers, whom the rabi was under the obligation to feed, and whose salary he had to pay for the duration of the trip.

The leader Samuel Moses Medina del Campo was quite indignant of the excessive democracy. He felt that authority primarily belonged to those acquitting themselves of the communal tax duty the *pesha*, thus to the *pesheros*. "Power to the *pesheros*" was his motto. This is in the same spirit as the popular Turkish saying *"Parayi veren düdüghü çalar"* (the one who gives the money is the one who is entitled to blow the whistle). The paupers, who did not pay taxes, but benefited from the tax collected from the *pesheros*, had nothing to do but to obey. One day, in the community Medina was directing, some indigents errupted into the room where the *Maamad* (communal council) was holding its session, they disrespectfully expressed themselves, and elevated their voices, making menaces. In very hard terms, Medina disapproved their misconduct, and did not fail to remind them of their subordinate condition and role as obliged to their benefactors. To prevent the repetition of such infractions in the future, on Medina's advice the rulers emitted an ordinance into forbidding those administered to penetrate the deliberation hall, unless expressly convoked.

Towards 1558, a scission took place in the Apulian community, leading to the birth of the *Neve Shalom* synagogue, itself later the theater of a new litigation, leading to the creation of a third Apulian synagogue, called *Neve Tsedek*.

After the catastrophic Salonica fire of 1545 (13), the Calabrese community which until then had been a focus of peace and tranquillity, was reorganized thereafter, and gave birth to the community of *Klana*, very well organized in a reconstructed quarter. Its leader, Jacob bar Samuel, said *Smouit* was at the outcome of a great disagreement with the faithful regarding the promulgation of an *ascama* against delators (those apppealing to State authorities on matters concerning litigations between Jews, *which were expected to be resolved by rabbinical courts only*).

Towards the middle of the sixteenth century a new synagogue was founded in Salonica under the propitious name of *Shalom* (66). Its adherents included Romaniots, Italiots, Catalans, Castilans and later fugitives from Ragusa as well as authentic Marranos. The synagogue had an interesting particularity. In its basement, a comfortable pool had been constructed for the major ablutions. Access to the pool was through a door hidden under the pulpit. The pool area provided a safe hiding place for the unfortunates hunted by the military from the infantry or cavalry (Janissaries and Spahis), both equally feared because of their depredations and plunderous thefts.

In 1537, the Jews of Otranto seeing their numbers increase with new arrivals, after the Turks lost the city to the Venetians, formed a new community. A few years later a group of dissidents formed the synagogue of *Astrouc* or *Estroug*, named after their leader.

A group of Sicilians, the *Syracuses*, because of a strange similarity of names resemblance, joined the Saragossians, to form the *Beth Aaaron* synagogue, with its own *Pourim* of Syracuse, also called the *Pourim* of Saragossa, In the Sicilian tradition it was said that around 1488 the Jews of Syracuse being obliged to take part in the Catholic procession were accustomed to hold the coffers containing the Torah scrolls at the head of their ranks. It was their practice to empty the coffers before the procession in the greatest secrecy in order to protect their venerated scrolls from a possible profanation or sacrilegious promiscuities. Having been secretly informed of this subterfuge the King decided to catch the Jews red handed and punish them in an exemplary way. However, by miraculously way the leaders of the Jewish community were informed of the danger. They came to the procession well equipped to the discomfiture of the informers. The Jews of Syracuse instituted a special *Pourim* to remember their salvation, and this holiday was observed for long years in Salonica the eighteenth day of *Shevat* every year.

In the Sixteenth Century, during the reign of Süleyman I, the Jews of Salonica had to face the prowess of the Knights of Malta. The Knights were primary promoters of piracy. The towers of their galleons were trained slaves treated with remarkable cruelty. The Knights captured vessels, and returned to their rocky shores without any respect for the monastic robes they wore. Their most prized capture was that of

Jewish merchants from the Orient who were bound to bring a rich ransom. *Esclavo judeo non hay* (Jewish slaves, there are none) was the proud dictum of the Sephardim. In Salonica the name of Knight of Malta was synonymous with brigand. Whenever speaking about these malefactors of the Mediterranean, the Salonician Jews never omitted the curse: *May their names and their descendants be exterminated! Amen!*."

In 1552, the Knights of Malta accomplished a master stroke. Their galleons encounterd of a vessel coming from Salonica with seventy Jewish passengers on board. The Jews were brought captive to Malta together with a large booty. Four among them were selected as delegates and brought a ransom demand for 10,000 ducats to Salonica, plus compensation for the maintenance and return expenses of the captives. The amount was exorbitant, and could not be met even after emptying the coffers. Whatever could be collected was delivered to the emissaries from the captured group, together with a mandate from Salonica rulers addressed to sister-communities for collection of the residual part of the ransom. The sister-communities generously contributed. The captives were freed.

When Rabbi Escapa arrived in Izmir in 1628 (14) there were six synagogues in the city. A small document found in the book of *Bate Kenessiot* (the Beth Kenesets, the synagogues) of Abraham Benezra, who died 1761, states that in former times there was a synagogue in Izmir, in which the Turks did the *namaz* (prayer five times a day, the face turned towards Mecca), so that the Jews could not pray there anymore. This is not exactly the case in the Turkish Moslem enlightened tradition, according to which a Turk can pray in any of the prayer places of the *People of the Book*, be it a synagogue or a church. President Sadat of Egypt entertained the dream to build in the Sinai a sanctuary where Moslerm, or Christian, or Jew could pray. There is also in the author's family experience the example of a Moslem Turk participating with excellent good faith in a *meldar* (yearly commemorative prayer for the dead of Sephardic Jewish families) to the point of even following the ritual davening of the Jews whose bodies should be swaying back and forth like "the cypress trees swaying with the wind."

The Hamon dynasty rose to even greater power under Suleyman I. Like his father, Sultan Süleyman also was surrounded by Jewish physicians. The growth in number of Jewish court physicians is well reflected in several official documents (15). One register dated 1536-1537, records four or five Jewish practitioners along with thirteen to fifteen Muslim colleagues. Twelve years later (1548-1549) a similar register mentions thirteen or fourteen Jewish doctors and seventeen Muslim doctors. The official post of *Hekimbashi* (Chief Physician) was traditionally given to a Muslim, regardless of his professionasl qualifications. The positions and qualifications of his colleagues were reflected in their respective salaries.

His Jewish physicians accompanied the Sultan on all his trips, including the battlefront. The most famous of them were Joseph Hamon the Elder's son Moses, Tam Ebn Iahya and his son. Moses Hamon (born in 1590 died about 1565) was the physician of Sultan Süleyman. On account of his skill and manly, determined character, he enjoyed even higher influence and reputation than his father. Moses Hamon, in the mid-1530s was the highest paid Jewish doctor, he received 45 *aktches* (aspers) daily which was less than one half of the pay of the Muslim *Hekimbashi*. Twelve years later Hamon's salary had increased to 75 aspers as almost nearing the Hekimbashi's pay. In 1536-1537 Moses, although listed the fourth in the hierarchy of court physicians, received the highest salary. The other Jewish court physicians including Moses' son and other relatives, were paid much less, down to 8 aspers a day. Presumably these low paid physicians acted as assistants until they grew into maturity and secured higher posts on their own. The junior physicians resided at court where they were provided free housing, food and many services, so that they could lead a comfortable life with their families. Moses Hamon and family, on the other hand, occupied a large mansion in the Jewish quarter, probably because they preferred to live among their correligionists and close to their synagogue. It is likely that some of the court physicians were allowed to have a private practice in addition to their official duties.

Moses accompanied the Sultan on his War expeditions, and brought back from Persia, where he had followed Süleyman on a triumphal progress, a learned man, Jacob Tus or Tavs (about 1535) who translated the Pentateuch into Persian. This version accompanied by Chaldean [Aramaic (from Onkelos) and Arabic (from Saadia ha-Gaon) translations], was afterwards printed at Hamon's expense.

Moses Hamon's treatise on *Diseases of the Mouth* was the earliest essay on dentistry ever written in Turkey. It was composed not very long after the publication of a similar work in the West. Moses Hamon was an accomplished linguist, perfectly versed in Hebrew, Arabic, Turkish and Persian. He authored commentaries on the Pentateuch written in Persian. Among his most precious possessions was a manuscript of the first Greek Treatise on drugs by Pedenius Dioscorides, which already had been of great interest to Hasdai ibn Shaprute, a participant in its new Arabic translatiion in Tenth Century Cordoba.

Moses was a philanthropist on the pattern of his father. He maintained in his surroundings a plethora of scholars. A contemporary author, Salomon Athia, wrote about Moses Hamon: "In Constantinople Moses is very powerful under Sultan Soliman. This means that he has rendered eminent services which deserve to be mentioned and cited in every city, every family, for all times to come... He has assembled a group of scholars, and erected an academy; he had an edifice built for that purpose...There people continuously study. In addition, his charity towards his correligionaries is inexhaustible, and his intercession for them, is exerted every day, in such a way that he continually is their support and refuge. At the head of his academy are placed the very knowledgeable rabbi Joseph Tasitzk and the very estimaable rabbi Samuel Shakhan."

Moses Hamon was successful in persuading Süleyman to intervene on behalf of Dona Gracia, a Marrano, when, during her temporary stay in Venice, her entire property was threatened with confiscation because of her secret adherence to Judaism. Within a few years (in 1552) Gracia Mendes would arrive in Constantinople via Dubrovnilk and Salonica. She had previously had a remarkable career in Flanders, England, France and Venice. In Ferrara she had demonstrated her Jewish spirit through numerous benefactions to Jewish cultural efforts.

Dona Gracia Mendes was the Sephardi Grand Dame of Suleyman I's reign. She was the Biblical and Apocryphal Miriam, Deborah, Esther and Judith, all at once. Partly under her inspiration the poet Samuel Usque published his classical Portuguese volume *Consolaçoes as Tribulaçoes do Israel* (Consolations for the Tribulations of Israel). In his dedication Usque called Dona Gracia "the heart of our people". He also compared her with the ancient Jewish heroines, Miriam, Deborah, Esther and Judith. Her son-in-law Joseph Nasi (82) was to become the legendary Duke of Naxos.

As to Dona Gracia's protector, Moses Hamon, his medical ministrations received the praise of foreign visitors such as Nicolas Nicolay who had accompanied the French ambassador to Istanbul in 1551-1552. However, all the foreign comments about Jewish physicians in Turkey were not laudatory. A German observer, Hans Derschwam, on his journey through the Middle East (1552-1553), generally blamed these doctors for their unfamiliarity with Western medicine. Moses Hamon's downfall soon followed but his death may have come from palace intrigues which led to the temporary removal (1553) of the pro-Jewish Rüstem Pasha, the Sultan's son-in-law and grand vizier since 1544. All of this did not prevent Moses' son Joseph the Younger from continuing in the family tradition to serve as a physician at the courts of Süleyman I and his son Selim II. Joseph the Younger secured in 1560 the Sultan's renewal of the wide-ranging Privilege of Settlement applied for by the Salonica Community's delegation to the Ottoman capital. Like his father, Joseph also acted as the patron of Hebrew poets.

His son Isaac was to become a fourth genration court physician. Isaac's incorruptibility was recorded in connection with a Spanish envoy's futile effort to bribe him to intervene in favor of a truce between Spain and the Ottoman Empire.

Another of Soliman's physicians Tam Ebn Iahya, was a native of Portugal, who had come to Constantinople with his father the scholar David Ebn Iahya. The family had been known in Spain for the last six centuries before the Exile, through its vast lineage of poets, philosophers and philanthropists. It is probable that Solomon Ibn Gabirol (1021-1078) figures among the ancestors of this remarkable dynasty. Don David Salomon Ebn Iahya (1450-1504) renowned for his vast knowledge had been deprived of all his fortune for allegedly helping Marranos to reenter the realm of Judaism. He was highly versed in Moslem jurisprudence, advising Moslem judges in their most difficult cases. He authored numerous works but very few escaped the flames of a fire. His son, Jacob ben Yahya, called Tam (1465-1541), the ancestor of the Turkish branch of the Yahyas in Turkey, lived in Constantinople up to a very advanced age. He published in 1510 the *Josippon* or Pseudo-Joseph.

An illustrious family of Maecenas, the Yahyas gave very effective encouragement to the *belles lettres* and favored the development of numerous talents. In Turkey Tam was to rapidly rebuild the family fortune. Tam's son Guedalia, a physician by profession came to establish residency in Salonica towards the mid-fifteenth century (16). He used his vast resources to indiscriminately extend charitable help to Jew, Greek and Turk alike. Till his death in 1575 under Murad III's reign, his home remained the meeting point of scientists and men of letters. It is in his house that Amatus Lusitanus, escaping Italy had found asylum. Guedalia's two sons Moses and Tam II were to inherit an opulent patrimony.

The Spanish born Abraham ha-Levi Ebn Megas was another of Soliman's physicians. He also was a participant in military campains, accompanying to Syria Soliman's victorious army. He left beautiful memorabilia in arts and sciences. There is a letter from the Jewish community in Damascus, inviting him to settle there. Only one of Ebn Megas' works, a sort of travelogue of his peregrinations through the Orient, printed in Constantinople in 1585, has survived.

Abraham Nahmias was a contemporary physician in Constantinople, author of several medical treatises, two of which on hemoptysia and on cerebral fever were translated into Latin, and published in Venice in 1591 and 1604.

The most spectacular accomplishment of Jewish medicine in the sixteenth century consisted of the published work of the Salonica Hippocrates, Portuguese-born Amatus Lusitanus (Amato Lusitano, 16, 17), the author of the *Jewish-Sephardic Hippocratic Oath.* Jean Rodriguez by his real name he was born *ca.* 1510 in Castello-Bianco. As one of the *bona fide* physicians of all times his path brought him to Salamanca where he completed his studies and obtained the first prize. Amatus while in Salamanca was also trained in surgery which he practiced in the hospitals of that city. He continued his practice of surgery in Lisbon. He had already completed when he was sixteen a commentary on Dioscorides, greek physician from the time of Nero and author of *Materia Medica,* the source of therapeutic knowledge in the Christian and Moslem world for fifteen centuries. At the age of eighteen he started the writing of an important work in seven volumes, *The Centuries* or more exactly *Curatiom Medicinalium Centuriae Septem*, the elements of which he would continue collecting during his life full of movement. He recorded in it as they occurred the observations suggested by the practice of his medical art, noting for seven hundred medical and surgical cases, judiciously selected, the diagnostics, the clinical evolution, the symptoms and the most effective treatments. He composed the seven volumes which make *The Centuries* in the different cities where he lived: Ferrare (1533), Ragusa (1558), Salonica (1561) getting the books published one after another in Vienna, Lyon, Barcelona, Bordeaux, Paris, Frankfurt, depending on the occasional friendships and benefactors of the moment. Thus the different volumes are dedicated as it happened to the duke Cosmas of Medicis, the cardinal Hyppolyte d' Este, the ambassador of Portugal in Rome Alphonse de Lancastre, Don Joseph Nassi and the senators of Ragusa, Guedalia Yahya. *The Centuries* brought Amatus an immense reputation.

As early as 1532 Amatus did not feel safe any longer in Portugal. After escaping the Inquisition in the Iberian peninsula, he travelled through France, Holland and Italy, teaching in Ferrara, and retired to Ancona (a haven for Jews). During his peregrinations, Amatus took care in Venice of high ranking personalities, and he also made the acquaintance of Joseph Mandino (Salomon Molho's nemesis who persuaded Charles Quintus to let the Inquisition take care of him). Mandino was quite a celebrity in his time, as the translator of works in Arabic to Hebrew. Amatus maintained life-long cordial relations with him. Amatus had settled in Ancona in 1549. He was more interested in having an opportunity to practice the faith of his fathers, which he could do under Pope Jules III (1550-1555) whose physician he became. In the fall of 1555. his protector having died, the terrible Caraffa (Paul IV) ascended the the papal throne. Starting to feel unsafe despite his verbal return to Catholicism to assuage the furor of the Inquisition, Amatus first sent his wife to Salonica, and then came perilously close to be included in the group of Repentant Marranos being shipped to Malta for slave service on the galleys. Owing his escape to his celebrity, Amatus spent some time in Pesaro first, then Ragusa. While still in Italy, he received offers from the King of Poland and the Republic of Ragusa, even from Pope Paul IV who sought his medical services.

Towards 1559, Amatus finally joined his wife and settled in Salonica. He returned there to the open practice of Judaism, also adopting the family patronym of *Habip ha-Sefardi,* the Hebrew name equivalent to Amato. He came under the protection of Guedalia Ibn Yahya, poet and orator which should not be confused with his homonym the physician. Guedalia was the son of Jacob Tam, the ancestor of the Turkish branch of the Yahya. Amatus dedicated to his benefactor his seven *Centuries.* He survived his benefactor by one year only, passing away at the age of fifty-one. In Salonica, Amatus became a close friend of the physician and philosopher, Aron Afia, who became his daily companion. The very cultivated Marrano, Flavio Jacobo from Evora, also was a close companion.

In 1565 a great plague epidemic ravaged Salonica. Amatus' hippocratic principle was always to adhere to the most needy, to those in the greatest suffering, in total disregard of any risk to his person. Himself contaminated while caring for his patients, Amatus died in his host Yahya's house, victim of his professional dedication, on January 25, 1568, aged 51. An epitaph in Latin hexameters by his old friend, Pyrrho Lusitano (89), was inscribed on his grave: "Amato Lusitano, who has provided life to princes and kings, to the rich and to the poor, died far away from his country and rests in the land of Macedonia."

A sagacious and ingenious observer, Amatus had brought an important contribution to physiology and surgical medicine. Despite the prejudices of his time, he was one of the first to dissect human cadavers to develop the exact science of anatomy. Medical science owes him the discovery of the role of veinous valves and their function in blood circulation.

Amatus had composed in Salonica his own Hippocratic oath, called *the Physician's Oath* (08), and a reminder of Maimonides' Oath. The Oath could not be published in full in Christian Europe because it referred to an oath in the Ten Commandments and spoke of impartially serving all persons whatever their religious beliefs. Here is the uncensored Oath:

"I swear by God the Almighty and Eternal and by his most holy Ten Commandments given on Mount Sinai by the hand of Moses the Lawgiver, after the People of Israel had been freed from the bondage of Egypt that I have never in my medical practice departed from what has been handed down in good faith to us

and posterity; that I have never practiced deception. I have never overstated or made charges for the sake of gain; that I have praised no one, nor censured anyone, to indulge private interests, but only when the truth demanded it. If I speak of falsehood, may God and his Angel Raphael punish me with Their eternal wrath and may no one henceforth place trust in me. I have not been desirous for remuneration for my medical services and have treated many without accepting any fee, but with no less care. I have often unselfishly and firmly refused remuneration that was offered, preferring through diligent care to restore the patient to health, rather than be enriched by his generosity. I have given my services in equal manner to all, to Hebrews, Christians and Moslems. Loftiness of situation has never influenced me and I have accorded the same care to the poor as to those of exalted rank. I have never produced disease. In stating my opinion, I have always told what I believed to be true. I have favored no druggist unless he exceeded others in skill in his art and in character. In prescribing drugs I have exercised moderation, guided only by the physical condition of the invalid. I have never revealed a secret entrusted to me. I have never given a fatal dose. No woman has ever brought an abortion with my aid. Never have I been guilty of base conduct in a home which I entered for medical service. In short, I have done nothing which might be considered unbecoming an honorable and distinguished physician, having always held Hippocrates and Galen before me as examples worthy of imitation and not having scorned the precepts of many excellent practitioners of our art. I have been diligent and have allowed nothing to divert me from the study of good authors. I have endured the loss of private fortune, and have suffered frequent and dangerous journeys and even exile with calmness and unflagging courage, as befits a philosopher. The many students who have come to me have all been regarded as though they were my sons. I have used my best efforts to instruct them and urge them to good conduct. I have published my medical works, not to satisfy ambition, but that I might, in some measure, contribute to the furtherance of the health of mankind, I leave to others the judgement as to whether I have succeded; such at least has always been my aim and ever had the foremost place in my prayers.
    Given in Thessalonica in the year 5319 (1559)."

Amatus Lusitanus' major works published in Latin are in addition to *Curationum medicinalium centurias septem*:
1. Commentatio de introitu Medici ad aegrotantem.
2. De Crisi et Diebus decretrotoriis, Venice 1557.
3. In Dioscoridis Anazarbaei de materia Medica Libros V.
4. Enurationes eruditissimo, Venice 1553.

Amatus had encountered in Salonica a large number of highly esteemed physicians on whom he had exerted an enormous influence. Perahia ha-Cohen, the Italian who had died in 1548, had formed a "pléiade" (distinguished group) of disciples quite proficient in experimental methods. Specifically the lineage of Perahia remained famous. His two sons, Moses and Daniel (the latter dead in 1575, under Murad III), his grandsons and even his great grandsons formed a true dynasty dedicated to the medical art. Benjamin Halevy said about Salonica that its illustrious physicians formed above the city like "a crown of glory". The French traveler Nicolas de Nicolay noticing the considerable number of Jewish physicians in Salonica writes: "among them there are quite a few scholars in the theoretical and also well experienced in the practice." Another French traveler Belon writes: "It is easy for these practitioners to deeply dwell in the secrets of science, because independently from Hebrew works, they have the commodity of Greek and Arabic books which have been translated into their language, such as those of Hippocrates, Galenus, Avicenna, Almansour, Srapios and others. The Turkish authority holds Jewish physicians and druggists in very high esteem".

Plague hit Salonica in 1553. At the time of this catastrophy, the famous Joseph Caro was in Salonica and lost within a few days three of his children (18). In the following plague, Benjamin Halevi Eskenazi saw the death of a daughter and a son, mourned in a magnificent elegy preserved up to our times. The violent fire of 1543 destroyed some of most populous streets of Jewish Salonica,

Under Suleyman, Salonica also had a Jewish Tyrant, Kehaya Baruch, Communal Representative under the Ottoman authorities. Almost worse than the plagues and the fires, was the tyrannical and disastrous rule of Barouch which started in 1539. Barouch, a native of Portugal, arrived very young in Salonica with the first contingent of Marranos. He gained power by befriending the Turkish authorities, and became the supplier of the Turkish army in Macedonia. He cemented his acquired friendships by generous *peshkeshs* (presents). He obtained from the Turkish authorities the title of *kehaya* (Imperial Comissioner supervising the juridical relations of the Jews with the authority). In Salonica this function had been until the advent of Barouh a weak sinecure. Barouh was not satisfied. He wanted to use his title as a means to establish power over his correligionists. He proved tyrannical by interfering in the repartition of tax duty, favoring sycophants and his own cronies, penalizing those displeasing to him. He pretented that he was empowered to impose the nomination of spiritual leaders, the members of the communal council (*Maamad*) and salaried communal employees. He maintained a paid escort of ruffians to impose his rule and terrify any recalcitrants. He was seconded by a certain Elijah, as unscrupulous as his master. The Jewish market of Salonica was treated as if it was Barouh's private hunting and trading ground. Nobody could set up a counter at the *Kapan*, the central bazaar for the trade of food products without first obtaining an express authorization from Barouh.

Terror reigned in the Jewish quarter. The most venerated rabbis, the proudest notables trembled before him. Like a czar he pronounced his ukases. His corpulent, larger than real, figure loomed over and every one. A quartet of rabbis supported him, the most distinguished of them being Rabbi Ibn Hasson who had some credibility as a talmudist.

Rabbi Benjamin Halevi Eskenazi, the true spiritual leader of the Jewish community and the philanthropist David Benveniste decided to seek the help of Moses Amon, the powerful physician of Sultan Süleyman in Constantinople. First Amon tried to act on Barouh by persuasion and kindness. Then, he engaged Salonician friends to draw a complete act of accusations which would justify the launching of a *herem*.

Amon advised that Benjamin Halevi Eskenazi should threaten Barouch with the worst chastisement by the authority of the Sublime Porte, if he does not modify his conduct. He further advised: "Do not be frightened by the venom of the wicked...To violence, answer with violence. I will fight with all my strength to have justice triumph."

Upon Amon's request the Grand Vizier Rüstem Pasha ordered the *cadi* of Salonica to dispatch Barouch to Constantinople. Away from his center of power, Barouch felt a new kind of fear for the first time. In Constantinople, a highly angered Rüstem Pasha was speaking of no less than the death penalty. Out of compassion, Benjamin, the leader of the Salonica delegation having asked Amon to intercede for a pardon, the *Kehaya* was able to leave for Salonica with all his following.

Barouh once in Salonica became his same old self as he rapidly regained his basis of power. The Grand Vizier sent a commission of inquiry to Salonica consisting of a *cadi* (judge) and a *tchaouch* (uniformed official messenger). The members of the imperial commission of inquiry were skillfully circumvented by Barouh and his friends in high places. He ended up exonerated and even more arrogant.

Finally Barouh met an opponent of his own class in the person of rabbi Joseph, son of David ben Lev, physically a shrimp of a man, quite small and frail, but a giant in intellect, will power and devotion to truth. Joseph ben Lev responded to the attempts to ridicule him with the energy of a lion. Barouh's supporter Rabbi Ibn Hasson, in violation of rabbinical ethics, entered the *yeshiva* room in which, Joseph ben Lev was in full exercise of his teaching, and he pronounced against him the formula of malediction and *herem*.

An even graver offense took place when Barouh encountered Joseph Ben Lev in the midst of the market, in front of the rich apothecary shop of Abraham Catalano. After violent reproaches, ultimate outrage, Barouch slapped the respected scholar in the face. None of the stunned crowd dared to intervene. Joseph ben Lev uttered: "Grieve, O Skies, at this spectacle; if the men did not punish this brainless, may God take care of it and accomplish His works."

The news reached Constantinople with lightning speed, but at that point the course of events drew attention to more pressing emergencies. An epidemic of plague started, followed by the great fire of Salonica. In the midst of the catastrophies Barouch seems to have vanished. During the plague epidemic Joseph ben Lev had sought refuge with his family in a remote village out of Salonica. Barouch's supporters assassinated his son, a promising young rabbi of twenty-eight, in an ambush. Joseph ben Lev unable to find any safe corner in Salonica moved to Constantinople where he was taken under the protection of Amon who warmly recommended him to Dona Gracia. She arranged the creation for him of a well endowed *yeshiva* and confided to him its rectorate.

In the night of July 13, 1545 (4 Av 5305) came the great fire. It started in the Apothecary shop of Abraham Catalano, precisely at the site in front of which the brutal outrage of Barouh to the person of Joseph ben Lev had taken place. Later in the popular legend, it would be said that the incident of the "slap in the face" had taken place on the eve of the great fire. Thus, the divine punishment and the expiation had very quickly followed the supreme outrage of the malefactor. In the night from Sunday to Monday, the apothecary Abraham Catalano, lamp in hand was chasing a mouse which had been running among his drugs. He accidentally fell, the contents of the lamp pouring around on poultices, resins and other inflammable substances filling hia apothecary shop. The fire activated by the winds of the Vardar which were frenetically blowing and by the summer drought rapidly spread. Within six hours more then five thousand houses and eighteen synagogues had disappeared. The seminars, the rich libraries full of manuscripts and printed collections, among others those of Don Sameuel Benveniste, Ovadia Alconstantini, Don Juan Senor Benveniste were all in ashes. "*Dies irae* (The divine anger) is unleashed against this population" exclaimed the chronicler Joseph ha-Cohen. Salonica had turned into Sodom and Gomorrha. Benjamin Halevi Eskenazi wrote an elegy which was incorporated into the ritual of the Ashkenazis and which it was customary to recite, in a tone of complaint, on the 9 Av of each year: "Innumerable misfortunes, are drawing screams of pain in Salonica. This city, the elegant adornment of the country...had welcomed scholars who made additions to the Talmud and who were skillful in resolving the thoughest problems. The Torah was like pouring out of this city..The abundance was fully flowing around, in peace and security...Those that have fallen were proud like poplars. And, us, the survivors, the poor remnants, we are from now on condemned to the ruin, without guides, leaders and priests. Our lodgings and our riches have perished, and we are wandering without resideence, and without fortune, without clothes and foodstuffs."

Salonica finally learned to live again. The commerce recommenced to flourish. The Jewish merchants in Salonica afar held the reins of commerce in the Aegean and the Balkans. The architect of the recovery of Salonica was Benjamin Halevi Ashkenazi, who belonged to an illustrious lineage of rabbis. His father fleeing Germany, resided successively in Nicopolis, Plevna and Sofia. During a stay in Istanbul Benjamin Halevi had gained the friendship of Amon. He settled in Salonica in 1530, and assumed the spiritual leadership of the Ashkenazite synagogue. In 1555 he lovingly got the *Mahzor* (festival prayer book) of the Ashkenazite community published, at his own expense, with excellent lexicographic clarifications. Benjamin accomplished the prodigy of being the Ashkenazite codifier of the Sephardic communities. He died towards 1560 still during the reign of Süleyman I.

The Turkish Judaism felt secure enough under Ottoman rule to enter the game of international politics on a grand scale, when the Ottoman Jews launched the boycott of Ancona (18). For a long time Ancona had been an independent republic. In 1532, it was incorporated into the Papal States. Its harbor, located in between two promontories, was one of the safest in the Adriatic. Ancona was a formidable competitor for Salonica and the Republic of Saint Mark (Venice). Merchandise from all parts of the world were to be found there, including all the goods of exchange coming from Turkish locations, such as grain, hemp, hides, varnished leather, silk products, oil, soup, cables and leather straps. In exchange for these goods arriving from Turkey, the traders from Constantinople would acquire the excellent drapes of the region, much coveited by the wealthy classes, specially in Macedonia.

Starting from the highest antiquity the city of Ancona had always had a Jewish community. From the mid-fifteenth century on a large number of Jews from Salonica and other cities under Turkish rule had established residence in Ancona for business purposes. The Marranos arrived in 1540 had received express authorization to openly practice their Judaism. They had remained under the protection of Popes Clement VII (1523-1534), Paul III (1534-1549) and Jules III (1550-1555). The powerful banking and high level trading enterprise of the Nassi family was represented in Ancona by the Marrano Joseph Morro, who had under his control large warehouses always filled with stores of merchandise, all for the account of the central house in Constantinople. Together with their Levantine correligionists and conationals, the numerous Jews of Salonica, were the true arbiters of Ancona's fortune. Some of these Jews, by force of habit or true conviction had preferred to remain Catholics or reintegrate Catholicism, leaving around the most intricate matrimonial or successorial complications.

Ancona suddenly moved from prosperity to martyrdom with the rise to the pontifical throne of the notorious fanatic and rabble rouser Jean Pierre Caraffa, already eighty, under the name of Paul IV. For the new Pope heresy was really *la bête noire* (the black beast) to be fought everywhere, at all costs, by all means. Under Paul IV's leadership the Holy Office of the Inquisition gained a tremendous momentum and the Talmud went into the fire by carriage loads. This was the year 1555. The rabbis, remembering that Caraffa was, together with Gaetan de Thiene, the founder of the order of the *Theatins,* drew enjoyment by calling him *Theatin.* The *Gematria*, their science of numerology told them that the name *Theatin* and the name *Haman* in the Book of Esther, had the same numerical value: 95.

Paul IV, was set on the "Annihilation of the Jews of Ancona". Marranos were specially targeted. Even some of the Jews with Ottoman citizenship were despoiled of their fortune. Twenty four men and one woman, recognized as uncurable cases of "Relapse into Judaism" were turned in to the secular arm of the Inquisition for retribution. The trial of the "Relapses" lasted several months, judges and their henchmen unsparingly submitting their victims to the horrors of the ordinary and extraordinary questioning. At the instigation of Dona Gracia Mendes and her son-in-law Don Joseph Nassi, on March 1556 Sultan Süleyman I dispatched a threatening message To Paul IV, who was nothing more than small fry in the eyes of the Ottoman sovereign. Süleyman asked for the immediate release of all Jewish Ottoman subjects detained in jail, and for the immediate restitution of all their goods, under the threat of extermination of the Christians within his Empire.

The letter of Süleyman was followed by Dona Gracia's emissaries, with the additional notice that if prompt satisfaction was not given, their masters and all the traders of Turkey would enter in a league to launch the boycott of Ancona. Written in March the Sultan's letter would not reach ther Pope's hands before mid-May. By that time the pyres were blazing; already a month earlier, of the twenty-five condemned, thirteen had been delivered to the flames from April 13 to 16, in a spectacular celebration drawing crowds of thousands who had come from all over Italy to join the local populace. The famed plaza, Campo della Mostra, had been totally cleared as the theater for the macabre drama.

When the Sultan's letter reached him Pope Paul had a full political and diplomatic crisis blowing in his face. As the Commander of the Faithful, Süleyman I, Caliph and Sultan, was the much sought arbiter of the European Kings and Princes, every sovereign going after his alliance. On the other hand, alarmed by Dona Gracia's threat of boycott, the Senate of Ancona was imploring the Pope to take into consideration the city's economic interests. Pope IV wrote in June a cautious and amiable letter. He drew a line between Levantine Jews, protegees of the Sultan and the Portuguese Marranos. The former were all set free and their property was returned to them. The Portuguese Marranos were considered unrepentant relapses liable to receive the death penalty. As to Jacob Morro, the agent of the Nassis, he was a Marrano hardened in the error, an inveterate Relapse. Thus Paul IV with deep regret could not pardon him. In what concerns the goods administered by Morro they would be restituted in the hands of the new representatives.

Just to get over with all the possibilities of new troublesome interventions, the last twelve survivors were divided into groups, and on the days of Monday June 15, and Saturday June 20, they were brought to Campo della Mostra, hanged and thrown on the pyre. The memory of the twenty-five martyrs would be perpetuated for centuries, in an elegy written by a local poet Jacob de Fano.

The hecatomb of Ancona plunged the Jewish community of Turkey into consternation. The Marranos all over were thirsting for revenge. The most militant of them were in Pesaro, a locality on the Adriatic shore, located on the road from Ancona to Bologna. For half a century, Pesaro was under the sovereignty of the dukes della Rovera d' Urbino. These Renaissance dukes had made of Pesaro one of the literary centers of Italy. The reigning duke Guidubaldo had extended a joyful welcome to the refugees of Ancona. In the vengeful Marrano minds, the idea was born to divert the maritime traffic from Satanic Ancona to Angelic Pesaro. Guidubaldo enthusiastically proclaimed Pesaro a free port. Pesaro was a narrow harbor, poorly protected. It did not present all the extraordinary advantages and facilities of Ancona. Guidubaldo was prepared to decree the agrandizement of the Pesaro harbor and he planned to have built a massive structure laid in the sea as a pier or breakwater to protect the enlarged port.

The last flames of Ancona had not been extinguished for more than two weeks when Faradj, the delegate of Pesaro Jews, stopped in Salonica. He gave his message at the Talmud Tora before a huge crowd. He spoke about the martyrs of Ancona: these men and women who the rope around their neck, face to the hanging pole, face to the pyre, had professed with all their strength their eternal credo *Shema Israel!* (Listen Israel!). The moment had come that the victims must strike their executioners at the vulnerable spot of their armor.

In haste, the federated council of Salonica prepared an *ascama* proclaiming the *herem* against Ancona. With considerable enthusiasm all the Salonica shipowners issued the required orders making sure that Ancona would not receive even one ounce from their shipments destined to Italy. The resolution was urgently communicated to all parts of Turkey, Constantinople, Bursa, Adrianople as well as to the Morea, and even to the smallest localities under the Sultan's rule where Jews would be living.

From one day to the next Ancona was deserted. The Pesaro proposal delighted Dona Gracia. She ordered her Agents to move to Pesaro. Despite all the initial enthusiasm for the economic boycott, after the emotions started to cool more sobering considerations came forward. Ancona had become a cursed and criminal city, but this did not stop her from having everything needed for an international harbor, port security, the required commercial and building installations, the complete network of correspondents and excellent credit facilities which made transactions smooth. Compared to all of this, Pesaro was nothing more than a desolate, almost worthless, second rate port with negligible maritime traffic. In afterthought, many merchants realized that they had considerable business interests in Ancona. They had made a first try at Pesaro but they were not satisfied. The cargos discharged in this port had remained unsold. Furthermore the Pesaro bay was quite unsatisfactory in itself, was often inapproachable, and the accidents, disasters which had taken place were of such a nature to shake the will of the best intentioned. The Duke of Urbino was still holding to his promise of having the harbor improved, but the completion of the works, was still a long way ahead, and in the meantime who was to guarantee the cargoes and the ships.

The strongest opposition came from localities which did not have Marranos. such as Bursa and even the Constantinople traders' support for the boycott was wavering.

As the Jews of Ancona were threatened in their livelihood and existence, their old and venerated rabbi Moses Bourasssa, who enjoyed considerable prestige wrote a compelling letter to his correligionists in Salonica. He expressed the view that even if the boycott of Ancona were abandoned the Jews of Pesaro were in no danger of reprisal from the Duke Giudubaldo. The latter was known as an enlightened and generous prince, and the hospitality he had extended to the Marranos had solely been on humanitarian grounds. The matter was quite different with the Pope. Infuriated by the ostracization of Ancona he would not hesitate to exterminate all the Jews of the Papal states. Bourassa was asking in consequence the immediate ceasing of the boycott.

Copies of Bourassa's letter had reached many Jewish communities. In Constantinople the community had become polarized. On one side were the supporters of the boycott ardently propounded by Dona Gracia and Joseph Nassi, on the other hand the anti-boycott dissidents primarily led by the spiritual leaders of the Italiots and Ashkenaze communities. The duel between the pro-boycott party and the dissenters was now to assume epic proportions.

With the Constantinople rabbinate divided, the Nassis did not abandon their commitment to the boycott. Moved by their vindictiveness above other considerations Dona Gracia and Joseph Nasi tried to obtain the sanctioning of *herem* from the rabbinical authorities of Safed. Joseph Caro and Moses Mitrani did not come forward and pursued a delaying and holding tactic, avoiding to make a clear pronouncement. The waverings in Constantinople and the reticence of Safed further reinforced the pro-Ancona camp. There was however one person who would not give in: Dona Gracia. She kept writing to all important communities. She went on promising that soon the new facilities of Pesaro would be operative. It seems that, moved by her passion, Dona Gracia was somehow losing touch with reality.

For two more years a large number of traders remained faithful to their first impulse. As resolute as ever Joseph Nassi tried to mobilize financial resources in favor of the Duke of Urbino to help him in the construction of the projected mole. Then, the adversaries of Pesaro brought to the public knowledge that contrary to what had been said before, the hatred of Jews was hereditary in the della Rovera family to which the duke belonged. His father, the first to have borne the title of Duke of Urbino, by the will of the Pope, was a Jew-hater. The same could be said about the actual duke. It was now reported that in 1552 he had allowed the populace to plunder the synagogue of Pesaro. He did not hide the repulsion he felt for the Marranos whom he considered worse than the plague. In short he made the figure of a sad sire, pusillanimous, prodigal, depraved and cruel. One could not be sure that in a fit of drunkness he would not deliver the Jews to the plebe, just on a whim or by any fantasy.

As progress in the renovation of the port was not apparent, the anti-Ancona league started to falter and disintegrate. The Jews of Pesaro wondered if they had not gone too far in their commitment. Soon the communal chest was empty, the last resources of the Jews of Pesaro having been exhausted in support of their correligionists from Ancona. Finally, two years had passed. The boycott was by now obviously useless, a failure. The Duke was starting to get bitter and restless with the failure of the subscription launched by Nassi. In the meantime he had on his hands an undesirable demographic problem. The Ancona Jews had been followed in the haven of the dukedom by masses of Marranos. Duke Giudubaldo was getting reproaches from the papal delegate on account of his culpable hospitality for all these unwanted Jews. The Duke yearned to get rid of it all. He decreed for June 9, 1558 the expulsion of all the Marranos. Many of the Jews of Pesaro ended in Turkey. Thus came the final act in the cycle of events started by the Boycott of Ancona.

Salonica's Jewish community had its uneasy contacts with the *Togar* (Turks). The leadership of Salonica had to take measures on an extremely delicate matter, the relationship with the Turks (19), which the Jews called the *Togar*. Contacts with the average Turk, the workers, the craftsman were rare. The Turk that the Jew the most often saw was the official who presented himself with the attributes of strength and power to impose tribute and ransom. This breed was of course the worst, far from being a majority, but the most visible. Such Turks could be accommodated with the appropriate *peshkesh* (bribe), but their tolerance for the *ghiaour* (non-Moslem) was nothing more than a disguised disdain. The specific Jew_taxes and the accompanying extorsion were imbedded in a system of government. It always was with unmitigated terror and concern that a Jew would meet the local *agha* or *cadi*. Any functionary who had a morsel of authority would use it to grab from the unfortunate Jew as much as he could. The Jews would tell themselves quietly: "*El hecho esta a la Puerta* (the business is at the Sublime Porte. *i.e.* in the hands of the State); this was a familiar local expression meaning that the business had taken a very alarming form and risked to become a source of troubles and calamities.

The average Turk was kindly and hard working. He was endowed with some of the best virtues, including frugality [surviving on yoghourt and onions (*cebollas*)]. Thus a common Sephardic dictum: "*cebolla dulce non hay* (there is no sweet onion, no sweet Turk)." Yet despite the dictum, it was a supreme injustice to say "There are no sweet Turks".

Moses Almosnino the *Marbitz Tora* of the Catalan synagogue, took action after mature meditation on the subject. On Wednesday November 3 1558 (9 Tevat 5318), all the religious and secular leaders of the Salonica Jewish community were invited at the Catalan synagogue. The plenary assembly promulgated an *ascama* law in which the formidable *herem* (excommunication tacitly implying the death penalty) was decreed against all those who under whatever pretense, would have recourse to Ottoman courts for litigation between the Jews on inheritance matters, on matrimonial matters or anything else. All litigations must be regulated according to Mosaic law, and it is a forfeiture of religious duties to attempt resolving these through Islamic legislation. The *herem* strikes not only the plaintiff, but also anyone assisting this party as witness.

Under Suleyman I, Ottoman Judaism twice experienced the nightmare of a blood libel. In 1561, a threatening matter had been the revival of the old myth of Jewish ritual murder (20). Curiously, the two blood libels recorded in the sixteenth century occurred in two Anatolian localities where the small Jewish presence had generally evoked few hostile reactions. Galante (21) reports: "A poor Armenian of Amasia who was in the habit of visiting Jewish houses, was sent away from the city by his correligionists; the Armenian women gave testimony before the *cadi* (judge) to the effect that he had been slaughtered by the Jews for their religious need, to make use of his blood for their unleavened bread on Passover. Under torture, some Jews confessed to the crime and were hanged; the physician Jacob Avayoub was burnt at the stake in the center of the city. Shortly after, the supposed-victim returned to the city and confessed that he had been sent away as part of a conspiracy. When Süleyman was informed of the matter, he ordered the punishment of the guilty, and they suffered the same fate as the innocent Jews. Some time later a similar slander was launched in Tokat and the slanderers were punished. Then, the Jewish community of Tokat addressed itself to Moses Hamon, chief physician of Süleyman the Magnificent, to demand protection. Rüstem Pasha, Grand-Vizier at that time, ordered the publication of a *firman* (imperial decree) issued by the Sultan, by the terms of which, any legal proceedings related to this slander could not be judged by the courts, but had to be referred directly to the head of the State. This *firman* was however lost (22).

As if the blood libels were not enough, Ottoman Judaism almost had to relive again the story of Esther in the Bible, with a new Haman at the Grand-Vizierate. During Süleyman's reign, his primary favorite and Grand Vizier Ibrahim Pasha assumed the role of Haman in Jewish history (23). Of Greek ancestry he harbored a deep-rooted anti-Jewish feeling. He was the Sultan's confident and intimate friend. He is the object of a legendary tale, circulated among the Jewish community, but there is no historical confirmation. Ibrahim Pasha tried to overcome by an artifice the Sultan's staunch resistance to the idea of expelling the Jews from the country. He arranged for a secret underground tunnel to be dug from his quarters to the Imperial bedchamber. On three successive nights he impersonated the prophet Mohammed and in the Messenger's alleged voice exhorted Süleyman to put an end to the Jewish people, Islam's inveterate enemy. Moise Hamon learned of the plot, the cabal was detected and the Grand Vizier was executed.

The actual motives of Ibrahim Pasha's disgrace and execution are more prosaic. First he had by various blunders provoked the hatred of Süleyman's favorite wife the Venetian Hürrem (Khurrem) Sultan (Roxalana). Swollen by vanity and arrogance, he had come to imagine that he could replace Süleyman on the throne. In 1536 at the conclusion of a banquet he was abandoned to the Sultan's deaf mute eunuch executioners, who tightened around his neck the customary thin but very lethal thread made of horse hair.

Again under Suleyman I, the Grand Rabbinate of Salonica experienced a constitutional crisis. The Grand Rabbi Elijah Mizrahi had acceeded to his function with the official confirmation of Sultan Beyazid II called *berat*. At his death, the Romaniots, the most ancient community of Constantinople were not prepared to accept the supremacy of the Sephardim (24). The rabbis of Istanbul opted for the choice as temporary *locum tenens* of rabbi Tam ben Yahya, a native of Portugal and court physician.

There is also the strange story of a French aristocrat in search of Biblical roots. At the time of Süleyman I, a French aristocrat by the name of Rouerie (25), the owner of at least three castles around Lyon, left with his two sons for Venice, where all three converted to the Mosaic faith. He later on came to Constantinople, where he was received by Joseph Nassi with all the due honors and consideration. However some unscrupulous Jews of Constantinople succeeded in embezzling from the all too trusting French nobleman. This did not affect his aim of adopting Judaism. French merchants in the Ottoman capital were at loss to understand how Rouerie could have come to share the fate of a people who had so abused him. Philosophically Rouerie answered: "I did not come to reach for the Hebrews, but rather for the God of the Hebrews and their Law."

With Selim I's conquest of the Mamluk Sultanate, gone was the last remnant of the Abbasid Caliphate, when its last representative in Cairo, Caliph Mutavakkil, was abruptly deposed by Selim and carried in exile to Constantinole. With the Caliph gone also was the office of last *Naguid* (Jewish supreme ruler in Egypt). But while the Caliph was irreversibly gone, the *Naguid* Rabbi David ben Shelomo ibn abi Zimra continued to function *de facto* until he decided to move to Jerusalem. Ibn Zimra, a native of the Kingdom of Castille (possibly from the city of Zamora) most likely born in 1479, arrived in Egypt shortly before 1514 (26). His family reached back Spanish Jewish memories as far as the thirteenth century. R. David ibn Zimra was one of the most commanding Jewish personalities of the sixteenth century in Egypt and Palestine. As his fame reached throughout the huge hinterland of Turkish-controlled territory, R. Zimri's *responsa* (commentaries in responses to addressed questions) provide a detailed social, economic and cultural study of Jewish life in the Ottoman Empire. He was hailed as the *Me'or Ha-Gola* (Light of the Exile) and as the *Mer Israel* (Light of Israel). R. Samuel Ha-Levi of Rhodes offers an appraisal of R. David's influence and place in his own day: "Now that the Lord has expanded the boundaries of the Exile and given unto us in the Empire of Turkey a refuge and remnant, He...sent unto us...this man of God, a offspring of the branch of wisdom and Torah, a twig from he roots of humility and holiness, a touch-stone and foundation stone..."

Rabbi Isaac Aqrish a scholar of note and a widely traveled man, having lived ten years in R. David's home, wrote after the latter's death and in anticipation of his own death: "Upon my coming to Egypt, which is a veritable Garden of the Lord for the Torah...There stood that great eagle (*i.e.* David ibn Zimra)...Upon his head were three crowns: the crown of noble lineage, the crown of the Torah...and above all three, the crown of fame...His countenance was like unto that of a lion, 'the lion that roared', who will not fear (Amos 3.8)."

R. Abraham Ha-Levi (114), in his volume of Responsa, *Givat Veradim* states that "in Egypt it was the practice to make according to R. David even if he contradicted Maimonides." For centuries in the heart of the Jewish Quarter of Cairo stood the "Synagogue of R. David ibn Zimra".

In Elul 1514 Zimra became a member of the highest Jewish juridical body, at the Beth-Din of the *Naguid* (Jewish supreme ruler in the Mamluk Sultanate of Egypt, Syria and Palestine) R. Isaac Solal. Ruled from the *Naguid's* siege in Cairo, Jerusalem's Jewish community had to follow suit. In 1517 when Selim I entered Cairo he abolished the office of the *Naguid.*

R. David was soon designated Chief Rabbi of the Jewish community of Cairo where he remained until 1533. In 1527 he pacified the recurrent conflicts arising between the *Musta'arabi* (native Jews) and *Mougrabi* (Western Jews from Spain and Morocco) living in Cairo. Another conflict between Sephardim and *Musta'arabi* on whether the Eighteen benedictions should be recited at public worship by the Reader only or by the congregation also was resolved by Zimra through a Solomonic judgement. R. David established the practice of having the congregation recite these prayers silently and having the Reader repeat them aloud. He further introduced calendar reform, a touchy issue between Karaite and Rabbanite Jews, consecrating the already accepted mode of reckoning from the Creation. R. Zimra was against the Jews adopting the epicurean lifestyle of the host country. He abolished the practice of having non-Jewish female entertainers (belly dancers) at weddings and other festive occasions. Sardanapalesque banqets were not part of the Jewish lore.

From Salonica came questions as to whether a Rabbi can compel his students to take an oath not to study with another teacher, or on who should succeed the Rabbi in the Congregation of Aragon. R. David writes in his notes: "Since my arrival over here (*i.e.* Cairo) so many documents from Safed written both by teachers and students arrive to me." From Damascus a student Gabriel Elijah sought clarification on several passages in Maimonides. From Tripoli a question was whether Jewish communal leaders were justified in their attempt to tax importers of silk and clothing in order to provide for the poor. Even Venice was on the hotline to R. Zimri with questions on the settlement of a will made out by Gentile notaries and attended by Gentile witnesses. R. David's opinions also held strong influence on the islands of Rhodes and Candia.

R. David on one occasion wrote: "I am so occupied with the burden of government affairs...". Even with the abolishing of the office of the *Nagui*, he was still the official representative of the Jews of Egypt. The situation became critical in 1529, when the Pasha of Egypt, Ahmed Sheitan, attempted to sever Egypt from the Ottoman Empire. Not getting support from the Jews he vented his rage on them by filling the jails of Cairo. Even if their Sultanate had vanished the Mamluks were still present. At the instigation of the Pasha they went rampaging and plundering in the Jewish quarter. Ahmed Sheitan further resorted to extorsion threatening by death the entire Jewish community unless an exorbitant sum was rapidly delivered to him. However, the Sultan's executioners were on the way. Ahmed Sheitan was betrayed, captured and summarily beheaded. With the Egyptian Haman gone, the Jews instituted the festival of the **Pourim' al-Mitsrayim** {the Egyptian Pourim).

Despite his forty years in Egypt, R. David wrote:

"It is the intention of all of us to return and to dwell in Eretz Israel for it is only on this ground that we permit ourselves to dwell in Egypt: for otherwise we would be violating the statement of the Torah 'Thou shall no more return by this way' (Deut. 17:6) for we are not to permanenly settle in Egypt but to dwell here temporarily and as soon as we will be able we shall go to Eretz Israel." Years later he explains why he delayed so long settling in Israel: "settling in Israel is very difficult. Who can live there without having to turn to others for relief?"

When he came to Jerusalem R. David was a man of great fame and fortune. The Jerusalem Jews invited him to become their Rabbi and Judge. He consented on the condition that he should not receive a salary. Accepting a salary would put him in an official rabbinical position to which the local Turkish authority would have objection and which would expose him to fine and punishment. He was thereupon given by the Jewish community an agreement duly signed by a number of Jewish representatives stating: "that he shall be their leader and Judge, that he shall judge and arbitrate in all matters... that should any loss, damage or expenditure be brought upon him for ny reason...they hold themselves fully responsible to make full restitution."

When on one occasion, R. David wanted to punish several transgressors, they went to government officials and informed them against R. David saying that he was in reality the Judge over the Jews: they also hinted at his considerable wealth. The chief government official questioned R. David as to whether he had a permit from the Sultan to act as leader of the Jewish community. Of course he had none. Twice, he was questioned and dismissed. The third time he was brought in chains. The government official spoke very harshly: "Who appointed you Judge over the Jews? If you are a leader of the Jewish community, then why haven't you called on me to pay your respects, as do all the heads of religious communities? One was then exposed to the irreverent spectacle of the venerable Rabbi dragged away by his beard and submitted to a bastinado with rods of wood. He was further threatened that his beard would be shaven and that he would be dragged through the streets of the city. It was however possible to mollify the irate official bent on extorsion, by recourse to considerable bribes.

R. David returned home grief stricken, but when he tried to obtain compensation for his financial losses, based in the agreemet signed by the leaders of the Jewish community, the Jewish communal leaders of Jerusalem reneged on their word. The rabbis of Safed were consulted. They fully sustained R. David's claim, but to no avail. R. Aqrish writes: "R. David's heart could no longer endure this evil. He therefore said to himself: "It is better to dwell in a corner of the housetop, than in a house in common with a contentious woman" (115). He therefore went to Safed.

In the mystical climate of Safed the legend had grown that the prophet Elijah appeared to R. David in Safed. He lived here to a very old age. On one occassion he writes: "For hoary age and advanced years have been sprinkled upon me." Some time in the early summer of 1573, he was called to the Academy on High aged 94 years. In 1742, a Jewish traveler to Safed noted that in Safed he saw "a cave filled with the graves of Tannaim whose names were not known; and in the entrance of the cave were the graves of R. R. David ibn Zimra, R. Moses di Trani and the author of *Darke No-am* (R. Mordecai Ha-Levi) of blessed memory."

Among the Kabbalistic works of R. David *Magen David* (Shield of David) is a mystical explnation of the alphabet. In another Kabbalistic work **Migdal David** (The Tower of David) R. David tells us: "In the days of my youth I wrote a book on the alphabet entitled *Magen David*." One other Kabbalistic work, the Bulwark of David, gives reasons for the 613 Commandments according to the four methods of explanation known as *Pardes* (Orchard). The *Migdal David* is composed of Kabbalistic homilies on the Song of Songs.

R. David was fond of poetry from the days of his youth but with advancing years he felt compelled to abandon it. He himself writes in poetic form: "It is a long time now since I have abandoned both the old and the new forms of fashioning Songs and Metaphors..." R. David's most famous poem is *Keter Malkouth* (the Crown of Royalty). It is a *Piyyout* (liturgical poem) for the Day of Atonement, and it is modeled after the famous poem of that name by Solomon Ibn Gabirol.

Even though the monogamous enactment of R. Gershom (960-1040) had been promulgated five hundred years before, polygamy was widely practiced among the

Jews of Northern Africa, Palestine and Turkey in the early part of the Sixtenth Century. The Responsa of R. David record many cases where men had two or even three wives, usually with a different residence and maid servants for each wife, when the husband was wealthy enough to be able to afford it.

R. David declares: "The Enactment of R. Gershom has not spread to our lands. I do not think it to be the prevailing practice in our midst. " But coexisting with polygamy there was also a growing tendency toward monogamy. It became the universal rule to have all *Ketuboth* (marriage contracts, marriage documents) contain the clause that he was not to take another wife during the lifetime of his first wife. Some Jewish women could not get their husbands to take vows of absolute monogamy, but they made them vow that if they wanted to take a second wife, they would not do so without the first wife's consent. In one instance such consent was purchased from the first wife at the cost of one hundred pieces of gold. The men who practiced monogamy were called "the men who acccepted the enactment of R. Gershom". They could be released from their oath in the case of the wife's sterility after ten years.

R. David had to rule in the case of "the rebellious woman" who refused her husband his conjugal rights. He advised that she should first be appeased and warned, and if she is still rebelling, her husband should be permitted to break his vow and remarry. About monogamy R. David made the following statement: "I do not consider this an established *Minhag* (Custom, Observance). Go and see how many men marry two wives and you readily will ascertain this fact. Further, because monogamy is not an established custom, they have to write this clause into the *Ketubba*. And there are many men who do not wish to accept this clause..."

The conquest of Rhodes

At the beginning of the sixteenth century, the Island of Rhodes was in the possession of the Christian Kights of St. John of Jerusalem. On June 10, 1522 (27) the Ottoman fleet, an armada of 300 vessels left the harbor of Istanbul with the course set for Rhodes. On August 1, the Knights' last stronghold in the Aegean was heavily surrounded. After two failed assaults, a third assault was started on September 13. A Jewish physician attempted to use an arrow to send a letter to the Turks. He was caught at the very moment and immediately torn to pieces. By December 21, the Grand Master was ready to surrender. On Christmas morning the *müezzin* (Moslem cleric) was calling to prayer the faithful from the bellfry of the Church of St. John. Ottoman music accompanied by drums was played from the Tower of St Nicholas.

The fall of Rhodes, was for the local Jews who had suffered persecution under the rule of the Knights, a blessed event. It is stated (28) that: "The Rhodian citizens, on becoming the Sultan's subjects, were to be allowed the free exercise of their religion...and no tribute was required from the island for five years..We learn from the Turkish rabbinical writer Benjamin Pontremoli that Süleyman was especially favorable to the Jews in many ways.

Most of the Jews lived in a quarter segregated from the non-Jews, with part of the Jewish section near the wharves and the shopping district. They were connected with the flourishing import and export business of the Island. The Jews were also largely engaged in the clothing industry and some were in the spice business. R. David denounced the practice of the Jews who were lending money at a fixed interest rate (*e.g.* 14%). Some Jews owned vineyards and other property.

The Jewish tax-farmers broke one night into the house of R. Juda Apomado, member of a distinguished family and a prominent man of the Jewish community. The intruders beat R. Judah Mercilessly, an act which incensed the community and brought from the *Parnas* (Notable of the community) R. Abrahem Mir a demand for their excommunication. With an over-confidence swollen by their influence in government circles, the tax-farmers went to the *Parnas* asking him not to put a *herem* on them. The *Dayyanim* (Judges) of Rhodes referred the case to R. David ibn Zimri, who wrote: "And it is clear that they are subject to so severe a punishment that it is even impssible to describe it. And I doubt if their sin will be forgiven them until the day of their death. Granted that he (R. Judah Apomado) can forgive them for the pain and loss of money, but who can ever forgive them for playing the part of informers?" R. David concluded that these evil-doers must first beg forgiveness from R. Judah and unless they do so he will excommunicate them with the greatest severity, and "even then, they will have to expiate their sins by deeds of repentance."

The microcosmos of Rhodes, provides some ideas about different modes of Jewish communal self-government. At one time the Jewish community of Rhodes was ruled by an autocratic leader. Disenchanted the Jews of Rhodes adopted a *Haskama* (communal Agreement) "that no Jew, shall ever be the leader of the community or any part of it, but instead that three *Parnasim* (notables) should be elected, that all matters should be decided and enacted by them and that no one should assume the right to depart from these decisions, unless by permissioon of the *Parnasim* and if a government official should want to put a *Kehaya* (Jewish Chief connected to the Ottoman authority) over them, that they should try with all their might that the will and agreement of the Community may prevail..." However, a Jew who had contact with the Government officials got the powerless (before the Turkish officials) *Parnassim* to declare him *Kehaya* and the *sole Parnas*! More exactly, he was *Kehaya* to the Government officials and *Parnas* to the Jews. The Jewish Community wrote to R. David ibn Zimri for advice about the Usurper. He answered that "if this man causes any damage or harm to any individual or to the Community and refuses to abdicate his position, then he is to be considered an informer." The Community is justified in spending funds for bribes in order that his influence be undermined and in order that he be removed. R. David further advised patience in case the Usurper would not turn out to be such a bad man. Subsequent questions addressed to R. David from Rhodes speak only of the *Parnasim* and the Usurper is never mentioned again.

In Rhodes at the time of R. David, there were two *Qehiloth* (communities centered around a synagogue), each with its own leaders and *Parnasim*. As the floors of the synagogues of Rhodes, were made of stones, R. Samuel ibn Verga inquired from R.

David whether it is permissible to pray on a stone flooring in the synagogue. R. David replied that it is not permitted, if during the service the worshipper kneels and his face touches the ground, because of the seeming possibility of idol-worship. For this reason it is the prevalent custom among all Jews to place mats or straw-coverings in these synagogues which have marble or stone floors, so to separate between the worshipper and the stone. If there is no such matting on the floor, the worshipper may recite his prayers, but under no circumstance shall he kneel in prayer in such a position or manner that his head shall touch the bare stone. In conclusion the Jews are not supposed to be "stone worshippers.

The existence of an anti-Rabbanite movement in Rhodes led by a preacher who taught that the "Generation of the Wilderness looked upon Moses as God" compelled R. Hayyim Alfoal to write on two different times to R. David. The letters called the teachings of this heresy sheer folly and a grave misinterpretation of the clear meaning of the Scriptures. The steps advised by R. David were first to show his refutations to the misguided anti-Rabbanite preaching the deification of Moses. If no amend was made upon the receipt of written testimony about this whole matter, R. David himself would excommunicate the heretic with the greatest severity.

Rhodes' R. Samuel ben Judah ibn Verga, also named R. Samuel Ha-Levi was in correspondence with R. David. R. Samuel's great admiration and reverence for R. David found expression in poetic introductions, as preludes to his question. Samuel's affection was reciprocated by the Great Master. R. Samuel consulted R. David from Safed on the practice of *Oriah* (Heb. Uncircumcised Fruit). *Oriah* deals with the law forbidding the use of the fruit of the the trees and vineyards for the first three years after planting. It says in Lev. XIX:23 "And when you shall enter in the country, and you will have planted there some fruit trees...the fruit will remain uncircumsized to you for three years, and it will not be eaten." R. David replied that the Rabbis of Palestine do well when they do not stringently interpret the law of *Oriah*, for, "when I dwelt in Jerusalem I did likewise. I did not refrain from eating the fruit of the land and so I observed the land and so I observed the practice of the elders of the generation, and with all their piety and righteousness they did not refrain from eating the fruit..."

CHAPTER 8

SELIM II: AND THE DUKE OF NAXOS WAS HIS WINE COMPANION!

At the ascension of Selim II (1566-1675) to the throne Joseph Nasi (1514-1579) was named Duke of Naxos and the Cyclades (1, 2). He was both the nephew and son-in-law of Dona Gracia, whose daughter Reyna he had married. Born in Lisbon, and known by the name of Joan Migues (Miques or Micas) he was the son of Agostinho (Samuel) who taught medicine at the University of Lisbon. He joined his aunt Dona Gracia in Flanders. At the University of Louvain he was a classmate of the future Holy Roman Emperor Maximilian II. For unknown reasons Joan joined the army in Flanders. As a dashing young cavalry captain, he cut quite a handsome figure in the entourage of Emperor. Years later in 1567 when Maximilian sent Bishop Anton Veranchich (Verantius) on a peace mission to Istanbul, the latter was carrier of a present from the Emperor for the new Duke of Naxos. The Bishop even found an excuse to praise the recently appointed duke, despite his conversion to Judaism which he attributed to a romantic urge, his love for Reyna; apparently Joan Migues had been lured away by the wealthy daughter of Dona Gracia. The Duke of Naxos gained further favor by mediating the Austro-Ottoman truce of February 17, 1568. On May 28 of the same year the Austrian mission was salvaged from a very embarassing position through an interest-free loan from the Duke. The same year Joseph Nasi was to receive from Maximilian an epistle which started with the line: "*Maximilianus Spectabilis et magnifice nobis dilecte salutam*".
The entry of Joao Migues into Constantinople had been quite a spectacle. Equipped with a formal safe-conduct and travelling on armed ship sent for him by his aunt, he safely crossed the Adriatic to Dubrovnik and proceeded in the company of Janissary bodyguards to the capital. In Istanbul he shortly thereafter underwent circumcision and assumed the Hebrew name of Joseph Nasi. The wedding ceremony to Reyna was followed by several months of festivities in honor of the newlyweds. There were some legal technicalities, and Joseph could have been accused of bigamy, but his purported "marriage" to a Beatrice Mendes at the cathedral of Ravenna, was conveniently overlooked and all forgotten. From the Jewish point of view his marriage to Reyna was not illegitimate. The Turkish

Sephardim, like their ancestors in Spain and Portugal, had never formaly accepted the ban against plural marriages issued in the Tenth Century by R. Gershom, the Light of the Exile. Furthermore all Marrano marriages in Christian countries, performed under the ever-present threat of the Inquisition, were considered null and void by the Turkish rabbinate, unless they were accompanied by other weddings in accordance with "the laws of Moses and Israel", and in the presence of ten adult Jewish witnesses. As to Beatrice, the first wife she subsequently married in Istanbul Joseph's younger brother Bernardo.

Andreas Laguna, the Spanish "littérateur", brought to Constantinople as a captive, gives the following account in his autobiographical *Viaje de Turquia*:

"The first days that Juan Mucas was living in Constantinople as a Christian, I went to him every day and begged him not to do such thing as to become converted to Judaism, for the sake of four *reals* of money, for one day the Devil would take them from him. I found him so firm (in his faith) that naturally I went consoled. For he assured he would not go to visit his aunt again, and that he wished to return (westward) at once. You can judge my surprise when I learned that he had already become one of the Devil's own. When I asked him why he had done so, he said that it was so that he should not remain subject to the Spanish Inquisition. I replied "You may as well know that you will come under it here much more so if you live, but I do not think that it will be for long, and ill and repentant at that."

Reyna, Nasi's bride had been unable to resist her cousin's handsome looks. Her dowry was immense (and exaggeration rumored it to be in the amount of 300,000 florins, which made it more than the fortune of the Medicis!) A more realistic figure might be 90,000. The climax was reached when on August 24, 1554 (Saint Bartholomow's Day), the French Ambassador M. d'Aramon (3) especially crossed over from Constantinole to Galata to congratulate the young couple.

Nasi's family's arrival in Constantinople coincided with a saddening and sanguinary dispute at the *Seraglio*, which, however, turned to the adventage of Don Joseph (4). While he was not himself directly involved in the bloodshed, he was a beneficiary of the bloody outcome. The heir-apparent to the Ottoman throne, had been Prince Mustafa, child of Süleyman's first wife, "The Rose of the Spring". The Crown Prince, was a superbly endowed heir, the darling of the Army and the People. Unfortunately, the favourite wife of Süleyman I, the wily Hürrem Sultan, known to the French Poets Marmontel and Favart, by the romanticized name Of Roxelana (Roxanna), had other designs, namely securing the throne for one of her own offspring, Selim or Bayezid. She obtained the complicity of her son-in-law, the Grand Vizier Rüstem Pasha. The elderly Sultan, already senile in his judgement, let himself be persuaded by the co-conspirators, Roxelana and Rüstem, that *Shehzade* (Imperial Prince) Mustafa was plotting with the Janissaries to seize the throne. During the course of the campaign against Persia in 1553, upon entering his father's tent the *Shehzade* was strangled.

When Nassi reached Constantinople the succession lay open between Selim and Bayezid. Selim, being the elder had priority; but Bayezid by his popularity with the military was more derserving to assume the succession. Nasi was on good terms with both. Selim, governor in Anatolia, treated Don Joseph with special favor, appointing him his *djevahirdji* (purveyor and jeweller). The politician in Nasi realized that if the military party gained the struggle, his lot, like that of the other aliens in Turkey could become precarious. He therefore decided to throw his lot decisively with Selim; he obtained the Sultan's permission to visit Selim at his provincial capital of Kütahya. Nasi arrived there with all the ressources to finance the dynastic contest. He took with him a magnificed gift of treasure, clothing, arms, horses (actually 50,000 ducats worth and 30,000 *in specie*).

In the summer of 1559, open hostilities broke out between the two brothers. Süleyman first remained impartial. Bayezid opened his attack with characteristic dash, but Selim was prepared to resist, he also had reserves of tenacity which were lacking in his brother. Bayezid (Bajazet) was decisively defeated at Konya and fled to Persia. The impartial Süleyman gave support to Selim after he gained the upper hand. In return for an enormous bribe, the unfortunate Bayezid was handed over for execution with his four sons. A fifth son met the same fate in Asia Minor. Even with his father still alive, Selim was already referred to as "Sultan".

Boxes filled with choice vintages packed at the order of Nasi, a connoisseur of wines started to reach Selim's castle in Magnesia, to satisfy the craving of the Prince-Emperor for the forbidden joys. It is certain that Selim, the *jouisseur* became deeply attached to Don Joseph, the *bon-vivant*. Cecil Roth (5) notes the analogy to the intimacy which developed three hundred years later between the future king Edwards VII of England, then Prince of Wales, and his Jewish *bon-vivant* friends, who similarly assisted him to escape the aggressively victorian austerity of the Court.

So close was the friendship between Selim and Joseph, that strange rumors began to circulate (5), on which Lamartine writes (6): "The intimacy of the young Moslem prince with the Jewish adventurer was such, that it was said in Constantinople, that Selim was not the son of Süleyman and Roxelana, but the son of a young sister of Don Miguez, whom a *Seraglio* intrigue had substituted in the harem for the stillborn son of the favorite. Money, pleasures, debauchery, everything was common between the two friends..."

In a country of teetotalers Nasi was running the wine monopoly (2), partially supplied from his own vineyards and the excellent wines of the Greek islands. Most of the production was for foreign European consumption. However, it is not for nothing that Selim II, earned his title of *Drunkard*. Selim II's drinking companion, the Duke of Naxos, is accused by Turkish historians to have been the *Great Corruptor*! For most Europeans, the "coloring" added to the Nasi-produced Turkish wines of the time enhanced "the appeal to sin".

The writer Bernschwam (3, 4) had little good to say about Nasi:

"He has been at the court of the Emperor of the Holy Roman Empire. Christian prisoners know him by sight...The Jews who are around him daily do not agree as to his name, in order that people should not learn to know such rogues...He is said to have been named Zuan Mykas, or Six; his father is said to have been a physician by the name of Samuel. This rogue whom I just mentioned came to Constantinople in 1554 with over twenty well-dressed Spanish servants. They attend him as if he were a prince. He himself wore silk clothes lined with sable. Before him went two

Janissaries with staves, as mounted lackeys, as is the Turkish custom, in order that nothing should happen to him. He had himself circumcised in the month of April 1554...He is a large person with a trimmed black beard..."

A chief customer of Nasi's wines was King Sigismund Augustus (2) of Poland to whom the Duke of Naxos had been introduced in 1562 by Süleyman I, in these words: "a gentleman worthy of all honor, faithful and favored by Us. Our servant and *mutafarik* (courtier)."

Don Joseph Nasi had about him almost a court (5). Contemporaries testify to his powerful build and his personal charm. His knowledge of the world was immense. The contemporary Jewish scholar Moses Almosnino spoke of him as "a great gentleman, of subtle intellect, most generous, a lover of justice and merciful, all in a high degree of perfection...". He also had in full measure, as Cecil Roth writes: "the defaults of his qualities...ingratiating enough when he pleased, it seems that he was overbearing and irascible with persons of lower status, flying into a passion and threatening summary vengeance if he were thwarted. But his anger seldom lasted and if his threats were implemented it was not for long. On the other hand, he never forgot or forgave what he and his family had suffered in the past, the grievances rankling for many years, until he found the opportunity for vengeance. For himself, he was highly ambitious, but he lacked fixity of purpose. He elaborated brilliant plans, but when prospects seemed brightest was beguiled by others still more brilliant and abandoned the first."

Don Joseph had the supreme dexterity to continue rising in power and wealth year after year despite the animosity of Grand Vizier Sokullu (2). The Grand Vizier could not help but realize the enormous services rendered by the duke of Naxos to the Ottoman State, via his international connections. Nasi was able to pay with political and diplomastic achievements the enormous price required to hold a sumptuous court in his Palace of Belvedere on the Bosphorus and yet survive with impunity.

According to the French ambassador Jean de la Vigny (2) Nasi "has the best means of hearing about anything happening in the West, better and earlier than anyone in the world; he immediately communicates these data to the Sultan." A near-contemporary French historian called Nasi "the greatest spy in the world." Nasi also had another asset much appreciated by the Sultan. With his keen perception of the existing realities and his precise knowledge of many leading individuals among the ruling circles of the Western lands, he was able to detect the most crucial information among the most often contradictory data suplied by the agents abroad. He functioned as a one man National Security Council, enabling the Ottoman **Divan** to make rapid and far-reaching decisions. The saying is attributed to Süleyman I (2) that for him Joseph "was the true mirror in which he saw all the developments in Christendom." Even the great Sokullu would not dare to break the Sultan's mirror.

A comment by a French visitor, Pierre Belon de Mans (2) written in 1547, before Joseph's arrival, has an unsettling tone: "they (the Jews) have taken over the traffic and commerce of Turkey to such an extent that the Turk's wealth and revenues are in their hands. They set the highest prices on the collection of tributes from the provinces and the harbor dues...I have often to make use of the Jews and keep company with them. Hence I have learned that theirs is the subtlest and most malicious of nations,"

In politics because of his hatred for Spain, Joseph maintained ties with the Dutch Protestants. He is said to have encouraged their rebellion against Spain (2) by asserting that "Philip the King of Spain, would become so involved in fighting the Ottoman Army that he would be unable to give much thought to the Belgian affairs". There is good evidence to show that the envoy sent to Istanbul by William of Orange, resided in Don Joseph's home and was apparently introduced by him to the Sultan.

Together with Sokullu, Nasi was instrumental in the decision by Selim II to attack Cyprus (2) then under Venetian rule. It was widely believed that Nasi had ambitioned the crown of Cyprus under Ottoman suzerainty. There were allegations that he was plannning its colonization as a Jewish state. The political climate of the time would not have tolerated a Jewish king and Grand Vizier Sokullu was aggressively opposed to the idea. The dukedom was as high as don Joseph could ever expect to reach.

All was not for the best at Nasi's Palace of Belvedere, his seigneural residence. Baron (2) reports a strange episode from the *Simancas archives*, relating the activities of Agostin Manuel, a renegade Jew from Istanbul, and also a mysterious letter in cipher addressed by Don Joseph to Philip II, in the aftermath of the battle of Lepanto, where the Turkish fleet was destroyed by the Venetians. Don Nasi who had been hawkish before the battle may have been afraid afterwards to be made a scapegoat. It seems that for a short while the Duke of Naxos was ready to change masters, to come to Spain and revert to Christianity. While the entire story could be a forgery, the facts are that on October 7, 1571, Selim II had left his capital for Adrianople. Sixteen days after when he learned about the defeat, Selim II returned to Istanbul in great anger. He hastened to dismiss Pertev Pasa, one of the two admirals who had commanded the Turkish navy. Pertev Pasha's entire property was confiscated. The matter, however, did not have serious consequences for Nasi and he soon returned to his senses.

A strange document, unique in history, is the Treaty exchanged in October 1569 between Selim II and Charles IX, king of France (1). This document, written by Joseph Nasi in Hebrew, remained until 1782 in the archives of the French Embassy in Istanbul, and was then sent to the French Foreign Ministry on November 12, 1782 by the Count of St. Priest, Ambassador of the French King in Istanbul. The document was translated from the Hebrew original by Domenico Olivery, interpreter of the King. It was then literally copied in 1783 by Gautpier de la Cayrone, to be inserted in the correspondence from Constantinople.

The Nasi family was the promoter of a Protozionist Experiment (2, 5). The original initiative came from Dona Gracia, who had been trying to find a permanent resting place for her husband in the valley of Jehoshapat. She had his remains exhumed and transported from Portugal to the Holy Land. According to the old Jewish tradition, burial of a body in holy soil was an assurance that it would be among the first to be resurrected. George Sandys (2), a poet adventurer, who visited the Holy Land in 1610-11, writes about shiploads filled with Jewish bones arriving in Jaffa: "They say that through that action they assure additional pleasure for their souls and that they would be the first to stand before the tribunal on the general Day of Judgment." Dona Gracia may have expected to follow her husband. Tiberias recommended itself as final resting place for various reasons. The much travelled John Sanderson (1681) claimed that he had never seen so impressive a landscape. The medicinally renowned warm springs annually attracted between 1,000 and 3,000 visitors. The work on the *Mishnah* and the *Palestinian Talmud* had been brought to fruition in Tiberias. Many pious Jews remembered R. Johannan's ancient saying that the end of the days will be ushered in from Tiberias.

By the sixteenth century the ruins of Tiberias were inhabited by snakes. With the local real estate devaluated it was not too difficult for Dona Gracia to approach Sultan Süleyman I (*ca.* 1560) and to ask for permission to colonize the city with Jews. Dona Gracia made the request with the promise that the region could bring in taxes far in excess of that the Treasury was collecting at that time.

After a short investigation Süleyman set aside a designated area around Tiberias which had numerous trees and land "appropriate for the cultivation of silk and the plantation of sugar cane." The Sultan formally transferred that area to a newly established *waqf* (charitable foundation) sponsoring a soup kitchen in Damascus (June 15, 1560). With this first step accomplished in concordance with Islamic Law and Islamic Charity, two days latter the property could be allotted to the Nasi family through a long-term lease under the protection of the Muslim authorities, religious and secular. The contemporary chronicler Joseph ha-Kohen wrote:

"The monarch (Süleyman) gave him (Don Joseph) the ruins of Tiberias and some adjacent villages making him chief and lord over there. Don Joseph sent there R. Joseph b. Ardit (Ibn Ardut), his employee, and ordered him to build a wall around the city. Ibn Ardut found favor in the eyes of the monarch's son (Selim) who gave him a salary of sixty piasters a day. He (the Sultan) also sent along eight men from his entourage and handed him (Ibn Ardut) a privilege signed...with the royal seal. He also recommended him to the Pasha of Damascus and to the district governor of Safed, ordering them 'to do everything that this man would ask them for.' Another order was issued on behalf of the Sultan commanding all builders and porters in the area to proceed to Tiberias and to work on construction there, under the sanction of severe punishment (for disobedience). They (the laborers) found there plenty of stones (for building)..."

The French ambassador, de Petremol (2) was writing in a letter dated September 13, 1563:

"In this way, it is believed, he (Nasi) plans to turn himself into the king of the Jews. That is why he urgently demands the money from France (in reference to debts incurred by King Henri II)."

Some scholars believed that the Duke of Naxos really contemplated establishing a Jewish principalty under the suzerainty of the Sultan but autonomously governed by himself. Under the prevailing conditions in the Ottoman Empire, semi-sovereign principalties were allowed only in the periphery of the Ottoman Empire, such as in Yemen or Transylvania, but not in a territory located in the middle of the Empire. The most that Selim II could agree to grant to his close friend Don Joseph was the establishment of a Jewish colony serving under a partially autonomous regime as a haven of refuge for exiles from Christian Europe.

There was the problem of the local Christians and Moslem "Palestinians"! Everybody hated everybody, according to Fray Pantaleo de Aveiro (1565), who also claimed that in Jerusalem the Jews were the most hated group of the population (2). Bonifacioi di Ragusa,, custodian of the Franciscan Order in the Holy Land complained to the Grand Vizier Rüstem Pasha that the Jews might appropriate the ancient Church of St Helena and convert it into a synagogue. In fact, the friar Eugene Roger who visited in 1630 mentioned the Tiberian synagogue as located in a warehouse.

An old Arab sheikh having overheard Jews speaking about the rabbinic tradition that the final salvation would spring from Tiberias, spread the rumor that he had found in an old book the prediction that, if Jews rebuild Tiberias, this event would mark the beginning of Islam's downfall. It seems that Don Joseph, who from Constantinople could act as a kingmaker for Poland, did not however qualify for expertise on the inner goings of the Holy Land.

When the construction of a wall around Tiberias was completed in the month of Kislev 5325 (November 5-December, 1564), close to Hanukah, this was accomplished by express order of the Pasha of Damascus who had mandated to the premises a detachment of soldiers. A small Jewish settlement rapidly followed: local Jewish fishermen living along the shores of the Sea of Galilee were persuaded to develop their trade in the new community. In the neighboring villages assigned to him Don Jodseph had many muleberry trees planted to feed silkworms; Jewish settlers, skilled in the production of silk and silk garments, were brought in. Don Joseph imported Spanish wool, and probably also merino sheep of high quality, so that a new textile industry could lay its foundation for a self-supporting Jewish community. The Duke protected the Jewish inhabitants of these villages against fiscal and other demands by local feudal lords and government officials. The Jewish population rapidly increased with newcomers from Italy escaping the persecution of Pope Paul IV.

The enthusiasm of Italian Jews for Tiberias is expressed in a letter addressed by the community of Cori in Campagna (2), the entire membership of which prepared to transplant itself to the new Palestinian settlement: "the Crown and glory and grace and honor of the prince, the lord and noble...Don Joseph to whom the Lord caused to be given the Land of Tiberias, wherein God chose him to be the sign and symbol for our redemption...We have indeed learned that many may have already set out and crossed the sea, with the assistance of the communities and the aforementioned Prince. It has been told us, moreover, that he seeks especially Jewish craftsmen, so that they may settle and establish the land on a proper basis.

The Jews of Cori were quite poor. Their circular among the Italian communities, asking for assistance, seems to have borne some fruit. In 1569, after the promulgation of the next Pope's (Pius VI) decree of expulsion, 700 refugees assembled in Pesaro and Senigaglia awaiting transshipment to the Holy Land.

At the beginning of the Tiberias settlement don Joseph was not still Duke of Naxos and the Cyclades. He was to reach that dignity only after the ascension of Selim II to the throne in 1566. The affairs of the new dukedom started to drain some of Don Joseph's attention away from the Tiberias adventure. The progress of colonization in Tiberias was very slow. Then came the Cypriot war, draining some of the Duke's energy. The last stroke was the affair of Safed. The city was no longer the mystical paradise of Luria, Vidal and the halakhic or cabbalistic sages! Even under the friendly regime of Selim II, the order of October 10, 1578 was issued for deportation to Cyprus of one thousand rich and prosperous Safed Jews with their families (see chapter on Safed). The Safed affair, plus other adverse factors, such as plagues, famines, hostility of local population, cast a pall on the Jewish immigration to the Holy Land, including Tiberias.

Cecil Roth writes that the question had apparently taken a secondary place in Don Joseph's fertile mind. With Dona Gracia's death in 1569 the idealistic force behind the experiment had waned. Also Nasi's enemies could have been at work, and warned the Sultan of the danger of permitting anything in the nature of a Jewish state from developing in Palestine. There is evidence in rabbinic sources of an outbreak of violence, probably about 1575, and in 1579, just before Don Joseph's death, there was a further Bedouin onslaught in the region. The response among the Jewish masses was not such as might have been hoped. Little practical encouragement could be forthcoming from rabbis, immersed in hair-splitting casuistry; or from mystics, convinced that the Redemption could only be hastened by permutations or combinations of the Divine Name.

Despite the gloom which had settled, the official scheme of building the Jewish colony was not revoked by the Ottoman government. The Tiberias *firman* originally issued by Süleyman the Magnificent, was cosigned by Selim, the heir apparent, and the latter's son Murad. In 1585, another Jewish diplomat, Solomon Ibn Ya'esh, duke of Mytilene, took interest in Tiberias. Even after Solomon's death the colony seems to have carried on for some time. On his visit *ca.* 1630, Eugene Roger (2) found within the walls of Tiberias only 10 to 12 Jewish families, alongside 25 Muslim families. The Jews were under the spiritual guidance of a rabbi coming from Safed once a week. According to Cecil Roth (5): "The Tiberias experiment was not a failure, but it certainly did not live up to the enthusiasstic hopes it had aroused." Yet the little flame of Judaism that remained flickering there continued to maintain a Jewish presence on the site and was somewhat contributory to the long term revival.

As to the personality of Don Joseph Nasi, one would like to know perhaps, how the wine companion of Selim II acted when he was at the palace Belvedere on the Bosphorus in his own circle. Cecil Roth relates that one day at the Belvedere palace, Don Joseph Nasi had a long discussion on various metaphysical problems with visiting Christian scholars (6). Talks drifted to astrology, to which the Duke declared himself utterly opposed. In vain the visitors adduced proofs from Arabic and Greek literature. Nasi went on that prophecy was essentially moral warning, rather than precise forecast; indeed, the prophets of Israel never tired to pointing out that the disasters and tribulations they foretold could be averted by true penitence. He recounted with gusto the story of the high Turkish dignitaries who carefully consulted the astrologers before building a fortification and followed their instructions to the last detail...only to find it was captured in the first assault...

The colloquy ended. The visitors kissed the Duke's hand and withdrew. The Duke received the congratulations of his interpreter, Rabbi Isaac Onkeneira, and bade him to record the arguments in writing. This culminated in a little work, *Ben Porath Joseph* [Joseph is a fruitful bough (main branch of a tree)] , see *Genesis* 49.22, published in Constantinople by Joseph Jabes in 1577. The choice of subject mentioned in Amatus Lusitanus' dedication of the *Fifth Centuries* to Joseph Nasi, illustrates Don Joseph's intellectual range. Joseph Nasi also accepted the dedication of the book *Yosef Lekah* (Cremona, 1576)--a commentary on the book of Esther by Eliezer Ashkenazi, the great Levantine talmudist, who possibly made the acquaintance of the Duke while passing through Constantinople. Eliezer Ashkenazi seems to have a James Bond-like second life, in Cyprus, where he might have been one of the Duke's agents.

Joseph Nasi patronized Jewish poetry and poets, *e.g.* the most gifted member of the Hebrew school of poetry, Saadia Longo of Salonica. Nasi's Belvedere palace was the gathering place of versifiers who vied among themselves in friendly compretition, the Duke defraying their sustenance with lavish donations. It is said that Nasi's *müterdjim* (translator) Isaac ben Samuel Onkoneira, having met in the street his cousin and namesake, Isaac Onkoneira, author of the poetical collection *Aijumah ha-Migdaloth* (Constantinople, 1571), the two went together on country walks, with a lad accompanying them and chanting for their delectation Hebrew poems by other writers, which they gaily tried to imitate or surpass.

Joseph Nasi may have had a certain amateurish glitter mixed with genuine gold. It is obvious that he did not have the time and maybe even the inclination to devote himself in depth to scholarly endeavors. According to Cecil Roth (6) "it was a point of honor to be interested in Hebrew literature..." The Duke, must have been a dilettante, the equivalent of Renaissance nobleman. It is suspected that the editor of *Don Porath Joseph*, added something of his own erudition to Nasi's composition.

Don Joseph was liberal-minded enough to admit Karaite sectarian compositions into his collection. It was from manuscripts owned by him that the *Gan Eden* of the Karaite scholar Aaron ben Elijah (often called the Karaite Maimonides) was transcribed in 1588. Another major Karaite book, the *Adereth Eliyahu* by Elijah Beschizi (Bashyazi) also was in the Nasi collection.

Nasi the Maecenas, obviously was a bibliophile. On one occasion, while discussing with scholars of his academy he produced an ancient manuscript which a "gray bird had given him...in the land of his enemies". The allusion may have been to a Persian campaign in which the Duke might have followed the Ottoman Court. It turned out that it was the book *Reumah* on the laws of ritual slaughter for food, wrongly ascribed to the ninth century's Gaon Nashshon.

During the reign of Selim II, at the Old Lisbon synagogue in Salonica (7), seven rich notables (*Oligarchs*) had succeeded in being appointed to assume full powers for a period of ten years. They started to appoint and revoke at will the commissioners, functionaries, professors and teachers. They were indifferent to the needs of the people and when a poor person died, with the *Hevra Kadisha* (pious organization in charge of collecting the dead and taking care of their funeral and burial) usually so punctual, absent, the family was obliged to carry the body on a man's back to its last residence. Finally, erupting in rebellion against the plutocracy, the indignant faithful of Old Lisbon created havoc in their synagogue on Passover Saturday, March 25, 1570 (19 Nissan 5330). By a crushing majority, the *ascama* conferring to the Council of Seven decennial powers was revoked. The absolutist regime was viewed then on *como testo roto* (as a broken pot), according to the picturesque expression used by the spokesman of the community. The appointees with decennial powers had proven to be "bad pastors". The democratic regime returned to the Sephardi synagogue of Old Lisbon.

Then followed Constitutionalism "Sephardi style" in Salonica. Under Selim II the appointed leader of the federated union of communities in Salonica, Samuel Medina del Campos (8) continued to face adversity and to experience bitterness. Thus, his signatures ratifying official acts were darkened by this dolorous mention added from his own hand: "*amargago y ansioso*" (embittered and anxious). Medina continued, remaining on the job from 1551 to 1581, declining titles, refusing praise. He modeled the constitutive framework of his community. The regulations, bylaws and structures he designed and built endured for three and a half centuries. In a way Medina was the mastermind of Jewish Salonica's "Constitution".

For this ultimate task which would be the crowning of his lifetime labor, Medina studied the *ascamoth of Toledo* and *reglementation of Valladolid*, plus all the ordinances passed in Salonica after the exile of 1492. By his care, the rabbis and administrators of all synagogues gathered at a synod on the Sunday November 19, 1564 (15 Kislev 5325) and decided that the *Marbitz Tora* is authorized to promulgate *ascamoth* and elaborate regulations strictly for internal affairs within his community. Any ascama of general order would be null and void if it did not emanate from the plenary assembly of rabbis convoked and gathered. Federal decisions would be by majority of those deliberating. Every rabbi, director of community or rector of seminary, was entitled for take the initiative of authoring an *ascama* destined to collective application, but to have it adopted, the author had first to submit it for express ratification to the totality of his colleagues.

Medina had one more task to complete. Helped by the federated council and most of the spiritual leaders, he had all the synagogues adopt the rite of Sephardic liturgy. This reform was more effective than any other in operating the psychological "rapprochement of the communities" and the factual fraternization of the faithful.

The two predominant rituals in Salonica at the time Medina started his liturgical reform were the Romaniot and the Sephrdic. Fundamentally, except for details, the two rituals were quite similar; they were a kind of anthology of sacred texts, with as common bond faith in the goodness of the Providence unique and all potent, belief in the redemptive mission of Israel and in the final deliverance of the Chosen People, and unshakable confidence in a better future and in a brilliant destiny for the human genus as a whole. The liturgy also reflected the aspirations of one hundred generations of wanderers, the martyrology of three milleniums.

The Romaniot *mahzor* (prayer book) was more ancient, having been printed for the first time in Constantinople in 1510. With some omissions and additions the Italian *mahzor* of "Rome" which Soncino had put to press in Italy in 1486 under the name *Sidurillo* was derived from the Romaniot, as also were the Sicilian, the Apulian, and the Ashkenazite. In the Romaniot *mahzor*, the poems of Eleazar Kalir, believed to have come from Babylonia and a disciple of the Palestinian Yannai are dominating. Before Kalir, the prayers were in prose; Kalir was the first to have introduced rime and rythm in the liturgy, towards the Eighth Century. Most of the work is due to the ancient liturgical author Jose ben Jose, said the Orphan. As to Kalir he only was the versifier of these liturgical gems.

The Sephardic *mahzor* was the *mahzor* of Castille, printed for the first time in Venice in 1524, and reedited in Salonica. The poems forming it are a superb flowering of the most beautiful Ibarian epoch, and they represent one of the most precious gems salvaged in the debacle of the exile. The *mahzor* was a receptacle of magnificent contributions by authors in the Golden Age of Spain: Joseph ben Abitur, the translator of the Talmud into Arabic and author of the service of Kipour; Moses Maimonides; Solomon Gabirol, the profound and sentimental; Juda Halevi, the bard of the synagogue and Moses ben Jacob ben Ezra.

In 1565, the renunciation by the faithful of the last vestiges of their special liturgies did not go very smoothly. There were clashes and opposition, nostalgical returns to the past, but the rarity and high price of special issues of *mahzorim* containing local liturgies, was a primary factor in rapidly imposing the uniformity of prayers for the whole Jewish population. The indigenous synagogues *Etz Haim* and *Etz Ha-Daath* and the various sections of the Italiot community residing in Salonica before the arrival of the exiles resisted for a while, but later joined. Sicilians and Apulians remained reluctant, but their rituals were only in manuscript form and they held for a while. Catalans and Aragones, too proud to submit to the Castillans kept their special *Rosh ha Shana* and *Kipour* services. The Ashkenzes remained obstinate. They held to their ancestral liturgy.

From its own side the Castillan ritual continued to draw upon diverse sources. It became a sort of amalgam of the other particular *mahzors*, which could only help in reducing the regrets of other groups who had to abandon their own *mahzor*.

His momentous work completed, Medina died at the age of eighty five, on October 12, 1589 during the reign of Murad III. His spartan epitaph bears his name followed by a Biblical verse: "Supreme peace to those who love the Law."

The federated Jewish community of Salonica had come up with a Constitution. All that was now needed was to have this Constitution endorsed by the Turkish authorities as a charter, which would also renew ancient privileges granted to the

Jewish community by the Ottoman Sultanate. During the reign of Süleyman I, the authorities did not seem well disposed to give their approval. Some of the Christian residents did not view with a friendly eye Salonica Jewry's attempts at concentration and their forming of a powerful federated union. They were worried that such a concentration would favor the progress of their Jewish competitors to the detriment of their own economic benefits. The majority of the Greeks lived in amiable and even fraternal terms with the Jews. The problem was that a handful of anti-Jewish agitators continuusly intrigued with the local Turkish authorities and stirred them up against recognizing the statute submitted by the federated Jewish council.

In the end the local Turkish authorities responded by a categorical refusal to the Jewish demand for a statute. What was worse, the whole position of the Jews in the region was again put in question, as if it only was temporary and subject to reassessment. All the communal privileges bestowed upon the Jews of Salonica seemed endangered, certainly a latent danger, but none the less grave. It was only the good pleasure of their masters which allowed the Jews to remain in the city, not a definitive and immutable right. Nothing that they had built there rested upon lasting foundations. Tomorrow an offended Pasha could declare unlawful their foundations and lay a hand on the funds required for their upkeep.

The Turkish administration of the time did not bother with naturalization charters and residency permits. It was only custom which gave sanction to what had been consecrated by usage and ancientness. Arbitrariness reigned supreme in the province, and the smallest government official, could, if he so fancied, put in question all the privileges gained in the course of generations, deny the Jews the most elementary rights. The Paradise chanted by Samuel Usque was only a Paradise by oblivion. It was a Paradise that could be revoked on a simple whim, to add a little *keyif* (merriment) to the *narguileh* (waterpipe) smoking of the Pasha of Salonica.

What followed led to the rise in Salonica of a quasi-autonomous *Müsselemlik* (practically the realization of a Jewish ministate in Ottoman Macedonia!). The Salonica community was not able to reassert by irrefutable proof the ancient privileges (8). The *firmans* of capital importance no longer existed in originals or copies. The Turkish functionaries, if they were ill-disposed could take adavantage of this situation. Those envious of the Jewish situation, having become aware that the Jews held no proof of their privileges, kept inciting the Pasha of Salonica and his cronies, that he should abolish such privileges.

All kinds of informers were at work, with abominable accusations and slanders aimed to further pressure the Jewish taxpayers. A number of individuals were denounced to the authorities under the accusation of hiding their fortune for the purpose of tax evasion.

Almosnino, Medina and all the notables directing the destinies of the Salonician Judaism took the matter in hand. In the spring of 1566, the last year of Süleyman I's reign, the decision was taken to send a delegation to Constantinople. Moses

Almosnino (8, 9), one of the scholars under Nasi's patronage was to lead the delegation. The mission sent to Constantinople was to procure confirmation of the privileges and exemptions granted in 1537 by Süleyman the Magnificent to the Jews of Salonica when he had visited the city. The original document of the charter had been lost in the great fire of 1545. With the charter forgotten the Jews of Salonica were exposed to outrageous impositions, including one to supply yearly the Imperial authorities with a herd of goats, at crushing expense. In an earlier trip to Constantinople, Almosnino had made the acquaintance of the Grand *Mufti* (highest Moslem religious authority in the Ottoman Empire), the cultured Abu Said el Amudi. In a scene reminiscent of the atmosphere under the Omeyyads in Andalusia, Abu Said, spectacles in hand, had propounded to Almosnino a problem in connection with the philosophical opinion of Aristoteles and Galenus.

In 1565 Almosnino stayed at Don Joseph Nasi's Belvedere palace where he befriended the Duke's brother Samuel Nasi. The Sultan was on his way to his last campaign in Hungary. The *Kaymakam* (Acting Representative and Governor of Constantinople) Iskender Pasha, the *de facto* Regent refused to take any responsibility. When the news of Süleyman's death at Zigetwar arrived, the matter was at a standstill, even though a number of influential Jews were called upon to help. Don Joseph Nasi, a supreme master in the art, suggested the inevitable *baksheesh,* in the amount of 1,000 ducats, to be made available. Almosnino had to extend his mission six times, but all he could obtain was a proposal for a fixed annual tribute of 50,000 aspri--far above the ability of the Salonica community. Bad tongues were accusing Almosnino to prolong his sojourn in the capital for a mercantile purpose: to benefit his personal businesses. As the negociations kept dragging on, Almosnino wrote in his diary: "*Polor dolor de korazon yo me topo aqui* [for heart ache I find myself here). Almost out of despair Almosnino followed the Court to Adrianople to recommence the negociations. According to his own recounting, Almosnino had one night a vivid dream. On the next day he was received by the Grand Vizier for the seventh time, in company of a master intrerpreter Abraham Salama, who had managed to enlist the interest of the Grand **Mufti**. The Grand Vizier Sokullu, perhaps understanding the issue clearly for the first time, proved more sympathetic, and agreed to recommend to the sultan the confirmation of the Charter with all the concessions contained. This, however, was to be at a price: an outright payment of 300,000 aspri in commutation of all extraordinary taxes (February 15, 1568). With the new Charter, the Salonica community was erected into a **Müsselemlik** (a self-governing political entity, independent of the city in which it was situated). Thus, by this precious document (8, 9), the Jewish Salonica now was a privileged administrative canton, and nobody anymore could touch to its statute conceded "at perpetuity" by the Sultan. The **Müsselemlik**, in effect, constituted a division, a district of the Empire. It was a region of lesser importance than a **Pashalik**, but of greater importance than an **Aghalik**. **Pashalik, Müsselemlik** and **Aghalik** were independent of each other. The **Pasha**, the **Müsellim** and the **Agha** were dignitaries on whom the Sultan directly rested his authority as explained by Félix-Beaujour in his *Tableau du*

Commerce de la Grèce (17). The duly mandated representative of the Jews had the title of **Müsselim**, he marched behind the **Pasha**, but had precedence over the **Agha**. It was true that the Jewish community of Salonica was included in the **Pashalik** of Salonica. However it was not submitted to the jurisdiction of the **Pasha** and the **Kadi** (Judge) who shared the power in Salonica. It had its own existence. It was considered as a quasi-autonomous territorial enclave. The *Pasha* limited himself to collect the taxes and the *Kadi* oversaw the judiciary order, but neither had the right to interfere in the internal affairs of the Jews. Only the Sovereign had the power to modify the assises on which from then on rested the constitutional liberties of the Jews of Salonica.

The *Müsselemlik* of Salonica, a Jewish autonomous ministate, with a Charter certified by an Imperial *firman* was to survive for several centuries. Almosnino had achieved for the first time in Jewish history since the Carolingians in France, a chartered autonomy almost reminiscent of the Jewish Kingdom of Narbonne (that is without the Prince-King) from Pépin le Bref and Charlemagne's time in the late VIIIth-early IXth century to the XIVth century under Philippe le bel.

Almosnino returned triumphant to Salonica, bearing with him the new *Magna Carta* of the Salonica Jewish Community established in *Müsselimlik*. A Thanksgiving service was held on February 22, 1568 (23 Adar 54290 at the *Talmud Tora* (15), and acknowledged by Almosnino, "among the twelve Jewish notables who had most helped the Salonician cause first and foremost, was the 'Prince, the Lord Don Joseph Nasi, Duke (may his might increase)' who helped us from the time we went to him, while the Sultan's father lived, from the beginning to the end."

Upon Almosnino's proposal, the federated assembly unanimously decided that for a period of ten years all the imports and exports made by the Jewish traders of Salonica would acquit a tax destined on one hand to amortize the debt of 300,000 aspers, and on the other side to ensure for the future, the preservation of the obtained franchises. The fund so created was to remain independent of all communal works, and it was forbidden to change it for any other purpose, or to distract for it under any pretext, even by a single asper.

This was a wise measure of indispensable foresight, when one should consider that in Turkey as well as in all the states of Christian Europe, collective as well as individual liberties were not an irrevocable constitutional right guaranteed as emanating from a natural right. All prerogatives bestowed upon anyone by the central power, as rewards for rendered services, or by pure royal grace, could be at once cancelled at a whim of the prince. What the sovereign gives the sovereign can take back. It is true that the Charter of Salonica, could not anymore be tampered with by the local Pasha or Agha. Any casual dealings with what had the Sultan's sanction might cost their heads to the inadvertent dignitaries...But the Sultan himself could do whatever pleases him, even tamper with the Charter. So one should be financially well prepared to open at great expense a gold-lined path to the Sublime Port, to "repurchase" the Charter in case it would happen to be endangered. The tax imposition propounded by Almosnino aimed to protect the perennity of the **Müsselemlik**.

While away from home, Almosnino (9) completed an extraordinary **magnum opus** of historical significance, *Extremas y Grandezas de Constantinople* (the Extremes and Grandeurs of Constantinople). The book in Ladino (Judeo-Spanish with Hebrew characters) was transliterated in Latin characters by a certain Jacob Cansino. "Vassal of his Catholic Majesty and his Interpreter in the Places of Oran" (*Interprete suyo en las plazasde Oran*). It was published in Madrid (CE 1638) with a dedication to the Conde d'Olivarez, Philip IV's all powerful Minister of State. The book describes the state of affairs in contemporary Constantinople, together with a Chronicle of Sultan Süleyman's reign, achievemets and death, and of Selim II's accession. Emphasis was placed on the paradoxical contrasts to be found in Constantinople-- extremes of heat and cold, of opulence and mysery, luxury and sobriety, bigotry and libertinism.

The other masterpiece of Almosino is *El Regimente de la Vida*, published in Salonica (CE 1564). While transcribed in Hebrew letters the book was written in pure Castillan. This book has been the **vade-mecum** of many generations. Though a believer in free will, Almosnino admits the influence of celestial bodies on human destiny. Appended to this book of religious morals, there is a Treatise on Dreams, *Tratado de los sueños*. In Almosnino's words, the Treatise was "composed at the request of the most illustrious señor, the señor Don Joseph Nasi, whom may God preserve and augment his prosperous state; Amen!" Almosnino was no Freud or Jung and his approach to dreams remained somehat unsophisticated. Yet the small book contains a resplendent description of Nasi's Belvedere palace from a twice repeated dream. From Cecil Roth (9):

"It was a feast-day, and Almosnino thought that he was in the *midrash*, or room of study, which Nasi had fitted up in his palace, where Divine Service was being held. Rich carpets hung on the walls and were strewn about the floor; there were two seats of honor. one for Don Joseph and the other for his brother, Don Samuel...the sacred Ark was opened, and the Scrolls of the Law were taken out; a raised bench accommodated the scholars who attended the service; and in an adjoining room, separate from the men, sat their two wives, Dona Reyna and Dona Gracia la chica, together with their respective daughters, the rest of the female members of the household and others from outside...It was apparently the Feast of Tabernacles, for the two brothers had in their hands the traditional lemon and palm-branch, and the prescribed psalms of praise were being sung..."

Almosnino's writings deal with an infinity of questions from religion to piety, defense of the faith (*Tefiloth-le-Moshe*), commentaries of the Bible, the Talmud, the writings of Ben-Ezra and of Rashi, of the works of various philosophers, ethics, logic, aristotelism, psychology, sacred eloquence, history, etiquette, hygene, practical law and formulation of contracts, natural sciences, cosmography and astronomy.

The master thought of Almosnino's life was the unification of the communities. He was the theoretician of an idea which found its realization through the constructive genious of Medina.

The wonderful news reached Salonica that the Duke of Naxos had obtained the Imperial authorization to restore Tiberias from the ruins (10). Soon the whole of Israel would be convoked to celebrate the inauguration of the Third Temple in Zion. Letters came from Tiberias announcing that this holy city had been rebuilt in the time of a few months. Suddenly more wonderful news arrived: The Duke of Naxos was on the verge of receiving the crown of Cyprus. Even the most skeptic and rational minds found it hard to continue doubting. Israel's salvation was in sight.

The most excited believers demanded that in the academies of Salonica, the *Kabbalah* and related topics become the sole matters of study. There was an insurrection against the rationalist teachings of Maimonides, severely banned at certain *yeshivoth,* by cabbalists, esoterists and occultists, "the mystagogues of Salonica", thus revealing the dark face of Judaism. It was just an expression of the innermost desires consuming the heart of every Jew, a part of the wishful thinking from which none could escape. It was a Freudian release or maybe a Jungian one, since it seemed to come from the depths of the collective unconscious, with the return of all the most sacred archetypes and a response to a more than millenarian longing.

The danger from this anti-rationalist streak in Judaism comes as stated by Barzilay, (11) from "their...demanding a total withdrawal from the pursuit of rational knowledge." By 1568, the extreme anti-rationalists were in control of even some of the most rationalist minds. The anti-rationalist streak, in great favor among the students of Joseph Taitacek in Salonica, did not stop with the martyrdom of Salomon Molho and David Reubeni. In the *yeshivoth* of Salonica all studies were centered on the miraculous *Zohar,* with everyone trying to penetrate its hidden meaning. Between Salonica and Safed, both upholding the mystical torch, there was a powerful wind of collective hallucination capable of inebriating even the most solidly made heads. Through a special set of circumstances, mainly based on "benign neglect" by the Ottoman authorities, Israel was king in both Salonica and Safed.

When the Salonician Joseph Saragossi had arrived in Safed he had first introduced there, together with an excellent administration, a vivid taste for scholarly studies, but the main trend in Safed was a vibrant mysticism. All the pioneers of esoterism, all the bards of mysticism and visionaries of Israel had converted this Palestinian city into their meeting ground. Joseph Caro was another prototype of the Jew waivering between reason and faith. Solomon Alkabetz, the powerful poet of *Lekah Dodi* left Salonica to share in the mystical Messianic dream of Safed. The two Usques, Samuel the chronicler-bard and Salomon the bard-merchant paid their visit to propagandize in Safed, and replenish therein their imagination.

In 1574 with the death of Selim II, and the ascent to the ottoman throne of the opium-addict Murad III, Joseph Nasi started to fall into oblivion if not total disgrace. In 1579 the Duke of Naxos was dead after considerable suffering due to kidney stones.

While Joseph Nasi's fame on the Jewish side neared the apotheosis and seemed a forerunner of Messianic times, throughout Christian States from France to Venice, the Magnate of the Jews had the reputation of a sinister, malevolent and diabolic figure. A vivid picture of Barabas, the Jew, is portrayed in *The Jew of Malta*, the masterpiece of the young brilliant playright Christopher Marlowe (6) produced in London in 1592. The main villain Barabas is a rich and famous Jew who lived in Malta, some time before the Turkish onslaught on the island. Maddened by persecution he turns into a monster. With his overpowering ambition, machiavellian schemings, anti-Christian bias, overwhelming wealth, widespread commercial relations with Florence, Venice, Antwerp, London, Seville, Frankford, Lubecke, Mosco and wherenot, his trade in "the wines of Greece", the Spanish words in his conversation, his intimacy with "Selim Calymath, son of the Grand Seignior, his rise to the rank of Governor of Malta, Barabas is the image of Joseph Nasi, Duke of Naxos. At the time of the Turkish onslaught on Malta Barabas attempts a horrible revenge and conspires with the Turks. The close of the play develops in a sequence of incredible evil. In the end Barabas falls victim to the plot he had prepared for his allies.

In a theory advanced by S. Sinsheimer in *Shylock: the History of a Character* (London, 1947), *the Jew Of Malta*, is not the only play inspired by such distorted image of Joseph Nassi. The English strolling players (*Englische Komoedianten*) who toured Germany had in their repetory a very popular play composed by Christopher Blueme, a Silesian student: *Der Jud von Venezien* (the Jew from Venice), also entitled *Von einem Koenig von Cypern und einem Herzog von Venedig* (About a King from Cyprus and a Doge from Venice). This play contains elements from both the Jew of Malta and the Merchant of Venice, with the tale of the three caskets (Malta) and the tale of the pound of flesh (Venice). The villain is again a Jew named Barabas. His life trajectory is that of the Duke of Naxos, but in reverse: starts with Cyprus ends with Venice. Barabas in Cyprus, dissimulates his faith and appears as Joseph, the Christian, in Venice.

Jews had penetrated the field of sesame oil production and soap manufacturing (12). A whole street of Salonica was occupied by potters called *cantareros*. A few specialists had brought from Mallorca a formula kept secret for the preparation of perfumed aqua vitae, famous in all the Orient. The Jews also were skilled in the raising of silkworms and they wove brilliantly colored silky fabrics.

Under Selim II, there also took place the wondrous saga of the Jewish miners of Siderocapso, with their mythical mascott *the metallar Demon of Siderocapso*. In the middle of the Sixteenth Century, Jews in the Macedonian hinterland, held a monopoly on the fabulously rich gold and silver mines of Sitrocapso (Siderocapso), in Chalcidiquia [the Chrysite of ancient times]. Located in the eastern extension of the Hortish mountain chain, the mines were at two days' walking distance from

Salonica. An important deposit of silver-bearing lead and gold-bearing minerals was layered in this mountainous region. The Jews used in the exploitation of the mine the most advanced metallurgical technology of the times. According to the report of the French traveler Belon (year 1548, see ref. 13), the miners formed a rainbow coalition of Jews, Albanians, Serbs, Greeks, Valachians, Bulgarians, Turks and Circassians. They were all busying themselves in the numerous shafts of the mines or around five to six hundred furnaces. An Armenian was employed to separate silver from gold by means of aqua forte. The Jews were so numerous that their Spanish language had become the most common means of communication among this heterogenous people. The mines were closed on Saturdays and Sundays, out of respect for the Shabbaths of the Jews and Christians.

The Sultan drew a respectable if not leonine share of 10,000 to 30,000 ducats, monthly, from the mines' exploitation. The Court felt an almost sensual attraction to this source of wealth and did not disdain an occasional vacation near the sites.

The metallurgical methods of exploitation seemed to have been imported by the Ashkenazites, who, despite the predominance of Ladino, had been able to impose their technical terminology on the tools and equipment which were in use. The region had its own malevolent creature, the belief of which was fed by popular imagination and superstitions. This rather whimsical creature was the "metallar demon", half devil and half gremlin, which appeared in the shape of a goat with golden horns, and amused itself by blocking the entry of mine pits, but when propitiated might indulge in directing the picks of the miners to the spots richest in auriferous deposits. Belon also relates that when unseemly dificulties would interfere with the work, the workers would prefer to stop mining activities for a few days, time enough to assuage the golden horned demon.

As to the gold and silver extracted in Siderocapso, they were sent to Vienna and Constantinople, to be converted into coins. Over the time the administration deteriorated and it stopped being cost-effective to operate the mines. They were abandoned, until the eighteenth century (14).

Foreign transactions took place in the golden ducats of Venice or the florins of Florence. By definition the ducat (ducato) was a coin with the Doge's portrait on it, weighing 2.20 grams. One ducat was worth 4.47 golden francs or 14 golden pounds of the time. The ducat corresponded to the *sultaniye* minted in Turkey. Before the Ottoman treasury started to tamper with the coinage, one ducat was equivalent to one florin or one *sultaniye* and each were worth on the average 50 aspers.

Within the Ottoman Empire the internal currency was the *kurush* (*groush*) or piaster in silver, divided into 120 aspers. For a long time the weight of the *groush* was kept at nine drams (drachmas) or about 30.47 grams. In the beginning of the Fifteenth Century it represented a little more than two and a half Venetian ducats. When after the discovery of silver in America, the metal flowing out of Spain started to flood Europe, there was an immediate monetary revolution all over the world which led to considerable depreciation of the *groush*. From the middle of the sixteenth century on, the value of the *groush* fluctuated between one a half ducat and three quarters of a ducat. For a certain time the *groush* enjoyed a reasonable stability, until the Ottoman treasury started to tamper with the coinage. It is noteworthy that even at the 10-15:1 equivalency in the Sixteenth Century, the value of silver in relation to gold stood much higher than in our days (with an equivalency of 100:1).

The monetary disorder, a major symptom of the fall in morality plaguing the Imperial Dynasty, marks the decadence of the Ottoman Empire. The fiancial anarchy was accompanied by a growing insubordination, lawlessness and agressivity of the Janissary militia. With the fall of the *groush*, the importers in Salonica faced disaster and bankrupycy. The Ottoman defeat at Lepanto in 1571 (15) brought temporary disaster to Salonica Jews. The Senate of the Venetian Republic ordered the suppression of all the favors being enjoyed by Jews of Ottoman citizenship. However soon commercial and economic considerations prevailed and trade with Salonica was resumed on a grand scale. The delegates of Salonica traders (16) were designated by the title of consuls or *fattori*, by analogy with the *feitores* or *factores* of Portugal and Spain. Half diplomats and half business agents, they also were precious informers.

The Jewish quarters of Salonica were subject to the enterprises of the crime lords, of the military and Janissaries or even plain soldiers gone on rampage after an unauthorized break out of their barracks. If a high rank Janissary would violently knock on the door of a Jewish house asking for a large *bakshish*, or a ransom for having spared the family by abstaining to play with their daggers, there was not much that could be done except obliging. With their coarse sense of humor, the Janissaries would then accept the due tribute, provided it was accompanied by appropriate demonstrations of respect, such as profuse genuflexions and deep bows (*salams*). The rest of the household, women, children, elderly folk would seek refuge in the subterranean caves reinforced with concrete, where they kept hidden their most precious belongings, jewelry, silk products, furs and rare books. During the reign of Selim II (1570), the Salonica notable Ruben Modiano perished while trying to defend his home.

In the narrow streets of the Salonica Jewish quarter, there were suspended tunnels hanging in the air, setting up an aerial labyrinthine network of communication between the houses for the purposes of warning in case of attacks by Janissaries (17). The Salonica men did not always accept to be sacrifical lambs. Butchers would lead in the organization of self-defense. A Janissary who had for too long made himself intolerable, would finally meet his equal and receive the ultimate punishment. As the cadaver of the once ferocious aggressor was moved in a bag through the mysterious passages opening into the river used for dumping, the password was *la Novia* (the Bride). Everybody had to open the way for the funeral convoy, in the same way as it is customary to do when the Bride crosses the street in the middle of the wedding procession. A road was opened for this not very *kosher* cargo.

In the populous streets, among the masses of peaceful citizens there were also occasional Jewish *kabadayis* (tough guys, swashbucklers) who by fanfaronade or bravado would play with their *navajas* (long and narrow knives). Very often after a show of noise and agitation, the play of the *navajas* would end without any bloodshed. It was more like an exercise in fantasy, in the style of a Moroccan *fantasia*. It was better not to ask the Turkish authorities to step inside the Jewish kingdom, where anyway they would not know what to do except stir up some trouble of their own.

THE KINGDOM OF MYSTICAL UTOPIA.CHAPTER 9

SAFED IN THE SIXTEENTH CENTURY
THE KINGDOM OF MYSTICAL UTOPIA

There were two Safeds: the mystical and the mercantile. One can start by a view of Safed, the capital of Jewish mysticism and talmudic studies in the XVIth century: "You find there (in Safed) plenty of *bottechi* (shops) of woollen clothes, for example *merceria* (textile wares) and spices. In all those three branches many shops belong to Jews; they bring the *merceria* and spices from Damascus and sell in town. With the *galeas* (galleys) they go to Beirut to buy clothes and other things... many (of the Jews) also earn by buying cotton, thread, wax, *salmonea* (a medicament) where prices are on the cheap side, and sell them at the proper time...Generally the country is much more *mercantandesca* (mercantile) than Italy, for Ishmaelites will much more willingly buy from Jews than from others. Throughout Eretz-Israel there are four worthwhile crafts: weavers, goldsmiths, shoemakers, tanners...But you cannot hope to be hired as a teacher or servant in a home or shop, and you cannot hope for charity, for there are many poor. Therefore let no one come out of Italy who has neither craft nor capital."

Moses Basola of Pesaro, Italy, writing in about 1523 (1).

Another view of the same landscape is through the dream of a mystic, Hayim Vidal (1543-1620):

"...Vital saw himself studying on top of the great mountain, west of Safed, amidst its two big peaks, which rise from Meron village. There he beheld the Messiah, saw ten of thousands of Jews flocking to him for battle, and after victory, the triumphant, avenging entry into the Temple" (1).

In another eschatological dream, Vidal sees himself "coming down from the khan of Safed on the *ha-sulam shel avanim* (stone ladder, stone steps) leading down to the market. There, at the butcher's bazaar two roads meet. On this crossroad, he meets various dead. In their company he goes to the Jewish street. {He) beheld a gathering of all Israel together there. The sun set at high noon; it was a pitch dark everywhere, in all the world, and in all Israel they were crying bitterly. And here was a man looking like the solitary dervishes, his clothes torn, his hair long, reaching its feet. He came from the west, by the way of the synagogue of the Aragonese, towards the above mentioned street. He was loudly chanting a sweet song; this song was made of several strophes...entirely dealing with *yibum mitzva* (levirate marriage commandment)...and the subject of Messiah and redemption as explained in the Zohar on the verse 'if he would redeem you, let him redeem. He came singing to where (Vidal) was; the sun shone again." (1)

Safed, a small city in the Upper Galilee, situated on a hill in a mountainous country, was the spot about which R. Joseph Caro (2) wrote in the sixteenth century: "After nearly fifteen hundred years of living in the exile and persecution, He (God) remembered unto his people his covenant with their fathers, and brought them back from captivity, one of a city and two of a family, from the corners of the earth to the land of glory, and they settled in the city of Safed, the desire of all lands,"

Schechter calls the Sixteenth Century Safed a "city of legists and mystics". For exiles from Spain and Portugal, the inducement to settle in Safed was an opportunity to be granted a total regeneration and renewal of heart. The attraction of Safed was a reenactment of the dream held by Judah Halevi in the twelfth century when he abandoned a medical career, fame and family in Spain with the unachieved hope to become a wanderer in the Holy Land. The preference given to Safed, a town with no scriptural reference to it in the Bible or the Talmud, over Jerusalem, may be accounted for the unfavorable conditions prevailing in Jerusalem at that time ." (2)

Jerusalem (*El Kuds* in Arabic), was also an important center for the Mohammedan population. A Jewish presence there tended to become too conspicuous and invited to extorsions by local officials or chieftains in the surrounding countryside. As the French say: *"Pour vivre heureux vivons cachés"* [To happily live, let us live hidden (unconspicuously)". Safed, never having had an important Jewish population in former times, Jewish settlers there were at advantage from a double standpoint: 1) the native Jewish community in Safed had no occasion to make regulations calculated to exploit the foreign Jews; 2) the non-Jewish population as in most places of low Jewish density throughout the world, had no prestablished prejudices and thus seemed more kindly disposed, sparing the new arrivals the heavy taxation which was the rule in Jerusalem.

In his famous letter dated 1489 (2) R. Obadiah de Bertinoro wrote: "They (Safed Jews) are mostly poor, spending their time in villages, going about peddling in houses and on farms. The Jews of Safed followed the old saying 'Love work and hate lordship (*i.e.* snobbery.' Those of less materialistic and more idealistic concerns...came to Safed to live the kind of life they enjoyed, one open to scholarly and other spiritual endeavors".

Shlomel of Moravia wrote in 1607 (2): among the citizens of Safed there were great scholars, saints and men of action, full of divine wisdom"...For Moravia what was most admirable about these men was the simplicity and humility of spirit which they possessed. He writes about them: "None among them, is ashamed to go to the well and draw water and carry home the pitcher on his shoulders, or go the market and buy bread, oil, and vegetables. All the work in house is done by themselves (without servants)."

Haim Vital Calabrese (1543-1620) was appointed by Luria as his spiritual heir. Vital had memorized and written down everything his teacher said.

On a visit to Egypt, it is alleged that Vital was called to Abu Suffa, the governor's office, who challenged him to rediscover the exact place of the aqueduct King Hezekiah had built in Jerusalem. Vital found safety in rapidly fleeing from Egypt at night. He resurfaced in Damascus where he completed a work on patriarch Abraham, filled with Cabbalistic incantations.

According to Vital (23) the old *Kabbalah* had outlived its time. The real *Kabbalah* was one taught by Isaac Luria and transcribed by him. With his proclaimed supernatural powers Vital also affirmed that Moses Cordevero appeared to him in dreams and disclosed many things to him. Thus was achieved the perfect continuity, between three generation of master cabbalists, Cordovero, Luria, Vital.

Nourished in mystical lore, Hayyim Vital became inebriated by his own self-reliance and fame to the point of proclaiming himself Messiah ben Joseph, who was supposed to appear before the real Messiah, a scion of the Davidic dynasty. He organized in Damascus, a circle of adherents, and freely lectured about his messianic dignity. He was vehemently opposed by the prominent rabbis, Menahem di Lonzano and Jacob Abulafia. Di Lonzano in his book *Imre Emet* (True Word) condemned him a an impostor. Vital left Safed and died in Damascus in 1620.

There were eminent perils in the way Luria's *Propositions* came to be written by hand of Vital (48). They were dangerous medicine. They led to pretenses such as those of Vital being Messiah ben Joseph, and Sabbatai Svi being Messiah ben David.

During an illness of Vital (51), notes on the Lurianic *Kabbalah* were extracted from their box, transcribed and published as *Etz Hayyim* (the Tree of Life). The book was left to the few initiates and exalted mystics, largely remaining ignored by the public at large. It nearly took two centuries until it appeared in print.

From the locality of Ein Zeitoun, near Safed, came *Sefer hayom*, authored by Moses ben Makhir, head of the Academy there. The work published in Hebrew (1599) is a compendium of liturgical and ritual practice. *Sefer hayom* includes a beautiful parable called "A Princess locked in a Tower.

In *Sefer hayom*, the princess was locked with her servant maidens in a tower that was completely closed at all times. Only by tremendous effort could one find an entrance, and one still had to search for the keys. After the initial outer opening, one found chambers within chambers, all of them locked. The king announced this challenge throughout his realm, and many came to the tower from the ends of the earth. They surrounded the tower at all hours with songs and praises to awaken the heart of the young woman. They used all their wits to find an opening. Candidates from east and west hoped to be able with their musical instruments and melodies to touch the young woman's heart, so that she might reveal herself to them through the holes and cracks. They left unuccessful and disappointed. At last an exceedingly poor lad, appeared thinking: "It is not possible that this tower was built without an opening to enter and leave. I will remain for forty days and forty nights if necessary until I find some opening or window through I shall be able to catch sight of the king's daughter and to speak to her. Then either she will grant my request or I will die because of her.''...At last, he found a window-like opening, which after scratching revealed a tiny hole. He then began to shout, calling the princess in a loud voice and pleading with her. When she saw that he had gone through so much trouble and labor, to seek her love, the princess' compassion was stirred. She began to speak words of encouragement. She disclosed to him the place where the keys were located. By virtue of his presence of mind and intelligence he opened all the doors, one by one. As the princess realized all the effort that he had expanded for her, she sent to inform her father. The king rejoiced and wanted his daughter to marry that man. He revealed other mysteries to him, gave him his daughter as wife. The young man succeedd in all his endeavors, and he became viceroy of the realm.

Wineman comments (24) "Like the suitor who found a very small hole in the tower, only after considerable effort, truth does not glare in the student's face but, rather, is found only through attention to the small holes and cracks in the tower, the seemingly insignificant details that may serve as keys by which to understand the real nature of one subject's of study."

In the early 1580's, there were some clouds over the Jewish community of Safed, which had flourished under Turkish rule, as it began to decline. The very prosperity of the community may have been a contributor, as it started to lose its original candor. The Jews of Safed originally were left in peace because they were inconspicuous. As they became icreasingly prosperous they started to attract criticism to them. A large trade in the weaving of wool and the manufacturing of clothes, was entirely in the hands of the Jews.

The Turkish conquest of Cyprus, originally plotted by the Duke of Naxos as a step towards his gaining the crown of the island, ironically turned to be a threat to the Jews of Safed. Under Selim II, Turkish orders were issued for the expulsion of a thousand Jewish families from Safed to Cyprus in 1576 and five hundred families in 1577 (25). Details about these events were extracted by Uriel Heyd (25) from the *Mühimme Defterleri* (Important Registers) today kept in the National Archives of Istanbul. Three years after the 1576 expulsion order, another document dealing with expulsion of Jews from Safed arose as a result of a possibly slanderous Jewish appeal to the Istanbul government. The matter is described in a letter signed by Rabbi Moshe Mitrani and Rabbi Israel Bar Meir, together with Joseph Caro, in person. The letter of the three rabbis was directed against a Jew from Safed who "wanted to be called *Maguid*". He is said to have informed on Jews to the authorities. His actions were ground for excommunication by the elders of Safed.

The bitter fruit of Nasi's dream of getting the Crown of Cyprus, was the Order of Expulsion of Safed Jews to Cyprus. In October 1576 and 1577 drastic orders were issued: the Jews of Safed with their families and possessions were to be expelled from Safed and its environs to Famagusta in Cyprus. That they could keep their possessions already showed a certain measure of leniency. Yet the orders were never executed. Skillfully an issue was raised which gained the support of the Muslim judge in Safed: expulsion of the Jews might lead to economic decline in the region. In the month of *Rabi'il* 986 (May 1578) the response came from

Istanbul that if it is decided to deport the Jews to Cyprus, the Public Revenue will lose a considerable amount of money and Safed will be on the verge of ruin. The Treasury of Damascus will suffer a loss of poll-tax and extraordinary levies. No buyers will be found for deserted Jewish houses. It was therefore commanded that the Judge of Safed should desist from deporting members of the Jewish community to Cyprus..."

The governor of Safed in collusion with his own clique of night watchmen, dragomans and other officials, including one Jew was involved in heavy racketeering and extorsion. There were violations of the Sabbath rest. When thieves attacked the house of a Jew and killed him, innocent members of the Jewish community were accused of murder, some were imprisoned and flogged, the governor demanding five-hundred gold pieces. The governor's soldiers broke into the Jewish homes one night, but again members of the Jewish community were imprisoned for the soldiers deeds, with an order to be administered seventy lashes. The night watchmen with a twisted sense of their mission, ambushed Jewish trade caravans passing betweeen Safed and Damascus, demanding one *para* (silver coin) for each animal.

In *Rajab* 985 (september 1577), an order was sent to the governor-general and the *defterdar* (treasurer) of that province, to enforce more effective comprehensive payment of the poll-tax by the Jews of Safed. Another surprising order was sent in June 1578 to the governor of Safed through the *kethüda* (his official agent in Istanbul) demanding that the Jews (and other subjects) in the Safed region be prevented from using rifles. Since the most irredentist elements in the region, and the most likely to use rifles were the Druzes, the measure must have been aimed to disarming them. However there was through the breaking down of Imperial authotity, a broad insecurity in the area and Jews often found themselves in mortal danger. In 1585-86, the Jews of Istanbul agreed to built a *khan* (a fortified courtyard) in Safed, within which the members of the community would be able to find refuge from "night bandits, armed thieves who come in the dark while they are in their homes."

A concern emerged that beyond a certain point Jewish prosperity might obscure the Islamic character of the city, as expressed in the following *firman* issued in *Dhu al Qa'da* 002 (November 1584):

"Order to the Governor-General and Judge of Damascus:
The judge of Safed has sent a letter to my Threshold of Felicity and has reported that in the town of Safed there are only seven sacred mosques. And the Jews (who) in olden times had three synagogues have now thirty-two synagogues, and they have made their buildings very high (which hurts the feelings of their Muslim neighbors). And they have bought much real estate and constituted it as pious foundations to their synagogues...

I have therefore ordered that you shall personally investigate the matter...according to the laws of the Noble *Sheri'a* (Moslem Law). You must faithfully report whether the above-mentioned synagogues are ancient...or newly established synagogues; if they are new, how (and) when they were established. Report (this) honestly, in detail...and bring the matter before me in truth. Beware of bringing the matter not in accordance with the facts."

CHAPTER 10

MURAD III: JEWISH INTERNATIONAL DIPLOMACY IN SEARCH OF PAX OTTOMANICA

Under Murad III, took place the episode of *Don Solomon Aben Yaeche*, Duke of Metelin, Knight, King-Maker and Exquisite Diplomat (1, 2, 3). In the afterglow of Joseph Nasi's death, around 1585, during the reign of Murad III (1574-1595), arrived in Turkey another Marrano, whose career was to follow the steps of the Duke of Naxos. His name was Solomon Aben Yaesh, born in Tavira, Portugal in 1520. His family assumed the name of Mendes and Solomon was called Alvaro Mendes. According to the historian Abraham Galante (1) he may have been apparented to the Mendes family to which belonged the Due of Naxos. However Cecil Roth (2), another biographer of the Duke of Naxos, holds the opinion that the connection with the great banking-house of Mendes with which Dona Gracia and Joseph Nasi were associated, does not on solid evidence. Salomon Aben Yaesh, as confirmed by both Galante and Roth, is a discovery of the historian Lucien Wolf (3).

The Ottoman Empire in which Salomon Aben Yaesh had arrived and assumed his new identity was ruled by Sultan Murad III (1574-1595), called *Amurat* by the French, see refs 1-5. The situation of the Sephardic Jews was prosperous with a plethora of liturgical writers and flourishing printing presses, despite some perturbing undercurrents. The Turkish annalist Danishmend attributes the Jewish influence (*Yahudi nüfuzu*) at the Seraglio to the Queen-Mother, Nour-Banou Sultan, a Jewess converted to Islam (*Yahudi dönmesi*) (6).

As to the beloved mother of Murad III, Nour-Banou, whose name means Woman of Splendor, Lamartine seduced by the consonance of the words, concluded that she was of Persian origin, but Turkish historians concord that she was of Jewish origin, including this author's history teacher at the French Lyceum of Saint-Benoît in Istanbul. Sultan Murad III had two great loves in his life: his mother Nour-Banou and his wife the Venetian Safiye Sultan. Nour Banou tried to find solace in her son's love for the infidelities and and inconsistencies of her husband Selim II.

She outlived Selim and wielded considerable power in the *Seraglio*, inaugurating in Ottoman history the fateful era called the Reign of Women (*Kadinlar Saltanati*).

The law of the Seraglio (*raison d'état*) or the dynastic canon of Mehmed II ordered the immolation for the crime of "public peril" of all the brothers of the Sultan ascending the throne. It is assured that Murad, influenced by the Venetian *Sultana* Safiye, his spouse, and by his own repugnance for innocent blood, had sworn to Safiye to revoke this State butchery, but the *Mufti* (highest Islamic authority) issued a *fetva* which forbade to the Sultan to show any pity. The ministers hastened to have the five princes strangled and their bodies thrown on the carpet of the *Divan* (Ministerial Council Chamber), under the eyes of Murad. The following day, Murad III mourned for his father, and went to cry next to the sepulchers of his five brothers.

The Sultan, together with eminent qualities, also had weaknesses of character which may have started the empire on the path of decadence. The twenty-eight year old sultan did not exhibit more than a faint resemblance to his illustrious ancestor Süleyman I. His long eyelashes, like those of a woman, had a Persian charm, but his red and sparse beard contrasted with the color of his hair, creating an unusual and depressing effect." Murad III had an excellent education, with administrative experience since the age of fifteen, as governor of a province in Western Anatolia. His literary *persona* was very strong. He left four collections of poems (*Divan*, in the literary sense), two in Turkish, one in Arabic, one in Persian. His collected works range from mystical writings to delicate and sensitive poems, signed *Muradi*, or Murad, according to the exigencies of the rhymes. He therefore had the intellect and culture to appreciate the qualities of Salomon Aben Yaesh. Unfortunately his physical and mental health were undermined by excesses in wine and the use of opium to which he had become addicted since an early age. The Turkish historian Münecim-Bashi writes: "he was so uniquely dominated by indulgence in pleasure (*Zevk-u-Sohbet*) that during all his reign there was no chance for him to leave Istanbul." Encouraged by the complacency of his mother, Murad III found solace in the harem, which became the main center of power politics. There was in the harem of the time a bitter-sweet power struggle between two main parties (5), that of the Queen-Mother Nour-Banou Sultan and that of the principal favorite Safiye Hatun, mother of the Crown Prince Mohammed (Mehmed). The most prominent adherents to Nour-Banou Sultan were Esma, the sister of Murad III, married to the Grand-Vizier Sokullu and the Lady-in-chief of the Harem (*Kethüda*), the famous Djanfeda (Canfeda). Nour Banou and Esma were finally able to introduce in the harem a Persian slave and a Hungarian slave, who succeeded in temporarily interrupting the sultanic idyl with Safiye. Soon there would be more than forty *Haseki Sultanas* (harem ladies, each of whom had mothered a son from the Sultan). The court historiographer Ali has left a portrait in verse of Nour-Banou, which makes her look no better than the Jezabel or Athalie of biblical times. It seems that in true priestess and princess from Sidon, Nour-Banou had been able to slander Safiyeh, accusing her of using magic spells against the fertility of the two rival slaves (the Persian and the Hungarian). Suspecting some Jewish women and other slaves to have entered into an imaginaruy conspiracy with the Venetian Sultana,

Nour-Banou had them tortured by the eunuchs, some of them being dumped and drowned in the Bosphorus by the ill-famed *mutes*, silent executioners greatly appreciated for their discrete services...

Nour-Banou ended probably poisoned by Safiye as the story goes (5a). Despite her failings, bitter rivalry and cruelty in accordance with harem mores of the time, the Turkish historian Danishmend has some words of praise for her due to her Moslem piety. Nour-Banou left behind her a number of good deeds, the most notable being the construction of the *Valide-i-Atik* mosque at Toptachi, in the district of Üsküdar (Istanbul-Asia), with on its ground a *medrese* (religious academy), lodgings and a charitable hospital. Dressed in mourning clothes Murad III attended the funeral service for Nour-Banou held on December 6, 1583 at the mosque of Fatih (6). Burial followed on the grounds of Santa Sophia in the *Türbe* (funeral crypt) of her husband Selim.

Don Joseph Nassi's widow, the Duchess Reyna continued to live at the Palace of Belvedere (7). She maintained her husband's great library, and was involved in active patronage of Hebrew and Ladino printing which started to flourish in Constantinople. Isaac Ascaloni, a scholar, presumably of Palestinian origin, prevailed on her to found a printing press herself. The books were emblazoned in glorious phrases: "Printed in the palace of the Duke Don Joseph Nasi, at Belvedere which is near Constantinople, under the rule of Sultan Murad." Among the works published were first *Gan shel Egozim* (the garden of Egozi) by Moses Egozi, homilies on the Pentateuch, *Torath Hesed* (a commentary on prophetical lessons by Moses Jabez); there was also a guidebook to the Holy Places in Palestine in Ladino, *libro intitulado Yichus ha-Zadikim*. After 1597, the press and perhaps Dona Reina's residence were moved from Belvedere to Kuruçeshme, a modest suburb on the Bosphorus. Among other productions were *Tapuhe Zahab* (the Golden Apple) by Moses Alsheikh, a scholastic edition of the tractate *Ketuboth* from the Babylonian Talmud and *Minhath Kohen* by the Sephardi writer Joseph Cohen. The press ceased to function in 1599.

Solomon Aben Yaesh (1-3, 8-9) was born in Tavira, Portugal around 1520. Throughout his career in the Ottoman Empire he was diplomat and King-Maker. He belonged to the peace party in contrast to the dashing Duke of Naxos who at one time dreamed of holding the crown of Cyprus, until Grand-Vizier Sokullu convinced the Sultan Selim II that no matter how exalted, a Jew, was not to reign over Turkish and Christian residents of the island...And so the dream of the Duke of Naxos was no more than a *narguileh* (water-pipe) rêverie. The Duke of Naxos by his passionate resentment of Venice and his regal ambitions had dragged the Ottoman Empire and the proud Republic of the Doge into a titanic confrontation, which renovated the fury of the Crusades ending in the disastrous defeat of the Ottoman fleet at Lepanto. On the opposite side, Solomon Aben Yaesh and his contemporary Salomon Ashkenazi (*Alamanonoglou* as the Turks called him), while working through different diplomatic channels, were the architects of a pax ottomanica. Solomon Aben Yaesh brillianly carried out what amounted to an alliance between Elizabethean England and the Ottoman Empire.

Solomon Aben Yaesh had been trained as a jeweller (1). Solomon (alias Alvaro Mendes, as he was called at the time), was around 1545, in charge of exploiting diamond mines in the kingdom of Narsinga, in the region of Madras, India. After his return to Europe he had a dazzling career in the royal and diplomatic circles of Portuguese, French, Italian and English courts. The person of the Portuguese Alvaro Mendes described in Cecil Roth's monograph *Men and Things Jewish Portuguese in Orient* was identical with Salomon Abenaes, Duke of Metelin, whose biography is treated at length in the study of Lucien Wolf (3) entitled *Jews in Elizabethean England.*

In Portugal, Alvaro Mendes, around 1555, gained the confidence of King John III, who bestowed upon him the Title of Knight of the Order of St. Jago of Compostella. After the death of John III, in 1564, he was reported to be in Florence and there is a somewhat apocryphal story that he may have visited his supposed relative the Duke of Naxos, then at the height of his career. Five years later he settled in Paris, with occasionnal trips to Antwerp, London, Lyons and Venice. He already was in the confidence of the two shrewdest and most ruthless of the leaders in Europe, Elizabeth, Queen of England and Catherine de Médicis, Queen-Mother of France. Under a glitter of glory and courtly refinement, the sophistication of the courts could not hide the barbaric customs of the time, as the head of a queen rolled under the axe of the executioner in Elizabethean England, and the nightmare of the Saint-Barthélémy massacre swept through Valois France.

In a letter to Sir Francis Walsington, Sir Henri Cobhan, English Ambassaor in France, was describing a Saturday dinner of King (Henri III) with the Portuguese Alvaro Lopez, in company of the Dukes of Lorraine, the Duke de Guise and his favorites. Soon after, practically all the participants in the royal banquet including the King himself were assassinated one after the other. Alvaro Mendes was still at the beginning of a long and splendid career (1). He had at the death of the cardinal-king Henri of Portugal, espoused the cause of the pretender Don Antonio born of a Jewish mother, Violante Gomez. He had to contend with Philip II, King of Spain, a grandson by his mother Elizabeth of King Manuel of Portugal. After Antonio's defeat at Alcantara, Alvaro put him in touch with Catherine de Médicis. His sponsorship of Antonio brought Alvaro Mendes in contact with the crown of England, through the intermediary of his brother-in-law Rodrigo Lopez, Physician-in-Chief of the Queen.

In the spring of 1585, Alvaro Mendes was to arrive in Salonica (1). Obviously Alvaro was on his way to a great dignity and his fame crossing the boundaries of the Ottoman Empire before his arrival already had reached the court of the Sultan. Upon arriving in Salonica and returning to Judaism with all his family, Alvaro Mendes assumed the ancestral patronymic Salomon Abenaish (Abenyaez) or Ibn Yaish which goes back to Don Yahya Aben Yaesh, treasurer of the first king of Portugal, who pretended to be of Davidic descent.

Aben Yaesh visited the embassies in Constantinople and had entry to the Sublime Porte, maintaining contacts with the *Divan* (Council of Viziers). He was appointed high commissioner at the Imperial Court. At that time he started to maintain an elaborate network of intelligence service all over Europe, using his connections in the diplomatic services (1). After gaining the confidence of Murad III, Don Solomon was bestowed the title of Duke of Metelin and he also gained concession of the town of Tiberias and the surrounding villages in Palestine (10). The fact that another duchy was created seems to indicate that there may already have been at the time a duke of Naxos, in the person of Joseph Passi (2). However gained the concession of Tiberias was extended to Solomon instead of Passi.

The island of Metelin, Mittilli or Midilli, which was a duchy became the fiefdom of Salomon is no other than the ancient Lesbos, home of the lyric poet Alcaeus and the poetess Sappho. The chief city, Mytilene, originally was a separate island, later linked by a causeway, and it was because of its good harbor that Mytilene became the capital (1). It was in 1354 the patrimony of the Genovese family Gattilusio, passing after the fall of Byzantium under Turkish rule.

It was not a casual decision which motivated Solomon Aben Yaesh to settle in Constantinople. He envisioned universal peace centered on a symbiosis of pax Ottomanica and pax Britannica. The sultan who wrote lyric poetry and was a classic of mystical writing certainly had the mind and also maybe the goodwill for Salomon, a man of destiny (1, 2). In Constantinople, Solomon started to work on a Turco-British alliance as a counterwight to Philip II of Spain. From her side, Queen Elizabeth of England was supporting the rebellion in the Netherlands, being also in alliance with the Moors. In 1587, a delicate matter developed between the two countries, as nine Englishmen were made prisoners on the coasts of Tripoli. The Turkish admiral graciously agreed to render them their liberty, but by delivering them not to Narbonne, the seat of a British ambassador with whom he was embroiled in a feud, but rather to Solomon, who then turned them to the British Embassy as a mark of consideration for the Queen.

In 1588, a new English ambassador, Lord Barton, arrived in Constantinople, who starting as a good friend of Solomon, later entered into a long-lasting controversy with him (1, 2). Solomon benefited from the trust of Queen Elizabeth of England, and she wrote to the Sultan a letter in his favor (1). It was a victory over Barton, who still embittered, continued to complain to Lord Burleigh, Queen Elizabeth's Minister, alluding to the fact that while Solomon was a declared Jew, his messengers Cormano and Sarfatim as well as Rodrigo Lopez were Crypto-Jews of London, the queen having received two of Solomon's messengers as if they were ambassadors of Christian princes.

In 1593, Solomon sent Serfatim to London, on a mission to ensure the benevolent neutrality of England, in the event of a war between Turkey and Hungary. When hostilities erupted, Barton accompanied the Ottoman army to the battlefied in Hungary, and was a witness to the crushing victory won by the Turks at the battle of Kereztes (Haç Ova).

The Solomon-Barton duel was continuing. In the meantime the Portuguese pretender Antonio who had broken up with Aben Yaesh after being denied a considerable loan, maintained in Constantinople an agent by the name of Passi. Passi was another prominent Sephardi, who may have been a nephew of the Sultan's physician Moses Amon or of Joseph Segura, his successor. He greatly influenced Turkish policy for this period (18). He was rumored to have been elevated to the rank of Duke of Naxos and the Archipelago, a position vacant since Joseph Nasi's death, six years earlier. The Venetians kept a close eye on him, and found his information reliable and trustworthy. The Spanish did their best to lure him to their side, and Spain's viceroy in Naples suggested that he should be given a regular allowance. Passi the agent visited Barton at the instigation of the Portuguese pretender to make insinuations about the way Don Solomon had acquired his fortune, but Passi's fate was soon to be sealed. He had a violent quarrel with his former patron, the Grand Vizier Sinan, conqueror of Tripoli, and great collector of manuscripts, but somewhat venal in other respects. An indiscretion in a letter to the chancellor of Poland, which may have seemed to the Grand-Vizier, as a betrayal and a breech of confidence, inasmuch as it affected the reliability of his conciliatory move towards Poland, may have been at th origin of the rift with Sinan Pasha which became very violent and life-threatening. After initially seeking refuge in the residence of the *Beylerbey* (Governor) the disgraced Duke of Naxos was chained and deported to Rhodes. Passi had some hand in the Sultan's finances, but the matter apparently turned to disaster in 1589. Moses Benveniste, another Jewish star of the time (11), made plenipotentiary, together with two Turks to open negocitions with Spain, arbitrarily exceeded his instructions. He was arrested with his colleagues and deported to Rhodes. Thus, arrests and deportations had broken the anti-Don Solomon party.

During the travel of Juda Serfatim to London in 1592 another tragedy had stricken, as the most valuable agent of Don Solomon, his brother-in-law Rodrigo Lopez fell victim to one of the many Elizabethean purges of the inflexible queen (2). Serfatim wrote a letter to Lord Burgleigh (Burgley, Privy Council of the Crown) requesting that the execution of Rodrigo Lopez be delayed, since he was "of the blood of Monseigneur le Duc", until Monseigneur may have a chance to communicate with the queen. The Privy Council answered "that the anger of the people was so great, that it was impossible to act on the request." Solomon had lost his primary channel of communication to the queen, but he still remained in control of a most powerful intelligence service.

A few years earlier, Don Solomon had achieved a feat in communications (see Galante 34). On October 9, 1588, Giovanni Moro, Venetian ambassador in Constantinople, was writing to the Doge and Senate:

"Alvaro Mendes was the first to announce that the Spanish Armada had been defeated by the English. The Ragusan representative declared the opposite. When the English representative went to see the Pashas to confirm to them the Spanish defeat, they simply answered 'May God grant that it be so', demonstrating in that way that they had their doubts."

The time was ripe for peacemaking between Barton and Solomon (2). The circumstances were due to a recurrent crisis in the Balkans, due to the restiveness of three local princes (*Voivodas*), namely the Voivods of Transylvania, Walachia and Moldavia. The death of Peter the Lame, Voivod of Moldavia precipitated the crisis. As the troops in Constantinople were in permanent rioting, the janissaries were seditious in Moldavia, offering the throne of the principalty to the highest bidder...It seems that a certain Pole of hypothetical Jewish extraction, Emanuel

Aron (12) [according to Lamartine, a Moldavian stable-hand (13)] was able to raise the most attractive *baksheesh* (bribe money), with the help of Barton, who guaranteed the amount needed, some 300,000 crowns, as the price went.

The story gets more complicated with involvement at one time or another of two Solomons!, the Duke of Metelin and Solomon Nathan Ashkenazi (Alamanoghlou) the doctor of the Grand-Vizier Sinan Pasha and the champion of peace with Venice. Both Barton and Solomon Ashkenazi favored the nomination of Aron. Barton aimed to enhance English influence in that area of the Balkans and Ashkenazi imagined that this would secure a more humane treatment for the Jews of the semi-autonomous principalty. After getting his appointment, Aron reneged on the debt, abandoning Barton to the mercy of the creditors. This was the moment chosen by Don Solomon for the rapprochement. He offered to the British Government an advance in the amount of 300,000 crowns.

Two years later Ashkenazi went to Jassy, the Moldavian capital to sollicit compensation for his efforts in favor of the Voivod Aron, which seem to have entailed some expenditures. Instead, he was handed over to the Voivod of Transylvania, and might have indefinitely languished in the jail, if it were not for the intervention of the British ambassador asking as a personal favor the release of the "Jew doctor of the Grand-Vizier Sinan Pasha", plus a generous ransom of 45,000 ducats.

In November 1594 at the urging of Pope Clement VIII the spirit of a new Crusade (*La Sainte League*, the Holy Alliance) inflamed the Balkans creating the Triple Alliance of the Three Voivods, the Transylvanian Prince Sigismond Bathory, the Moldavian Voivod Aron Tiranuj (Tyrant in Roumanian, also named *Zalim* by the Turks) and Michael Viteazul (the Brave) Voivod of Valachia. The chancellor of the Grand-Vizierate Ferhat Pasha ordered the dismissal of Aron and dispatched a new appointee, but he was turned back and the Turkish unit under the command of Mustafa Pasha was sent to rectify the situation. According to the Turkish Annalist Danishmend (14) November 13, 1594 was a bloody Sunday, with Michael Viteazul and Aron Tiranul ordering the massacre of Turkish and Greek creditors, all passed through by the sword.

A few months later (January 1595) Murad III was on his death bed. On January 1595 the public heralds and the cannon of the Seraglio announced to the Ottoman people the death of Murad III (15). Under Murad III the "Romanization" of the Ottoman Empire became more obvious with gigantic spectaculars lasting several days, such as the extravaganza enacted for the circumcision of Crown Prince Mehmed III (16). Since the capture of Constantinopler the sultans had on the whole followed a markedly pro-Jewish policy. Murad III, was the first Turkish ruler in whom there may be discerned a definite and consistent anti-Jewish bias (17). Two imperial orders promulgated by Murad III, stated the kind of sandals to be worn by the Jews and the color of their clothing. A 1577 *firman* insisted that it was prohibited for the *rayas* (non-Moslem minorities) to wear white or red sandals, silk clothes or clothing in fine dress, or in general to dress like the Moslems. The Sultan's order was announced on the squares and markets by the public herald. By the second *firman* of 1579, Jews and other *rayas* were prohibited to wear the turban, and had to wear instead a red hat. Mortal danger followed: according to the words of an informer, a Jewish woman had paraded in a carriage through the streets of Constantinople with an ostentateous display of jewelry. An offended and infuriated Murad III had issued a decree for the extermination of all the Jews in the Empire. The intervention of the Ashkenazi couple (Solomon ben Nathan and wife) seconded by the Grand Vizier and the latter's reference to the stipulations of the Koran were successful in averting the disaster, to the credit of the Ottoman system of government where the Sultan himself, despite his absolute power, could be brought to listen to the commands of a Higher Law. Ashkenazi asked the Sultan to alleviate the hard legislation codified against the Jews because of their lack of simplicity. Avoidance of ostentatious life for the Jews also included the prohibition of owning slaves.

Over the years, as Don Solomon continued to work towards a consolidation of the Turco-English alliance, a flurry of correspondence from Spanish and Venetian ambassadors followed (1).

In the words of Lucian Wolf, Aben Yaesh was the chief artisan of the Turkish-English alliance with its consequences on the European balance of power.

At the time that the Ottoman Empire was setting up with England trade relations which were soon to be turned to political exchanges under Sokullu, another European Commonwealth, Switzerland, started to maintain for the first time a Jewish agent in Constantinople to oversee its commercial interests there (18). Mehmed III maintained Don Solomon in all his privileges. He was to outlive this Sultan also...

Don Abenyaesh who died in 1603 at the age of eighty-three cannot be compared to the court Jews (*Hofjude*) who in the Seventeenth and Eighteenth century played a dominant role in many European Courts. The conditions in Turkey were quite different, in terms of benevolence, traditional generosity, enlightened hospitality, a kind of tolerance unequalled in those times, which was conducive to a true Golden Age and an authentic cultural flourishing of Jewish life. Abenyaesh was a statesman in the caliber of Talleyrand, Metternich or Disraeli with a broad world vision and a grasp of political as well as diplomatic life which affected the European balance of power.

Abenyaesh patronized Hebrew scholarship, but the only reference to him in Hebrew sources are panegyric prefixes in two talmudic tractates *Shabbath* and *Yoma* published in Constantinople. The prefix on the title page of the tractate *Shabbath* announces that: "he who engaged himself and assisted in the good deed with his means and his money, to enmerit the public, behold he is the Lord Don Samuel Aben Yaish..." (1, 2).

In Aben-Yaesh's time there took place a follow-up of the Tiberias experiment. This experiment, taken over by the Duke of Metelin (10) following an *interregnum* after the death of the Duke of Naxos, has been variously intrerpreted -- as a philanthropic venture, an experiment anticipating political Zionism, or an economic speculation...Probably it was all of that. The original plan may have been responsive to the old rabbinic adage, approvingly upheld by Maimonides in his great Code: "From Tiberias, the redemption will begin." Tiberias had been the last manifestation of Jewish military presence in ancient times, when the Jewish commander Benjamin of Tiberias collaborated with the Persians against the Byzantines...Tiberias was also the city where the last existence of Jewish independence had continued to flicker upon the extinction of the Patriarcate.

Solomon, the Knight and Monsignor, the Duke of Metelin was too much a gentleman and a man of the world to be a mystic. Therefore Tiberias where temporal and economic power could be applied to Jewish resettlement must have appeared more attractive to the realism of Don Solomon. The grant secured for Don Solomon was administered by his son Jacob (formerly Francisco). Jacob who settled in Tiberias must have been more of a Talmudist and a mystic than his father, who wrote to Rodrigo Lopez:

"Your servitor my son is in the Holy Land, persisting in his folly. He has spent some money in his ardor, without effecting anything, for not understanding well the people in the country. He is an honest man and of a good conscience; he spends all his time in *meldar* (study), and procures more for his soul than after the world. The Lord be for all."

After the death of Aben Yaesh, some continuity of tradition was maintained, with the place of worship founded by Dona Gracia (aunt of the Duke of Naxos) and called *Kahal de la Señora*. In 1748 Rabbi Hayim Aboulaffia of Smyrna settled in Tiberias with a number of Jews, enthusiastically renewing the work of colonization. From then on Tiberias was one of the Four "Holy Cities" together with Jerusalem, Safed and Hebron, towards where Hassidic revivalists continued to converge, and where the Law was studied uninterruptedly.

Contrasting to the Hebrew literary documents writing in illuminated characters the panegyrics of Don Nassi, Duke of Naxos, there is near total silence on Aben Yaesh. The explanation may be found in his sort of coolness towards the Judaic causes espoused by his son. Don Solomon was more of a *gentilhome* in the French sense of the word, than a Talmudic scholar and probably he would have been more at ease at the court of Henri III of France, or in the Elizabethean entourage, or in the *lokum* (Turkish delight) and rose-scented garden sessions of the Sultan and his companion the *Kaptan Pasha* (Grand Admiral) of the Sea, than he might have been comfortable in a rabbinical assembly.

A memorable Jewish biography from the time of Murad III is that of Solomon ben Nathan Ashkenazi (called by the Turks *Alamanoghlou*, son of a German), (11, 19, 20). He had first exerted his Hippocratic skills in Poland, as the physician of King Sigismund III. Then in 1564 he settled in Constantinople, in the service of the Venetian Embassy. Holding the dual titles of Rabbi and Physician, he truly had his heart set on diplomatic endeavors. From Venetisn service Solomon ben Nathan moved to the Ottoman *Divan* (Council of State) when he became special counselor to the Grand-Vizier Sokullu. He was to keep this position for thirty years. His grand act, an expression of Ottoman-sponsored "Jewish Grandeur", was an extraordinary ambassadorship to Venice, to conclude a peace treaty with the Republic. Sokollu knew that no victory was complete unless something was done to heal the searing wounds of the vainquished foe. Venice had been severely amputated if not mortally wounded by the loss of Cyprus at the time of Selim II. Sokollu undertook to ingratiate the *Serenissima Dominante* by proposing a Turkish-Venetian military alliance. The road would be open for the conquest of the Kingdom of Naples from Spain.

In 1574 the Grand Vizier dispatched Ashkenazi to Venice to lay the proposal before the *Signori*. The *bailo* (Venetian delegate, representative) Barbaro, in his dispatches from Constantinople, had recommended Ashkenazi in most cordial terms, as a "man of high ability, and in my opinion well disposed towards you". In the midst of the Venetian Senate there were voices of strong opposition against the approval of the Ottoman ambassadorship despite the favorable words of the Doge's Council of Ten. In the end the credentials of Solomon ben Nathan were approved.

On July 7, 1574, Ashkenazi officially appeared before the Doge and the dignitaries of the Republic, with all the pomp that the diplomatic protocol required (20). Any Venetian cold-shouldering of Ashkenazi, would have been considered as a slight to the Ottoman international prestige. The whole Senate, preceded by the Doge Alici Moncenigo, had gone to the encounter of the Ottoman ambassador, and along the road taken by Salomon, crowds had gathered with frantic applause. The peace treaty was signed at the Palace of the Doge. However, the *Signori* decided to announce that they were rejecting with friendly thanks the offer to help in undertaking a war against Spain. The master plan of dismembering the Spanish Empire was dead.

To the Jews of Venice, Solomon ben Nathan Ashkenazi was the Messiah incarnate. In the colophon to one of Rabbi Joseph Caro's works published in Venice the episode is described (20).

Solomon's two sons remained in Venice to be educated at the expense of the Venetian Republic.

Ashkenazi had been earlier (in 1572) a king-maker. His old benefactor King Sigismund II Augustus of Poland having died childless, five candidates were in line for the succession, among others, Maxilimian II Emperor of Germany, the tsar Ivan IV the Terrible, the Pope's nominee and France's Catherine de Médici's son

Henri de Valois (future Henri III of France), Duke of Anjou. The latter was to become Turkey's favorite when France sollicited Ottoman support by the intermediary of ambassador Francis of Noailles, Bishop of Aix (Acqus). Turkey certainly needed a friendly sovereign along its long frontier with Poland. After Henri de Valois was elected King of Poland, the Bishop of Acqus took all the credit for the successful outcome. A denial came from Solomon who wrote to Henri: "In the election, when Your Majesty was chosen to be King of Poland, it was I who was responsible for all (that was done here)."

In 1578 (21), the grand duke of Tuscany wished to resume diplomatic and commercial relations with Turkey. In a personal letter, sealed with the Shield of David, surrounded by a garland, Solomon ben Nathan Ashkenazi advised the Duke on proper diplomatic etiquette and procedure, matters of supreme importance when dealing with the Ottoman authorities.

There is the reported story of a Spanish bribe, and some confusion between two Jewish personages at the Ottoman court, Solomon Ashkenazi and "Rabbi" Isaac (22). Who was this mysterious "Rabbi" Isaac whose path overlapps with that of of Solomon ben Nathan Ashkenazi, in such an intricate way as to raise the question on whether two separate personages or the two Janus faces of a same personage are involved. Speaking of Rabbi Isaac Roth writes that he was very highly esteemed at the Court and also by all the foreign diplomatic representatives. The Venetians thought it important to gain his sympathy, in the hope that he would help them with Mustapha, the new Grand Vizier; the French ambassador used him as an intermediary in communicating with the same official and promised him a regular allowance of 100 ducats. It was reported by the secretary of the French Embassy as something noteworthy that "Rabbi" Isaac had refused a bribe from the Spanish agent to use his influence for an extension of the armistice between Spain and Turkey. He had good reason. The Spanish sovereign, he said, only wanted to gain time; thus it might have been possible for him to conquer Portugal, after which he would haven been able to turn with full strength against Turkey. If that had happened there would have been no hope for himself, or for any other Jew living there.

Another very influential Jewish physician was Moses Benveniste, mentioned together with David Passy, in reference to the anti-Solomon Aben Yaesh cabal in league with Ambassador Barton (23). He was known to the Turks as Hoca Musahibbi, in attendance on the Grand Vizier Siyavush Pasha. The description by Lamartine (24) has Shylockan overtones, no less filled with maleficence, where the unreal, the melodrama and the historical are blended in an horror tale. The adviser on the currency reform was Moses Benveniste, a frequent collaborator of Solomon Ashkenazi. In 1583 he advised on the currency reform, which had serious repercussions, when "The Jew Money" as it was called led to a Janissary revolt.

The *Darphane Mültezimi* (Director of the Mint) at this time was another Jew, the *chaus* (*çavush*) Hodja Nessimi [Nissim (25)]. The "Jew" (sic) offered the *Bash-Defterdar* (Head-Treasurer) Mahmud Pasha a present of two hundred thousand *aktche* [one *asper*, small silver coin, the base of the Ottoman coinage system, one third of a *para*, one hundred-twentieth of a *kurush* (*groush*)], if he would accept this debased coinage (as described by Lamartine) for the pay of the troops. The *Bash-Defterdar* declined this dishonorable offer. One of the favorites of Sultan Murad III, was the *Ermeni-Dönmesi* (Armenian convert to Islam) *Beylerbey* (Governor) Mohammed Pasha, the Sultan's *Doghandji* (Falconer), so nicknamed because of his function in the Seraglio. The Jew repeated his offer to the Falconer, who rapidly agreed to the present and daringly took upon himsef to make the pay of the troops in the capital with this (debased) money.

The Janissaries, indignant at the derisive money they were receiving, started to riot and to surround the palace, with their vociferous curses. Siyavush Pasha the Grand-Vizier and Ibrahim, the ex-favorite, who were jealous of the domineering position assumed by the *Doghandji* Mohammed, were secretly fomenting the sedition. The gates of the courtyard in the palace were smashed by sixty thousand Janissaries, their numbers swollen by soldiers from other units. The room of the *Divan*, where

Murad III was sitting in ministerial council with his viziers, was resounding with threats which did not even spare the sultan's head. Never, until that day, had a sedition dared to rise up to the sacred name of the Sultan.

"If the *Beylerbey* Mohammed, is not delivered to us", clamored the rioters, "then the Sultan should tremble for himsef. We will know how to arrive till him." Mountains of gold and silver, drawn from the swollen treasury of Murad III, were in vain piled in the courtyard under the hands of the janissaries. The rage was greater than their cupidity.

"The first among us", they roared, "who will consent to touch his pay, before the heads of the Falconer and the treasurer have fallen, let him be punished on the spot."

After having temporized and negociated for several hours to save his favorite, Murad III in tears, embraced him, removed his dagger and delivered him up to the Janissaries. The Falconer was cut to pieces before he had the time to come down from the steps of the *Divan*. The innocent and virtuous *Bash-Defterdar* Mahmoud Efendi, unjustly denounced to the troops, received the same fate which was only deserved by the one who had tempted him. Murad III suspected the Grand-Vizier Siyavush and Ibrahim to have fanned the sedition against his friend. "I was wrong", he said, when entering his harem, "not to have delivered all the viziers to the just vengeance of my slaves; the most guilty have not been stricken."

It appears from Selaniki Mustafa Effendi, a contemporary of the rebellion that the story was much more complicated (25); that the actual trouble had started five years earlier than the events in 1588-1589. It was a more or less complex state decision (which could not have simply emanated from a single Jew in the mint) to alter the silver content of the piaster. With the metal value of the piaster cut by half, speculators were quick in seizing the opportunity, and the entire rate of silver and gold was upset, the Janissaries ending with five gold pieces in pay instead of ten.

A year before the janissary sedition an official government decision was taken called *Tashihi-Sikke* (Correction of the Coinage, of the Mint) according to the chronicler Galib bey, the *Beylerbey* Mohammed the Falconer, an Armenian convert from Marash, was ordered to proceed. Several Ottoman sources are concordant that the Falconer had, to the contrary of the accusations made, started to take steps for the improvement of the coinage, but that he was killed before he he had sufficient time for action. It appears that the Sultan knew something about the inocence of the Falconer and the intrigues of his dignitaries.... He abruptly dismissed the Grand Vizier, the *sheikh-ül-Islam* (highest religious leader), and the whole set of dignitaries in the *Divan*.

As to Moses Benveniste the adviser of the ill-fated currency reform, he was closely associated with Turkish policy, domestic and foreign, for many years. It was his advocacy which had been responsible for the reinstatement of Peter the Lame as *Gospodar* (*Voivod*, Prince, Viceroy under Ottoman suzerainty) of Moldavia (23). Regarding the second Duke of Naxos, David Passi, who had some hand in the sultanic finance, in his book *Don Joseph Nasi* Cecil Roth (26) says that "when the incensed Janissaries invaded the Divan clamoring for the heads of those who were responsible for the debasing of the coinage, he was so severely wounded that he was reported dead. But he completely recovered." It seems that the Sultan very highly valued David Passi and Passi "...had slaves like the Grand Vizier in abundance".

The Merchant of Venice is not the only Elizabethean drama which depicts the Jewish stereotype of the time. The personality of Passy may have a bearing on the figure of the Jew in other Elizabethean drama (27).

Sultan Murad III who fathered one hundred children, maintained in his surrounding a retinue of dwarfs and midgets. He spent much of his leisure in witnessing buffoonic comedies which the Jews--famous at this time as play actors--were compelled to present for the potentate's delectation. At the time of Murad III, there was a Jewish dwarf who became very famous. His doom came, when inebriated by his fame, he used irreverent language about the women of the harem. He ended up banned from the palace.

Under Murad III and his predecessors, the highly respected Jewish Court physicians were exempted from several taxes, and could ride on horses, a privilege ordinarily reserved to the Believers only. At Constantinople, there was at the Court, under Murad III (1574-1565) forty-one appointed Jewish physicians of whom eight held the title of *Pasha*, ranking immediately under that of vizier. The Jewish *pashas* were entitled to the honor of wearing a kalpak of *samour* (*zibeline*), and also by respect for their rank, they wore, as the official rabbis silk *caftans* [an often striped ankle length garment with very long sleeves (from Arabic *shash* for muslin, in this case a band worn about the waist as a dress accessory that is very common in the Levant)] and yellow shoes. There is an echo of the fame of the Jewish physicians in the Sultan's service, but with the stereotyped Shylockan overtone in Robert Greene's play, *The Tragicall raigne of Selimus, sometimes emperor of the Turks*, produced in London between 1588 and 1592 (28). Abraham " a cunning Jew professing physicke" is portrayed, who is used by Selim for his nefarious purposes, but succumbs to them in the end.

In the summer of 1583, a maritime disaster filled with consternation the Jewish community of Salonica. Fifty-five Jews, having boarded a vessel with a Christian crew, were en route to Salonica. In the midst of the sea, *en la alta noche* (in the depths of the night), the crew jumped on the peaceful passengers, men, women and children, killing them all and dumping the cadavers in the sea. A lone survivor was able to reach Rhodes, where he gave a full description of the cowardly and tragic massacre. The assassins were forced to admit their crime to the *Cadi* (Judge). It does seem, however, that a proper punishment was not meeted out to them. In those times, pirates were treated in the popular imagination as court heroes.

Among the notable Salonica Talmudists who lived at the time of Murad III, one can cite Mordehai Matalon (1502-1589). Matalon was equally versed in the Talmud and profane sciences. He was the scion of a family devoted to all kinds of intellectual exercises. He only had a problem with the orthodox rabbinical authorities, who if they could do it, might have set a mini *auto-da-fe* for him. Matalon, because of his encyclopedical knowledge, had grown too liberal for his time.

Matalon's commentaries were still appreciated, and his sermons were favorably followed by the intellectual elite of the city.

Another Talmudist, Salomon Abraham ha-Cohen (38) was probably a native of Serres. He was a man of amenity, affability and goodness. Known under the name of *Mouarchach,* formed by his title and his Hebrew initials, he left a very important imprint in the annals of Salonician casuistics.

Salomon Lebeth Halevy II (38), surnamed the Old, after his death, was a grandson of the poet by the same name. He distinguished himself by his remarkable precociousness in following, for the Talmud, the teaching of Joseph ben Lev and for the profane sciences, the courses of Aaron Afia. A profuse writer, he composed several commentaries on *Avot* (Articles on Chapters of *Fathers*, a Tractate of the *Mishnah* in *Mezikin* having no Talmud commentary; it contains the sayings and religio-ethical teachings of the sages from the Third Century BCE to the Third Century CE). Salomon Lebeth was very knowledgeable of Greek philosophy and an admirer of Moses Maimonides. The influence of Maimonides' *More Mevouhim* (Guide of the Perplexed) is quite visible in his writings.

In the profane sciences, David Bensussan (39), who moved to Constantinople towards the end his life, was a magnificent example of this category of minds to whom no branch of human knowledge was alien. With such Renaissance men on the scene, it was quite natural, to educate the disciples at the *yeshiva* with enyclopedic knowledge in the *Shevath Hohmoth* (geography, history, natural history and physics, medicine and surgery, mathematics, astronomy and astrology, metaphysics.)

The scion of the Yahias, Tam II (40) had come from Constantinople in 1575 to definitely settle in Salonica, where he remained, exerting there till his last day (1594) the functions of *Marbitz Tora* at the Lisbon synagogue. A man of great culture, he surrounded himself with scholars. His brother Moses had served as physician at the Sultan's Court before coming to settle in Salonica. Emulating the death of Amatus Lusitanus during the plague of 1565, it was in taking care of the sick during the great 1595 epidemic that he found death.

The Midrash ha-Shir, the College of Poetry of the two Gedalias

Moses' second son Gedaliah (41) in the Yahia lineage was the founder of the *Midrash ha-Shir*, the College of Poetry. He organized an academy of rhetoric. The poet Longo celebrates the birth of Gedaliah who would become the animator of a great poetical movement after having studied hebrew prosody, syntax and grammary, acquiring in all these fields an uncontested mastery. He was influenced by the visit of a close relative and homonym from the Italian branch of the Yahias, Gedaliah ben Joseph (1515-1587), who had come in 1568 to Salonica to gather material for his great work *Shalshelet ha-Cabbala* (Chain of of Tradition). He wrote many historical works of which only *Shalshelet ha-Cabbala* has been published. This is a history of Jewish scholars, so replete in legendary elements that it was sarcastically dubbed a "Chain of Lies". Nevertheless it is considered of great importance for history as well as folklore. Gedaliah ben Joseph was a charmer. What exerted the greatest impression on the Salonician Gedaliah was the description by his Italian relative of the literary circles which were flowering in Rome, Florence, Naples, Ferrara, Modena, Genoa and Bologna (41). The young salonician may also have heard from other visitors about the ancient *Académie de Jeux Floraux* in Toulouse, this celebrated consistory of the *Maintenance du Gay Savoir* [Maintenance of the Gay (Merry) Knowledge] (41). The Toulouse Academy used to organize poetry tournaments largely attended by contesting poets in the hope of collecting the gold or silver flowers, attributed to the most beautiful poetry. Gedalish ben Yahia also was informed of the academy of poetry founded in the Ottoman capital, by the physician Joseph Amon. Members of Gedaliah's academy would gather once a month in the house of Moses, everyone reciting, in a declamatory style, the poetry he had written. Poets from neighboring or far away localities would join in. Discrete subsidies were available for the meritorious aspirants cultivating the Muses. There also were corresponding members, among them Saadia Longo and Israel Najara (42), the two *choryphées* of Sephardic letters (43).

CHAPTER 11

MEHMED III: A QUESTION OF DEBASED COINAGE

The decline of the Ottoman Empire was accelerated under Mehmed III (1595-1603) (1). Murat III had one hundred and two children from his wives, many concubines and slaves (2). In accordance with the traditional law of fratricide, the new Sultan Mehmed III inaugurated his reign with the immolation of nineteen brothers. The Queen-Mother, Sultana Safiye, Venetian birth and in touch with many Venetian and Christian princesses, had been nonetheless desensitized to the ferocious practices of the Ottoman court; she barely uttered a word! The Imperial tragedy is touchingly described by Lamartine (2).

The Balkan crisis was now spreading with Valachia in full uprising (3, 4). The army of the Grand Vizier Sinan Pasha met disaster in the swamps of Kalugeran on the outskirts of Bucarest. On October, 1595 a new disaster followed and the fortress of Tergovitz fell into the hands of Voivod Michael. It seems, if the story is not apocryphal, that after the fall of Tergovitz acts of cannibalism followed. The governor of Trebizond, Ali Pasha, and the governor of Amasya, Koçu Bey, who were among the captive, together with other dignitaries were all impaled and roasted on slow fire, then abandoned to the festivities of the troops.

Shortly before the Tergovitz disaster, a tragically unfolding drama had sealed the fate of Ferhad Pasha, son-in-law of Safiye and twice Grand-Vizier (4). While Ferhad Pasha was approaching the Danube as commander of the Valachian campaign, his archenemies at the court of Murad III's successor Mehmed III obtained the rescinding of his appointment. Ferhad Pasha, with a foreboding of his possible execution, delivered the seal of Imperial Authority (*Mühürü Hümayun*) to the newly appointed governor of Valachia Satirdji (Sword and Large Knife Maker) Mehmed Pasha, and tried to seek refuge in his farm of Litroz. At this juncture, the ubiquitous Solom Ashkenazi reappeared on the scene trying to save his friend Ferhad; he carried to Ibrahim Pasha, current *locum-tenens* of the Grand-Vizierate a very precious dagger with which he was able to obtain the issuance of a new *Hatti Sherif* (Decree) for Ferhad'd pardon. In the meantime an intrigue at the Sultan's stables aggravated the situation, thus triggering the hidden anger of Mehmed III, who resented the excessive protectiveness of his mother Safiye for her son-in-law Ferhad. The unfortunate ex-Grand Vizier was thrown into the dungeon of *Yedi-Kule* (the Seven Towers). Soon a new *Hatti-Sherif* was issued, this time with the death penalty and Ferhad died strangled. There is also a interesting retelling of Ferhad's drama by Lamartine, with the special romanticized flavor of the French author's style (5).

During the reign of Mehmed III a terrible tragedy concluded the wondrous story of the Seraglio Jewess Esther Kyra, (6-8). The Greek term *kyra* is the equivalent of the English Dame. The first Jewish *kyra* seems to have performed services for the ladies of the Sultan's Harem. Her services were considered beneficial to the state; Süleyman I issued a decree permanently exempting her and her descendants from various imposts. The decree was reconfirmed by Selim II, Murad III, Mehmed III, Ahmed I and Osman II. The first Jewish *kyra* adopted Islam in 1548 under the name of Fatma. It is said that she belonged to a Karaite family in Kaffa.

Far better known is Esther Kyra, known as the *Seraglio Jewess*, from the Rabbanite community and a master player at harem intrigues and international politics. She was the widow of Ribbi Elia Handali of Constantinople. The historian Solomon Rozanes (9) gives another explanation for the etymology of the word *Kyra* which must have been derived from the Spanish *querer* (to wish). When Galante was visiting some islands of the Aegan Archipelago as an inspector of the Turkish Ministry of Education, he observed that the terms *Kyra* and *Kyrassa* were given to ambulatory sales girls. Since Esther Handali had started at the palace as a sales woman, her appellation may have described her profession. In his *Tarih-i-Abu-el-Farouk*, the Turkish historian Mehmed Murad (10), has the name *Kyra* followed by that of *Dudu*, *Dudu* is indeed a female name, in use among Jewesses of the Orient.

Jewish influence in the *Seraglio* remained quite strong, as Lamartine, Galante, Danishmend and Cecil Roth have described, by the works of the legendary Esther Kyra, the famed woman merchant of the Great Bazar, through her commerce in fabrics and jewelry for the opulant *Sultana* Safiye, wife of Murad III and mother of Mehmed III.

The career of Esther Kyra spans a prodigious period from the reign of Süleyman the Magnificent to that of Mehmed III. Galante claimed to have obtained from the hands of Ahmed Saib Bey, a Turkish revolutionary publisher of the Young Turk newspaper *Shure-i-Ummet* a copy of the *firman* issued by Sultan Süleyman I, exempting Esther Kyra from taxes. It is likely that there is a confusion between the first Kyra and Esther. The latter was instrumental in the introduction of Dona Gracia Mendes and Don Joseph Nasi to the Court.

Under Murad III the harem women gained considerable political influence, which made the Turkish historians call this period the beginning of the Rule by Women (*Kadinlar Saltanati*). The actual Ottoman power was in the hands of the Queen Mother, Nour Banou and the Sultan's favorite Safiye. According to Cecil Roth when during the reign of Murad III, the women of the *Seraglio* began to direct the affairs of the Empire, it was Kyra who manipulated the women. Kyra who had unhindered entries to the palace established strong connections with the two ladies inside the *Seraglio's* walls and also extramurally with the foreign ambassadors in Galata. Esther Kyra was party to all the intrigues, whether love or ambition, in the palace. It was alleged that through her direct pipeline to the Queen and harem sources, as well as ties to diplomatic circles, she was informed of the most intimate state secrets, even before the Grand-Vizier himself.

When a Turkish ship coming from Algiers, with the governor Ramazan Pasha's wife on board, was captured by the Venetians, it was Esther Kyra who was entrusted by Safiye to carry out the delicate negociations. The French Queen Catherine de Médicis entertained a direct correspondence with Sultan Safiye to obtain assistance from the Ottoman fleet of Murad III against the Spanish Navy under Philip II. According to Galante, it seems that, being in the confidence of Safiye, Kyra obtained a copy of one of Médici's letters. She was indiscrete enough to reveal the correspondence to the ambassador of Venice, a compatriot of the Sultana. Playing a complex game of intrigues, and motivated by self-profit, Kyra was even able, under the protection of Safiye, to organize a lottery in Venice, being the first foreigner to obtain such permission.

There is a letter from Safiye Sultan to the Venetian ambassador to confirm the receipt of velvet she had ordered by the intrermediary of Esther. From velvet and women clothing Esther moved her intra- and extramural trade to the distribution of fiefdoms, not to the most meritorious but rather to the highest bidder. At the death of Murad III, as Queen mother, Safiye wielded immense power; her confident Esther Kyra accordingly became even more powerful.

Under Mehmet III, came the epilogue to the story of Esther Kyra, "the riot of the Spahis". Esther Kyra's tactlessness brought upon her the wrath of the *Ulemas* (Hierarchy of Theological scholars) in league with the proud *Spahis* (elite Cavalry). Both groups demanded from Mehmed III Esther's death. With Safiye in control, Esther still appeared untouchable, but she committed a fatal mistake in supporting one candidate to the command of the Spahis against another. The Turkish historian Mustafa Effendi Selaniki Zade (11) gives the following account of her demise:

"One Friday, the fifteenth of the month of Ramadhan 1008 (1592), the Janissaries went to the *Sheikh-ül-Islam* (highest Islamic juridical authority) Sun'Allah Effendi and asked him: 'Can the goods that we buy with bad coinage, which represents our *ulufe* (pay) be considered *hilal* (legitimate)?

The Sheikh-ül-Islam answered 'these goods are not considered hilal'. Upon this answer the Janissaries exclaimed 'They pay our salary with this ill-fated coinage, because the Jewess has control of the Customs...We shall smite her, give us a *fetva* (religious sentence)." The sheikh-ül-Islam told them that it is not allowed to kill *zimmis* (non-Muslims living in a Moslem country) and Jews. The Sheikh-ül-Islam advised them: "Make up a petition, mention your wishes there and I shall take charge to present it to his Imperial Majesty, who will answer you by a *Hatti-Hümayun* (Imperial declaration)." This proposition did not seem to satisfy the seditious Janissaries...who decided... to go... the next morning, on Saturday, to the residence of the *kaimakam* (*kaymakam*, district manager) Khalil (Halil) Pasha...they penetrated the courtyard of the Pasha...and shouted: "Naturally, if one

sells to the Jewess Kyra the government charges...then he must show himself
before!"...As nobody showed up, the Janissaries delegated the *tchaoush bashi*
(*çavush bashi*, sergent master, master sergeant) Ömer Aga and the *kapou kethüdasi*
(commander of the gate) Nassoub Aga to find out the places where they could
hide...in the midst of all this, the *tchaoush basshi* Ömer Aga suddenly appeared
dragging Esther Kyra which he forced on a horse. She had barely dismounted in the
courtyard of the Pasha, that the Spahis, impatient, rushed on her and killed her with
their daggers and they had her body tied to a rope dragged to the plaza of *At-
Meydan* (Hippodrome). Arrived at the plaza, the Spahis swore again on the Koran,
to gather in one place the children and relatives of Kyra to kill them. From the
plaza of *At-Meydan*, the Spahis went again to the Sheikh-ül-Islam, asking him to
sign their petition and to have it delivered to the Sultan. Zia-el-Abidin Effendi, the
ancient *Cadi* of Mecca and the preacher Seid Abdul Kerim Effendi interfered in the
matter, took the petition and reshaped the text in conformity with the dispositions
of the *Sheri* (religious law), and by the intermediary of the *Sheikh-ül-Islam* had it
addressed to the Sultan. The next day, Sunday, a great crowd returned to the palace
of the *Kaymakam-Pasha* and insisted that the relatives of the Jewess must be
delivered up to them...After many searches, they ended up finding the son of the
Jewess, who was brought before the mob, and stabbed...His cadaver, cut in several
pieces was dragged next to that of his mother. Kyra's younger son converted to
Islam. This conversion was accepted at the condition that he would discharge
himself of all the debts incurred against the government...A number of measures
were taken against the Jews. They were prohibited to dress in clothes made from
fine cloth, they had to wear red caps, they were prohibited from being involved in
the administration of government trusts. It was also decided that the value of the
coinage would be brought back to the original state. All these demands were
sanctioned by *Irade* (decree) of the Sultan. The *Kaymakam* Halil Pasha put at the
disposition of the government 100,000 ducats to be used to fix the value of the
coinage. The Imperial *Irade* affirming all these demands was read by the *Kazasker*
(Commander) of Rumelia, Hodja Zade Mehmed Effendi. The reading of this
document was religiously listened to by the Spahis who then felt vindicated. The
Spahis abstained from demanding the heads of the Bostandji-Bashi (*Bostanci-
Bashi*, officer commanding the Sultan's body-guards) and the *Kapou-Aghasi* (Chief
White Eunuch in the Imperial Palace) Gadanfer...After praying for the longevity of
the Sultan (*Padishahim çok yasha*, Long live the King), the Spahis dispersed...The
cadavers of the accursed, left without burial for some days...now partially devoured
by dogs, exhaled a foul odor wich incommodated the Muslims. The authorization
was asked to clear the plaza. The Spahis at the service of the *Mehter-Hane* (a
military band in the train of the Vizier) brought wood and burned the decayed
cadavers. Because of the ties that the accursed...had entertained with the Imperial
Harem and considering the profits she had drawn from the ministering of customs,
she had accumulated such a quantity of jewels that it was imposible to count or
weigh them...These jewels were sent to the Sultan as they were being found. In
addition to the value of these goods, Kyra's fortune in coins was calculated to be of
500 loads of aspers, disregarding one thousand bonds representing the *ulufe*

(soldiers' pay) bought from their owners, the value of the jewelry, the buildings she possessed in forty two different places, and the mechandise she had on ships. All this fortune was confiscated and the sale of some articles was entrusted to a man of integrity called Mustafa Effendi, who had previously been the *Mütevelli* (Coptroller) of Sultan Süleyman Khan.

The version rendered by the historian Mehmed Behmedmi Effendi (12) makes no mention of Janissaries. In this version it says that the *tchaoush bashi* Kazandji Ömer Pasha (went) to Kyra's residence and brought her with her sons to the palace of Halil Pasha. They had barely ascended the Palace's when they were killed by the Spahis. The Queen-Mother, indignant of Halil Pasha's action, dismissed him and replaced him by one of the eunuchs, Ahmed Pasha. In the version rendered by the Turkish historian Danishmend (9) Kyra (Kira, Kera) is called *Yahidiyye-i acuze* (Jewish old woman), *kocakari* (old woman, devilish hag). She is described as "the corrupting connection" of Mehmed III's mother called *Sedefi durr-i Hilafet* (Mother-of-pearl shell of the Caliphate).

Galante (13) renders the translation of the firman by Osman II related to Kyra (but there is some uncertainty about which Kyra), mentioning the services rendered by the Jewess Kyra to the Mother Sultana of one of his great ancestors the late Sultan Süleyman the Magnificent. One of the descendants of the aforementioned (Jewess) the Jew Cord, grandson of Elias, had addressed a petition to bring to the Imperial, knowledge the fact that the aforementioned Kyra, before embracing Islamism had sollicited a favor from the Mother Sultana. She had requested for herself, her grandsons Elia, son of Mosse (Moise) and Yossef, son of Mosse, their wives and descendants of both sexes, an exemption from all legal and local taxes and the granting of the right to have in their service slaves, who did not have the requirements for becoming converts to Islamism. Her demand having been graciously received by the Padishah (Sultan Süleyman) the latter had in his great benevolence exempted her grandsons, their wives as well their male and female descendants from the poll-tax, the land-tax, the tax on vineyards, on the pasture, the tax to be paid to the military class which is called *Segban* and which is attached to the Janissaries and the tax for the construction of fortifications. He (Sultan Süleyman) had ordered that none of his sons (the Sultan's children), descendants and relatives, as well as his ministers, chiefs, fiscal administrators and bailiffs for whatever reason should hinder the execution of his command, should interfere with it, or create embarassment or difficulties."

There is a brief Lamartine version of the Kyra story (14).

As Mehmed III ascended the throne, Solomon Usque (15), the poet, formerly a descendant of the House of Nasi, presented the English ambassador an interesting report on conditions at the Turkish court, which was straightaway sent to England and carefully studied by Lord Burleigh.

Mehmed III projected the construction of the great and beautiful mosque *Yeni Djami* (the New Mosque) at the mouth of the Golden Horn and the Bosphorus, at the head of the bridge connecting Istanbul to Galata. The site was occupied by Jewish houses which were expropriated. The construction was supported by the

Queen-Mother Safiye Sultan; the project was abandoned at the death of Mehmed III, to be taken up again half a century later.

In the period extending from Murad III to Ahmed I, the Golden Age of scholarship in Salonica had continued (16, 17) with Samuel de Medina and Solomon Abraham ha-Cohen (*Mouarshah*), who was considered on the level of Jacob ben Asher (1288-1340) or Asheri, the *Rosh ha Turim*, author of *Arba Turim* (the four Rows, Jewish code book before Caro[s *Shulkhan 'Aruk*). Both Medina and Mouarshah took a very strong stand against those devaluating and debasing the silver *aktche* and the gold ducat, by reducing the content of silver and gold in the coinage. Volume two of Mouarshah's *responsa* contains a precious commentary on Maimonides' *Hilhot Geroushim*, which is a fervent plea for sympathy for Jews forced to renounce their faith.

CHAPTER 12

AHMED I: WONDROUS HEALING BY THE ASHKENAZI WIDOW

Ahmed I (1603-1617) ascended the throne at the age of 14. Soon after he was in the throes of illness. Solomon Ashkenazi's second wife and widow, Bula Iqshati became the wondrous healer of the Sultan. She undertook to treat him with the skills she had acquired while assisting her husband's ministrations. Baron (1) calls the illness *Veroli* (syphilis). For Galante (2) the illness was smallpox (*la petite vérole*)...From that date on, Bula had free access to the Imperial Palace and used it when required to intervene in favor of her correligionists.

The peace with the Christian powers was beclouded by a Jesuit incident (3, 4). The French Jesuits established in Istanbul. at the Church of Saint-Benoît, since 1582 were under the protection of the King of France. The Jesuits were able to force the conversion of several Jewish children in 1609. Upon an intervention by Ashkenazi's widow, the sultan ordered five of these Jesuits to appear before the *Divan* where they were arrested. Baron Salignac, Ambassador of France, intervened in turn. The Jesuits were freed. Lamartine's version is somewhat different.

For the Jews of the Ottoman Empire, Sultanic bias and Spahi riots cast a shadow on the Jewish Golden Age. With the growing power of the Moslem theologian-jurists (the *Ulemas*), and of the *Grand Mufti* (Chief Moslem Ecclesiastical Officer), the anti-Jewish bias of Murad III and the anti-Jewish Spahi riots during Mehmed III, the Golden Age of Turkish Judaism was in decline. It was followed by an era of incipient stagnation, with the dream of "Paradise Retrieved" gone. According to the Polish envoy in Istanbul, in the new political climate, the *muftis*, as a class were bigoted; their animosity towards the "infidels" also colored their attitude towards the Jews.

When Sultan Ahmed I, wishing to duplicate his mother's construction of a mosque in Istanbul, built another one called the *Ahmedia* at the annual cost of 1,000,000 *scudi*, the Imperial Treasury was nearly empty. The Sultan's munificence had raised the specter of insolvency. Yet during the reign of Ahmed I, Turkey had still a long lease of vitality. As Baron comments (1): "It really was a testimonial of the intrinsic vitality of the Turkish masses and the vigor of the legal and administrative system established by earlier sultans and fully reorganized under Süleyman the "Lawgiver" (*Kanuni Sultan Süleyman*) that the Empire survived without suffering even greater damage."

Despite the great resilience of the Ottoman Empire, something of the original flavor of the Jewish life in Turkey, the joy of having at last found "a land of happiness", as praised by the poet Samuel Usque, must have been lost. Even the greatly lionized Prince of Judaism, Joseph Nasi, after years of glory, suffered a certain ostracism from Murad III. The fortune accumulated by Esther Kyra vanished in a weekend of riots. The Jews still had tremendous opportunities, but their fortunes remained exposed to arbitrariness, be it from the side of the *ulemas*, the Janissaries or a simple whim of the Sultan. The hubris of Jewish individuals, also, whether in the administration of the mint or participation in palace intrigues brought its own seeds of corruption.

The poet Abtalion (5) went on with his work, as a continuator of Najara, through the reign of Ahmed I. His Odes chanted in practically all the families of Salonica and elsewhere were modeled on Najara's poetry. At Adrianople where he had settled, Abtalion enjoyed the friendship of the Dervishes who held him in high esteem. He was so popular among the Sufism-oriented Turks that they surnamed him *Küçük Hoca (Hodja) Haham Abtalion* [Little Hodja (Teacher) Rabbi Abtslion].

In the Turkish-Jewish interaction music played a crucial role, as the Sephardim were fascinated by the tunes of Turkish music and the Turks enjoyed the creativity of Jewish composers and the performance of Jewish cantors.

In Ahmed I's time the Jewish mystics-dervish connection, seems to derive from the link between the Sufi stream and the Kabbalah (6, 7).

Music also played its role. The body-mind movements of the Whirling Dervishes (12), coupled with the reed-pipe music to which they were performed, are the product of a special method designed to bring the Seeker into affinity with the Mystical Current, in order to be transformed by it.

Thus, the poet-cantor Abtalion could indeed find some common ground with the Dervishes of Adrianople. When one looks at the *Tales of the Dervishes* (13, 14) and also to the stories of the Turkish folk hero Nasreddin Hodja, at the stories of the *Bektashi* Dervishes, one can find considerable analogies with the *Tales of the Jewish Sages and Gaonim*, as if they are all parts of a common culture. Poets like Abtalion who belonged to the circle of Yahia, the *Midrash ha-Shir* (5) had concern for harmony. In general they respected the metric science and followed with care the rules of poetry in vigor during the Golden Age of Judaism in Spain. The compositions often were on such profane themes that the rigorists of the time prohibited their reading during the holidays which had to be spent in holy meditation.

Next to their obsequiousness, the Salonician poets had other failings, not the least of which was their proclivity for excesive formalism, flowery language and embellishments deprived of substance. Nothing can better express it than a half English, half Swedish sentence used by a famous Stockholm Professor when faced with a manuscript with too many words and too little substance: "Too much *lingon* and not enough *kött!*" (too much lingonberry used as a sauce and not enough meat!). The poets of the circle indulged a little too often in banal rhetoric.

The poems read in the course of sessions at the Gedaliah's College, were chanted on different airs, Turkish, Spanish or Greek. Hebrew was the usual language. A few Marranos tried Latin verses without much appreciation from their entourage.

There was a special brand of poetry reserved for grave stones. Some of the engraved stones were beautiful marbles, such as the tombs of Isaac Serres and Israel Menahem, both dead in 1570, and are authentic pieces of anthology.

Few of the works produced by the *Midrash ha-Shir* were published, and very little remained from this literary effervescence except rare manuscripts scattered through European University libraries, such as at Oxford.

The lessons learned from the Spanish Inquisition did not seem to prevent anti-Marrano bigotry, among the Salonica Sephardim (15). Two Marranos, father and son, had come from Portugal to Salonica in 1597. They belonged to the lineage of the *Kohanim*. According to the traditional right of their lineage, they never failed to stand every *Rosh ha Shana* and *Kipour* at the place of honor near to the holy ark and to fulfill with the appropriate mystical fervor the sacerdotal services which are the charge and privilege of their cast. One day the Marrano son happened to engage in a quarrel with another Jew who threw at his face insolently: *"Kistiano, hijo de Kistiano y todos los Portugueses son Kistianos!* (Christian, son of Christian and all the Portuguese are Christians!). The son and the father felt mortally outraged and referred the matter to Rabbi Salomon ben Hasson, famous for his science and devotion. Ben Hasson expressed the following opinion:

"The person who made the insult is very reprehensible. and should be inflicted with a hard punishment. It is a grave sin to remind a "repentant" of his past errors, so as to make him suffer...In chapter 87 of his *Ilkhat Teshouva*, Maimonides taught that those who convert by constraint cannot be held responsible for their apostasy."

Thus some of the doctors of the Torah, were full of indulgence for the Marranos, and did not hesitate to proclaim that these "repentants' were better Jews than the most pious of the Jews, better even the *tsadikim*, the just ones with an established and consecrated reputation.

In 1649, the two sons of a pious repentant, Samuel and Joseph, as well as his grandson David, son of Samuel, quit Salonica to receive the baptism in Venice. The time bomb of another faith, planted by the mystique of the Church's seduction had finally exploded. Samuel, assuming the name of Giulio Morasni (1612-1687), rapidly gained a high rank in the hierarchy of the Church. Appointed librarian of the Vatican, then lecturer at the Collegium propaganda fidae (seminary to train missionaries to the Orient), he was in charge of delivering speeches in a polemic style against his old coreligionists. He authored a book entitled *Dereh Emouna* (the

Road to the Faith), translated into Italian under the title *Via della fede demonatrata*, where he attacks Judaism.

During the reign of Ahmed I, a terrible murder took place in Salonica in the year 1614, which sent tremors for a while throughout the Jewish community (16). Moses de Medina, the son of the famous Salonica leader of the sixtenth century, Samuel de Medina was himself quite a scholar. When he died in 1608 he left an impressive fortune to his two sons, Juda said Comprado, a man of law and letters, and Chemaya, very well versed in profane and religious sciences.

If there was a man who did not compromise on matters of principle, that was Juda Comprado de Medina, *dayan* (judge) at the synagogue of Portugal. Juda divided his time between the practice of medicine, his charges as a judge and his personal scholarly studies. Like his father Samuel, he financed the printing of various literary works, among others *Sheerith Yehouda* of Juda Taitacek (Salonica 1599).

A Jew of Verria had accumulated a large fortune. Fearing the cupidity of the authorities and especially the detestable vigilance of the stool pigeons for the *Agha* and the *Cadi*, he was trying to keep his wealth discrete. He established an inventory of his possesions, had it recorded in a register by his secretary and convoked at his home a group of trusted persons. He revealed to these that he was in possession of 80 to 90 *pesos* (a *peso* being worth 2,000 ducats, with each ducat being equivalent to 7.47 gold franks), of which eleven were to go to the sons of his brother, and the rest to his own single son. His nephews and his son, all being minors, he designated a trustee to run the estate. He then signed his will in the presence of all and asked each one of the present to take an oath that they will keep the most absolute secret on the numbers which he had made known to them.

Dazzled by the "treasures of Ali Baba", now under their control, trustee and his secretary did not hesitate to despoil the inheritors. When the time came to give account on their "trust fund", the two fiduciaries arranged to have the bulk of the fortune vanish, but made sure to obtain from the unexperienced and trusting inheritors a quittance stating that they had been remitted their due inheritance.

The inheritors first enjoyed their situation, but soon they were without resources, an object of pity. The trusted family friends who had knowledge about the true numbers soon understood that they were in presence of a large scale embezzlement. The trustee and secretary had powerful friends among Turkish functionaries bought by generous gifts.

Before Salonica's rabbis, the two dishonest trusties displayed their duly signed quittance; the document looked impeccable. As the rabbis were temporizing, and claims and counterclaims went dragging on, the plaintiffs proposed the arbitration of Juda Comprado. It was not long before the perspicacious magistrate in Juda Comprado discovered the imposture. Juda asked the dishonest trustees to produce the testament, the register of the inventory and the management accounts. The two thieves went into a grossly distorted account of the "huge" sums they had spent for the education of the minors. As to the old inventory, register and account books, they did not have them anymore. Why should they still have have these documents when they already were in possession of the document showing that they had been duly discharged of all their obligations?

Despite a mounting wave of hostility against him and the formation of a cabal, Juda Comprado remained adamant. When the defendants failed to produce the documents he had demanded within a set time period, he condemned them without any ambiguity and pronounced a verdict ordering the restitution of all the stolen goods. Tremendous agitation ensued, with the two partners stirring up violent demonstrations against Medina, even at the synagogues. Medina maintained his sentence, on the strength of the oath taken by the two defendants to abide by his arbitration. He received support from an uncontested authority. The Grand Rabbi of Constantinople, Mitrani, having studied the litigation in its details, confirmed the condemnation. Knowing that they could not win their case anymore by legal means, the two malefctors hired a few ruffians, who surprising Juda in the street administered him a ferocious beating, nearly killing him. It took Juda a long time to recuperate, but his will remained unflinching.

The bandits then tried to stir up the Turkish authorities against Medina by the generous use of *bakshishes*, denouncing him as some kind of rebel, an enemy of law and order, a dangerous disturber of the peace. They almost succeeded in obtaining his incarceration and the confiscation of his property...But Juda also had friends. His party also was able to buy favors. Medina's rich family contributed enough *bakshishes* to assuage the authorities.

The partners were getting impatient and they decided on the ultimate solution. They had to use a hired killer. On thursday January 2, 1614, as the noble *dayan* was leaving his home, the killer made his move plunging his dagger into Medina more than once killing him. The murderer was rapidly executed on a hanging pole, next to Juda's house and close to the spot still stained by the blood of his victim.

Shemaya, the younger brother of Juda Medina, swore revenge. Still unrepentant, the instigators together with their friends continued to maneuver, denouncing Shemaya to the Turkish authorities as a dangerous and revolutionary malefactor. They continued to harass Shemaya in every possible way, making his life bitter and unbearable. For two years Shemaya relentlessly worked to obtain justice, but his partisans were getting tired, while his adversaries for whom the stakes were too high did not disarm. As the Salonica leaders were interested only in one thing, the return of peace and tranquillity, rather than the accomplishment of justice, Shemaya's adversaries had a free game, and get off scot free. At the beginning of 1616, at their insistance, the Turkish authority in Salonica, expelled Shemaya from the city. He abandoned Turkey, and settled in Venice, for the salvation of his soul, as he himself says, in the preface of a book entitled *Ben Shemuel*, printed in Mantoua in 1622. In the preface, he added, as a consolation, that the divine punishment had fallen upon the authors of the crime, both of them having found a premature death in the course of the eight years which had followeed his brother's murder.

During the reign of Ahmed I (1603-1617) the culture of tobacco imported from America gained more ground. It became first acclimatized in Bulgaria, then in Thrace (25). The sandy valleys, all exposed along the Aegean coastal network, constituted a very favorable terrain for raising tobacco. This also remained true for the centuries to follow, and the encounter between tobacco and the Aegean territory became a real love match. Nowhere in the world did this delicate plant find such a minutious and assiduous care as it received in the Turkish provinces, where the peasant, with an untiring patience sollicituously proceeded to the choice of leaves and to the multiple manipulations necessitated by this luxury product. The Turkish tobacco began to acquire a growing reputation. Considerable quantities started to be exported at an early date to all central and occidental Europe. The agents behind this success story were the Jewish traders who encouraged the production of tobacco, by providing before the harvest, large advances to tobacco growers; they also knew how to advertise their product, how to make it known and appreciated in foreign lands, through their multiple correspondents, on the big international markets. The penetration of the European consumer market took place through Venice where the Salonica traders held a preponderant position through their Levantine colony. Towards 1657 during the reign of Mehmed IV, the monopoly of tobacco was already in the hands of the Marranos returned to judaism.

The Jews of Macedonia, in the hinterland of Salonica, had also brought to the level of an art the preparation of succulent cheeses (17), among others the *ricotta*, the *queso fresco* (fresh cheese) and the *cashcaval* which is a variety of cooked cheese highly appreciated in the Balkans. The milk was collected by diligent care in the sheep farms of the region and transformed on the spot. This industry was managed strictly in conformity with the delicate conditions required for ritual purity.

 Rabbi Joseph Isaac ben Ezra (18), a native of Constantinople (1560-1620), came to Salonica at the age of seventeen and was a student of Medina. Later he formed at the Portuguese *yeshiva* of *Yahia* his own "pléiade" of disciples. His work *Atamoth Yosef*, which had three editions, in 1767, 1790 and 1836 in different countries, enjoyed a great vogue among rabbis, particularly Ashkenaze rabbis. An important section of this work, *Mase Meleh* (Royal Charge) contains valuable information on the nature and repartition of fiscal impositions in Salonica. Another section is dedicated to the thirteen Talmudic principles and a commmentary on the treatise of *Kedoushim*. The two works separately paginated were printed in 1601, during the reign of Mehmed III, much before the rest of *Atamoth Yosef*. Joseph ben Ezra was a wanderer, occupying the position of spiritual leader, first in Larissas, then in Sofia. Towards the end of his life he retired to his birthplace, Constantinople, dedicating his last days to teaching.

CHAPTER 13

OSMAN II: THE FIRST REGICIDE

Ahmed I was succeded by his imbecile brother Mustafa I. Brought in a daze from his dungeon in the *Seraglio*, where he had languished for fourteen years, he was considered a holy man, halfway between a madman and a fool. One of his delusions while in captivity was to throw pieces of gold to the fishes in the Bosphorus (1, 2). The seditious military were in control of the capital and with Mustafa deposed, Ahmed's fouteen year old son Osman II (1618-1622) was placed on the throne (1).

Jews, even in Istanbul, were often chosen targets for pillage by Janissaries (3). With every change of the regime another opportunity arose for an assault on the Jewish quarters and extorsions of ransom from Jewish leaders.

Encouraged by a preliminary victory against Poland (1), Osman, donning a suit of mail that belonged to his ancestor Süleyman I, crossed the Danube pushing to the banks of the Dniester. He was forced to retreat with heavy losses. From the British envoy's report dispatched to London: "The Grand Signor entered the city Istanbul the First of January, clothed like a common soldier, without great train, and less pomp. His losses in the war have been extremely great, especially of horses." Osman, then, was only eighteen.

Janissaries had to risk their own head to bring the head of an enemy severed in battle, but their reward was no more than one ducat per head (4). The Sultan Osman also had another unsettling habit: prowling through the streets of the city, by night and in disguise, with a few palace officials, "peering into houses and taverns, to detect infractions of his laws against the conumption of wine. He ordered arrests and punishments which ranged from being flung into the Bosphorus to consignment to the galleys. With growing discontent among the Janissaries, the Sultan was planning the suppression of the by now restless and militarily inefficient "elite" corps.

The Janissaries and Spahis were quick to suspect ulterior motives. They massed together in the Hippodrome. They broke into the *Seraglio* itself, the Sultan's mainly largely defended by Osman's gardeners. The rebels were ready for regicide.

The Grand Vizier and the Chief of the Black eunuchs were torn to pieces. Mustafa was once more enthroned. His mother, the *Sultana Valide*, took charge, seeking to soothe the terrified weakling:

--Come, my Lion!"

Osman II was caught in his hiding place, only wearing an undergarment and a skullcap. From a window the distraught Osman made a final oration: My *Aghas* of the *Sipahis*, and you!, the *Elders of the Janissaries*, who are my fathers, with a young man's imprudence I have lent an ear to bad advice. Why do you humiliate me in this way? Do you want me no longer?"

An unanimous clamor answered him: "We want neither your rule nor your blood." Osman was then conducted to the dreaded prison of *Yedi Kule* (Seven Towers). Awakened in his cell by the Grand Vizier Daud (Davud) Pasha, and three henchmen, Osman put up a good fight, but he was overpowered, struck on the head with an axe and strangled.

Anarchy followed (5). Three Grand Viziers went by in succession. The civil and military elements called upon the mad Mustafa to renounce the throne. Mustafa obliged "with much joy". Osman's younger brother (Murad IV), "the true heir" was then chosen as Sultan, proving acceptable to both Janissaries and Spahis.

A Jewish document dated from 1610 (6) states that at that time 40 Jewish physicians were employed in the service of the Palace. These doctors continued to serve under Murad IV. At the time of Murad IV's ascension to the throne, the Grand Rabbi Yahiel Bassan who had acceded to his position under Murad III was still in function.

Under Osman II, Rabbi Joseph Escapa (7), was invited to Izmir by the Salonician Jews having established residence there. There were six synagogues in Izmir when Escapa arrived. He was appointed rabbi for three of these. The other synagogues kept Ribbi Isaac Levi as their spiritual leader.

Towards the end of the sixteenth century, in the years around Osman II's period, the bankers and money changers were all Jews (8). They advanced money to the exporters and shipowners. In the same way as they gave loans to the Turks who usually were incautious and free spenders, they also did not hesitate to borrow from the Turks large capitals at fixed interest rates for major business transactions such as the financing of hide and leather shipments to Ancona, Ragusa and other ports. The annual interest rates of the time were 20 to 25% which were considered quite reasonable, since interest rates in contemporary Europe were no less than 40 to 45%. Hasday ha-Chen, a contemporary author, very well informed, writes that if the creditor or debtor came to die, the sum lost was lost. The inheritors of the debtor were rarely inclined to pay the debt of the defunct. On the other hand, the debtor often did not hesitate to contest the credit titles held by the inheritors of the defunct's estate. Ruins, bankruptcies and financial discomfitures were widespread.

Any dealing with state functionaries was a very delicate matter, and their intervention was feared. The most a leader could achieve is to order the temporary incarceration of the debtor regardless who there was innocent or recalcitrant. They did not seriously try to enforce the acquitting of debts. Thus, it became convenient for some debtors to accept three months of jail, after which time they were freed of any obligation.

A further risk for the creditor was the constant depreciation of money. Already in 1582 and 1590 (under Murad III) the *groush* had been altered at the Mint House to the profit of the Imperial Treasury. In 1603, under Ahmed I, the Porte had tried to alleviate its financial problems by further decreasing the value of the *groush*. In 1820, under Osman II, diluted money was minted and put in circulation under the name of *groush*.

The Rabbinical jurisprudence, in these matters, remained guided by a single principle. Whatever name is given to the coinage by mperial decree cannot change the intrinsic value. Every coin is worth only according to whatever metal content it has. All pretenses laid on a special symbol or image were to be disregarded, null and void. Interior transactions were to be run in the same way as foreign transactions, the intrinsic value of coinage being solely dependent on weight and precious metal content. The only consideration was to be the intrinsic value and not fictive value. The rabbinical view was that financial transactions between honest traders were to remain independent of arbitrary variations. Thus, in the liquidation of entreprises, the share of capital contributed by each associate was evaluated according to its equivalent in gold weight.

The Salonician rabbinical jurisprudence established that all long term operations had to be carried out in "real value" and not in depreciated coinage. The same applied to the return of dowries stipulated in *Ketoubas* (Marriage contracts),

In the practical domain sometimes a compromise sum was decided upon at an average price between the value in gold and current value. As an example, three of the grand masters of Salonician jurisprudence said, that when as a result of successive depreciations, the *groush* valued at 120 aspers had fallen to 80, the obligation contracted before the financial upheavals had to be acquitted at 100 aspers per *groush*.

Joshua Joseph Handali, the scion of an old family, reputed for its scholars and physicians, compiled all the   decisions on monetary conflicts in an excellent compendium, which was annexed, to *Pene Yoshuah*, a collection of *responsa* by the same author.

The Salonician traders (9) participated in huge commercial enterprises through the intermediary of their commissioners and agents abroad. They were able to buy huge cargoes of wheat in all the granaries of the world, from Crimea, Apulia, Sicily to Tunisia, as well as mountains of salt from Istria, and invaluable barrels of fish salted and smoked at Azov.

Maritime travel was not without danger. The vessels which went into the Adriatic were often subject to attacks from another sector, the *Uscoques,* Slave bandits chased from their territories by the Ottoman conquests and now entrenched in Venetian territory, in the labyrinthine hideouts of the Dalmatian coast. These redoubtable corsairs, animated by an unextinguisable hatred against the Turks, were celebrated as heroes equal to the *Haidouts* [*Hayduts* (Bandits, Brigands)], in the popular Serbian lieds. They were equally the darlings of Venice and the terror of the Jews who constituted for the *Uscoques* a high ransom-yielding prey of choice. The *Uscoques* did not even hesitate to purchase Jews from the Venetian vessels on which they were embarked, not neglecting in the process to confiscate all their merchandise. They could then expect that these Jews would generally be purchased through the funds provided by the *Pidyon Shevouyim* (communal funds for the Redemption of Captives).

In the middle of the Sixteenth Century, the fortune of Isaac ben Habip, an enormously wealthy scholar, seems to have grown despite wars and raids. He was, however, an exception, as the province of Macedonia was nearing its downfall. The time had come to open *ferceles* (safe deposit chests) protected by solid locks, and empty the cellars, where the family treasures had been safeguarded by earlier generations in better days. When reserves also were exhausted, loans became necessary and houses were temporarily mortgaged. The loan givers, however, were not Jews, they were Moslems, master of great fortunes. Some of these nababs, applying the magnificent principles of their religion, would abstain from charging interest.

In hard times, all kinds of shady transactions took place, in the form of what was called fallacious "drafts of complacency" which created the illusion of funds not really existant.

In Osman's time, the greatest Talmudist of all, particularly in the Macedonian metropolis, who maintained his supremacy for half a century, was Haim Sabatay known under the pseudonym of Mouarshah, which according to the rabbinical usage gives in its last two letters the initial *het* and *shin* of his name. *Mouarshah* quite early was appointed *Marbitz* at the *Yeshiva* of the *Shalom* Synagogue, to which the rapidly conferred a splendor with no counterpart. Most of the Talmudic masters who belong to the roster of honor in Haim Sabetay's century, were brought up as his direct disciples. For among these Aaron Cupino, founded a brilliant rabbinical school in Istanbul, and Aaron Joshuah Eskenazi was a highly successful professor of theology in Izmir.

Haim Sabetay who kept his functions at the *Shalom* Synagogue for forty years, had only one failing, his floundering health. From 1612 on he started to complain of a nervous affliction causing tremor in his limbs. Despite all his ailments, everything gained life at his contact, he was the animator, the inspirer of wills and intelligences. This frail and quasi moribund old man comunicated all around himself courage, condidence, enthusiasm and optimism. He maintained excellent relations with great erudites of his time, Isaac Lebeth Halevy (died in 1623) and Juda Benveniste (died in 1647). His *responsa* to many consultations were subsequently published in four volumes under the title *Torath Haim* (Salonica 1713-1722). Being an artist in caligraphy, he continued to exert his art in handling the *calam* (*kalam*, pen) until crippled by senility. He particularly excelled in Hebrew square letter composition.

A particularity of Salonica was the *Moghrabi Synagogue* (North-African Synagogue) of Tunisian origin. It was often designated by the name *Caal (Kal) de la Silla* (Temple of the Chair) because at *Simhat Tora* (Holiday marking the completion of the annual reading of the Pentateuch), the *Hatan Tora* (Bridegroom of the Law, *i.e.* the worshipper who reads the last section of the Deuteronomy) is triumphally carried on large armchair which all year remains hung from the ceiling of the temple. At *Simhat Tora* it is customary to take out all the Scrolls of the Law and to carry them seven times or more around the Synagogue sometimes with dances which may be continued for hours. All male worshippers are called up for *aliyyah* (ascent), a "calling up" to read the Scroll of the Law at the synagogue. The last section of the Deuteronomy is read by (or for) the Bridegroom the Law. He is followed by the Bridegroom of Genesis (*Hatan Bereshit*) who reads (or has read for him) the first verses of the Genesis. Sweets are usually distributed to the children and the "Bridegrooms" act as hosts to the community.

Among the families affiliated to the *Moghrabi* congregation, those with names Cabili, Hiskia, Ecayos, Senor, and Toledano, must have lived for various lengths of time in the district, of *Maghzen*, very frequently the site of terrible religious persecutions.

Numerous disenchanted worshippers from other synagogues had joined the *Moghrabi* congregation, as could be detected from their surnames such as Joseph, Pinhas, Nehama, Uziel, Ovadia. The greatest infusion of worshippers into the *Moghrabi* congregation came from the Italian communications. After the great Salonica fire of 1620, during the reign of Osman II, a few Aragonese (the Benrubis) and a few Catalans (the Esformes) also passed to the *Moghrabi* congregation.

The true Calabrese and the autochtonous Ashkenaze Italiots throughout the Orient did not adopt family names like the Sephardim had done. It was customary among them, to complete their names by that of their father: *e.g.* Joseph ben Abraham. or simply Joseph Abraham. In some instances, the name of the immediate predecessor was adopted as the definitive patronymic name for the descendance; this patronym was called the *alcunia.* Thus, Joseph Abraham would keep his name as before, but his son Isaac would be called Isaac Abraham. Like all their relatives the Ashkenazis of Salonica did not have surnames, but in time they adopted, in imitation of their Sephardic correligionists, either the name of an ascendant or a professional appellative.

If the male forenames were all Biblical, the female forenames were curious reminders of Spain: Buena, Paciencia, Dona, Señora, Vida, Estrella, Sol, Luna, Flor, Rosa, Joya, Oro, Plata, Perla, Diamante, Esmeralda.

By the seventeenth century (10) the *telar* (hand-loom of textile weavers) being fully active, the *albasha* (distribution of costumes) to the students of the *Talmud Tora* had become a great annual festivity at Salonica. It attracted the attention of non-resident passersby by the solemnity of its celebration. It was traditional, as customary throughout Sephardic communicaties (and later in Amsterdam), to have the children play a small Biblical drama: Joseph sold by his brothers and found later by them on the throne of the Viceroy of Egypt.

CHAPTER 14

MURAD IV: THE CONQUEROR OF BAGHDAD

When Sultan Murad IV (1623-1640) made his first solemn entry into Istanbul (1), he was another fourteen year old boy, like Osman II. He almost singlehandedly accomplished more than several of his predecessors put together from Mehmed II on. Murad IV, gave to his realm a new lease of power and life. He justified the words of Sokullu to the Venetian Ambassador after the naval disaster at Lepanto, of the resiliency of the Ottoman Empire.

During her years of regency (1623-1633) Murad IV's mother Kösem Sultan had to deal with the loss of Baghdad and Erivan to the Persians, the rebellion of tribes in Lebanon, the wavering allegiances of governors in Egypt and other provinces, the assertion of independence by the Barbary states, a revolt of Tatars in Crimea, and raids by marauding Cossacks to the coasts of the Black Sea. At the end of ten years of regency by his mother, Murad IV had turned into an athletic, well made young man so boastful of his muscular strength, that he was a redoubtable wrestler, "like Prophet Muhammed himself" (1). Still in 1632 he had to confront Spahi mutineers, breaking into the first and second courtyards of the *Seraglio,* then swarming up to the hall of the *Divan,* with the words *"Better the head of the Grand Vizier than that of the Sultan."* Murad IV's beloved brother-in-law and ex-grand Vizier Hafiz Pasha met his death at the hands of the mutineers.

From then on, the now mature Sultan took matters into his hand. The treacherous Grand Vizier Rejeb Pasha who had succeeded Hafiz, was executed by the dreaded Black Eunuchs. After this final act of emancipation, Murad IV, obtained the unconditional loyalty of his Janissaries and Spahis. One among his summoned judges declared: *"My Padishah* (Sultan, King) *the only remedy against these abuses is the scimitar."*

Traitors or ringleaders of rebellion were executed with sword or bowstring, their corpses flung in the Bosphorus. To prevent seditious assemblies all coffee-houses and wineshops were closed. Smoking of tobacco was made illegal. Offenders caught at night smoking a pipe, drinking coffee, or flushed with wine might instantly be hanged or impaled, and their bodies cast into the street as a warning.

Steeped in the corruption of bloodshed, Murad IV turned to killing for the sake of killing. Disturbed by the boisterous merriment of a party of women dancing on a meadow, he had them all seized and drowned. He beheaded his chief musician for singing a Persian air, and so honoring the enemies of the Empire.

So went the epigram (2): "Chase the eunuchs who give us sleepless nights, by crossing the streets the glaive in hand, and closing our houses to the licit pleasures; before prohibiting the *negro* (designation for the coffee seed) and before prohibiting the innocent smoke that rises to the sky, dissipate, O tyrant, the vapor of blood which you make everyday rise from the hearts of those opposed to your executioners."

The *imams* and the *sheikhs* in the mosques disguised their transparent criticism of the momarch's cruelty by resorting to the tales from the folk hero, the very popular Nasreddin Hodja:

"A man was working in the field with two oxen, one fat and strong, the other small and weak, both tied to the same yoke; the little one being unable to pull his weight, the ploughman struke the fat one. A man passing by asked: 'Why are you striking the one who is pulling his weight and sparing the one who is unable to pull?' 'It is to set an example' answered the ploughman. 'The small one would never have wanted to pull the plough if he did not have next to him the example of the obedience and efforts of the big one.' The moral of the story was that one who wants obedience from the small people must not hesitate to strike on the powerful, who are usually spared."

Murad IV was the cruel tyrant necessary at that juncture to counter the seditious tyranny of the armed forces and the venality of their civil confederates. In Racine's famous tragedy *Bajazet*, about the execution of Amurat (Murad IV)'s brother Bayezid (3), the Sultan is described as "le cruel Amurat" (4). The wily Amurat did not resolve on the execution of Bajazat, a high spirited prince, until after his victory over the Shah in Babylonia, as he feared that were he, Murad, to die in the battle, the Empire would fall into the hands of the last of the Ottoman, his imbecile brother Ibrahim.

The Judeo-Salonician historian Nehama calls Murad IV "*Ce monstre couronné*" (This crowned monster) (5). He also was animated by an insatiable greed. Any occasion was good for him which would provide a pretext for laying hands on the wealth of his subjects. In 1636, he confiscated the jewels of the Jews in the capital. Since 1627, the fiscal charges had enormously increased, doubled, tripled, quadrupled or even decuplated. Since his access to the throne Murad IV was entirely ruthless in the taxation of the *rayas* (non-Moslems).

Despite his initial enforcement of anti-drinking legislation, Murad paradoxically was himself in a perpetual state of daze and drunkenness. Haunted by his nighhtmares he kept running high on his execution binge. The number of his victims is estimated from 25,000 to 100,000. One sad merit, Murad IV's cruelty was totally indiscriminate, striking left and right, Jew as well as Moslem, Armenian as well as Greek. Among the roster of his victims: the *Sheikh-ül-Islam* (Muhammed's substitute on earth), C.E. 1643; the revered Sheikh Sakaria (C.E.

July 6, 1638); and a month later the illustrious Greek Ecumenical Patriarch Cyrillus Lucario (death by strangulation, followed by dumping of the cadaver into the sea).

Murad IV first had observed the rules of abstinence from alcohol (2). His mother worried much less about competition from odalisques in the *Seraglio*, than the young Sultan's voluptuous inclinations for Greek pages. Mustafa Bekri, grandson of a poet by the same name, was a young courtier famous for his depravity, and the brilliance of his humorous replies. He gradually drew the Sultan into heavy drinking.

Under Murad IV, taxation was heavy because of considerable war expenses (6) and the Jewish community often compared these heavy taxes to the plagues of Egypt. Murad IV had no patience for leisurely or benevolent *defterdars* [heads of the financial department of a **vilayet** (province, administrative district headed by a *Vali* or *Kaymakam* also called *Pasha*, Governor). Suspected of negligence, the *defterdar* of Adrianople first, and then that of Salonica were recalled to to the Sultan's presence in Constantinople and decapitated in succession.

According to the *Revue des Études Juives* (7, 8) a blood libel on ritual murder took place in Istanbul, during the reign of Murad IV. An Arab manuscript (9) at the end of a prayer book brought from San'a, Yemen, constitutes the unique document dealing with this libel. As it emerges from this text, in 1633, two janissarus, of Christian origin, decided to accuse the Jews of ritual murder. One of them killed his own child and threw him, during the night on the eve of Passover, in the year 5393 of the Hebrew calendar, into the Jewish quarter. This action came to the attention of the Grand Vizier Redjeb Pasha, who communicated it the next day to the Sultan. An inquiry was ordered, which proved the culpability of the two Janissaries; they were executed.

Under Murad IV, the Jewish population of Istanbul was twice as numerous as the Greek population. In the words of Evliya Tchelebi (Çelebi): "the *Mahalles* (quarters) of the Jews, in the year 1048 of the Hegira were in the number of 637; those of the Greeks in the number of 304; those of the Armenians in the number of 27 and those of the Franks in the number of 17."

Before the Baghdad campaign which took place towards 1638. Murad IV held a review of all the corporations in Istanbul, among these, the corporation of the *yüzlemedji* [(*yüzlemeci*) makers and sellers of honey *beignets* (flat pastries in honey syrup)]. The Jewish *yüzlemedjis* were escorted by rabbis, who controlled the *kosherout* (ritual purity) of the article. In the same parade, the corporation of the Jewish tavern-keepers, formed, again for reasons of *kosherout,* a separate section.

Under Sultan Murad IV, 40 Jewish physicians were on the payroll of the court. There was still, under the reign of Murad IV, a renowned physician, Ribbi Moses Amaradji, a native of Salonica, who had come to settle in Istanbul. His medical fame ended up penetrating the highest official spheres. Ricaut (7), who was then residing in Istanbul, cites the case of a Jewish physician, Moses Amaraggi (5) who was timidly trying to advise Murad IV to moderate his orgies, because of the Sultan's tendency to suffer from gout. The Sultan indulged in wine and did not take well the exhortations of the Jewish physician. Amaraggi was, despite his intent to save the Sultan, or just because of that, banned from the *Seraglio*. There is also a Lamartine version, typical of Murad IV's attitude towards his physicians (10).

The tenure system by which governor-generals or viceroys (*e.g.* in Egypt and Algeria), the so-called *beylerbeyi* held their positions, throughout the Ottoman realm, was at the origin of mismanagement from which other populations of the Empire, as well as the Jews suffered (11-12). The tenure of the *beylerbeyi* lasted usually no longer than three years. Similar brief tenure also existed in the offices of provincial governors in Damascus, Aleppo and elsewhere. Most of the officials tried to accumulate as much wealth as they could during their short term of office. In 1625, during Murad IV's reign, the governor of Jerusalem, Mehmed ibn Farukh, succeeded in extorting money from the Jewish inhabitants under all sorts of trumped up charges. He imprisoned some of the outstanding rabbis, including th highly revered sage, R. Isaiah Horowitz, and held them for ransom. To comply, the Jewish community had to borrow 60,000 aspers from their Moslem neighbors. Although the *sheria* (Moslem law) prohibits the charging of interest, the prohibition was waived. The Jewish community was charged interest. The debt to the Muslim neighbors quickly increased by an annual interest of 10,000 aspers. When governor Ibn Farukh went away for a while to lead a caravan of pilgrims to Mecca, he left as surrogate his brother Osman Anas, who, now had the opportunity to enrich himself at Jewish expense for only a few months. He had to proceed at a much accelerated pace in extorting and ransoming. It required persistant efforts of the Jewish leadership in Damascus and Istanbul before Ibn Farukh was deposed on the order of Murad IV who hated corruption.

There also was the episode of Governor Bibir Pasha (13), the extortionist of Damascus. To extort funds from the Jewish community, he placed the city's gallows in front of the synagogue and had a common criminal hanged there. He allowed the corpse to dangle three days and three nights in the hot Syrian climate until the Jewish community secured its removal by an enormous gift. Not content with that, Mehmet Bibir Pasha allowed his son, whom he appointed chief of police, to make intensive searches in Jewish homes to discover the source of wine generously consumed by the Moslems in violation of their religious law. On such occasions, the vice squads of the chief of police were able not only to confiscate the containers of wine but also to rob the owners of other possessions for their own and their boss's benefit. Bibir Mehmed Pasha overplayed his hand when he ventured to similar extorsions from the Moslem majority. Murad IV ordered the governor's execution (October 5, 1623).

In 1638, under Murad IV, Ribbi Azaria Yehoshoua Eskenazi, a native of Salonica came to Izmir (15). By that time the aging grand rabbi Isaac Levi had lost his sight. An inquiry was submitted to the rabbis of Constantinople on whether Ribbi Isaac Levi could continue to fulfill his functions under such conditions. The answer was affirmative. Shortly thereafter Issac Levi died, and was succeeded by Ribbi Azaria Yehoshoua. The Jewish community of Izmir was split between the supporters of

Rabbi Escapa and those of Rabbi Azaria Yehoshoua. The mediation of the Constantinople rabbinate became necessary. The Turkey of Murad IV was the Turkey of authoritarianism, and nobody would dare to oppose the great autocrat Murad IV. However, in the realm of the Constantinople and Izmir rabbinates, this was not the case. The Yehoshoua-Escapa quarrel continued to drag on for a year without any solution in sight. In 1631, the two rival rabbis signed jointly a *haskama* (communal regulation). In 1638, Rabbi Azaria Yehoshoua died and Escapa became the Grand Rabbi of the whole Jewish community of Izmir. When Murad IV died in 1648, Escapa continued to be Grand-Rabbi under Ibrahim and Mehmed IV.

The darkest episode clouding the lives of Salonica Jews under Murad IV, was the tragedy of Juda Covo and *the Kalb Çuha* (Faulty Textiles) of Salonica. In the last years of Murad IV's reign, the financial distress had reached a culminating point. In Salonica (16) the Jewish communal administration had no more funds to pay the textile workers. Due to lack of means, the fabrics produced were not uniform any longer. In addition to the fabrics directly produced by the textile workers, there were other tissues contributed as payment in kind for communl taxes. Innumerable families in those days of financial distress kept their weaving machines operating practically at all times including the moments of leisure. Everyone was busy weaving to pay the *haradj* (tax owed by the non-Moslem *zimmis*) to the Turkish state. Since money was extremely scarce, the textiles produced or acquired were practically the sole currency in use. The problem was that the textiles used for fiscal payments *in lieu* of money started to lack the required quality and standardization. Faulty quality, delays and inefficiencies in deliveries led to the complaints from governmental authorities that the community of Salonica was not sufficiently complying to the payment of taxes to be collected in kind. The *Ambardji*, the Ottoman official charged to collect and store the tissues delivered as taxes, was becoming more and more irate. The Jews of Salonica were terrified thinking of possible reactions of the Man in the *Seraglio* (the Sultan) as he kept receiving through his subordinates in Constantinople bad reports from the officials in Salonica. Draconian orders were transmitted from the capital, commanding the Jewish community in Salonica to shape up once and for all, to immediately comply with old delayed deliveries, and to pay an indemnity for the past delivery of faulty tissues.

Any further whim of the Sultan could result in annihilation of the Jewish community there. Until then the Jews of Salonica had benefited from the benevolence and tolerance of Kuleli Safer, the *Defterdar* (General Tax Perceptor of Salonica). Suddenly, Kuleli Safer was placed under tight surveillance. The new *Cadi* (judge), the Egyptian Arab Shehab, a theologian favored by the Court, who had been transferred from Gümülcine to Salonica, was a true Cerberus. Soon the Jews had no more protector. In the spring of 1637, Safer was taken to the capital and brought to the presence of the Sultan who ordered his decapitation.

The pressure on the Salonica Jews intensified. The Army no longer found the Salonica textiles to its liking. The Jewish leaders of Salonica were summoned by Imperial *firman* to appear in Constantinople to justify themselves.

For three months a plenary assembly of rabbis and notables deliberated. Finally on Friday, February 28, 1637, the deliberations were condensed in an *(h)askama*:
"We, the undersigned, residents of Salonica, tried by an adversity of a kind that we never had experienced until recent times, we are obliged by firman to send a delegation to Constantinople for the litigation relative to the confection of military tissues. We have decided to entrust the mission to Juda Covo, Isaac ben Nahmias, Joseph Aaron Cohen Naar, Samuel Melamed, Zacharia Sullam and Joseph Lobel...We are giving them full powers to undertake all the required expenditures for the account of our Community, up to the sum of 30 **torbas** (purses) of money, each purse of 1,000 aspers being equivalent to 20 ducats...We are, in addition, engaging ourselves to reimburse them for any damage or expenditure that they might incur account of the Community, until concurrence of 30 purses. We wish them success and favor in their undertaking."

The delegates departed. Their leader, Juda Covo, was accompanied by his seventeen year old son Eliyahu, who wanted to take this opportunity to see the capital of the Sultans. The delegates had taken with them a lot of the best fabrics which they intended to directly deliver for the satisfaction of the account. When they reached destination without delay, they deposited their cargo at the Supply House of the Janissaries. Because of the Sabbath, the Jewish delegates could not be present, when a commission of functionaries, made on that day, the perfunctory examination of the tissues delivered. The experts' conclusion was unanimous: the tissues were faulty and they were rapidly put to sale by auction. Because of little competition, the sale was concluded at a very low price.

Without any appeal possible, the tissues were officially declared of low quality and, therefore, a much larger quantity had to be delivered to comply with the tax requirement. Covo and his companions were flabbergasted. They were aware that they were confronting an unfair and biased resolution. They knew that the condemnation of the tissues, which were in reality of the best quality, was made in absolute bad faith. They requested a second examination to be carried out in a detailed and analytical manner, taking into account all the required variables, such as price of wools, dyes and salaries of textile workers.

The delegates knew that the Sultan was inflexible. Yet they tried to defend the vital interests of their community. The most passionate and restless negociator was Covo. The tissues had been sold, but still they had not been delivered to the buyers and the bales half-opened were still in the warehouse. An expert examination was still feasible. Covo tried to get inside help, to build friendships and sympahty. His efforts were to no avail. Covo feared that even if payments and additionl deliveries were made for the present batch, there still remained the threat of retroactive claims for past deliveries. Such claims would be totally destructive for the Salonica community. Additionaly as Covo persisted more and more in his endeavors, he also became a suspect.

The suspicion arose that he might attempt to corrupt court officials. Those approached by Covo started to get frightened. They were afraid to get compromised, and to be under suspicion of conspiring to the detriment of the

Treasury. It became convenient to avoid Covo, and even to try getting rid of him. His most innocent words were purposefully altered, as invitations to culpable actions. The head of the Salonica delegation was finally denounced for attempting to corrupt officials. By Imperial orders, all members of the Salonica delegation were apprehended and bound with chains, fetters on the feet, handcuffs on the wrists. They were jailed like criminals. On the day of Sabbath, by derision, to add to the disgrace they were paraded under escort, through the streets of the capital. The Jews of Constantinople had no power to interfere, as they practically had no inside men at the court. The Jewish physicians at the court had recently fallen into disgrace, after having the audacity to advise the Sultan, stricken with gout, to quit drinking strong alcoholic beverages.

A sinister parody of justice took place. The delegates were dragged before a pretended court. It was a kangaroo trial. The judges had already set their sentence from the beginning. Covo was condemned to death for having delivered faulty tissues. All the efforts to save him were futile. The sovereign was inaccessible to pity. He was inexorable. The life of a man did not count for him.

The execution had been fixed for Saturday September 5, 1637. The arms tied, all the delegates, got on the way towards the site of execution in a macabre procession. Juda Covo, bare chested, walked in front of the others. He was preceded by a herald announcing in a loud and clear voice: "*Kalb tchouha eden budur!*" (Here is the maker of counterfeit tissue!).

After Juda's hanging, the other delegates experienced an unexpected reprieve. They were without a word of explanation freed of their chains and set free.

Afterwards, the survivors gave under oath before the rabbinical authorities a full description of all they had experienced. Then they hastened to comply with all the payments and demands of the authorities. The settlement achieved, they returned to Salonica.

Covo's widow asked an indemnity from the community, in the form of a pension *ad vitam* (for life). She had most of the rabbis on her side, but the lay leaders were hesitant. Covo could, they said, have been less stubborn and intransigeant. In the end, the Rabbinate of Constantinople delivered its opinion on the *Bigde ha-Meleh* (Drapes of the King). The Jewish population of Salonica must be considered as a vast association of which all members are united by bonds of solidarity. Any damage happening to one of the members by the fact of actions in this association must be supported by all. The accusation of counterfeit textiles, or faulty textiles, which has caused the juridical murder of Covo, falls upon all the population which must assume the responsibility and the consequences. Covo had been sacrificed as the expiatory victim for an incrimination brought upon the Jewish population of Salonica. The Jewish leaders agreed with the opinion of the Constantinople Rabbinate. Covo's widow obtained satisfaction.

Covo's son Eliyahu, disconsolate at the loss of his father, had refused to return with the rest of the delegation. The Jewish leadership in Constantinople took him under its care, while he completed his studies in the yeshivoth. Eliyahu became an accomplished talmudist. He continued living in Istanbul and finally resolved to return to Salonica after a thirty year absence.

After the tragic death of Covo, the Jewish community in Salonica implemented steps aimed to prevent the repetition of such a tragedy. To achieve a uniformity in production of tissues, a regime of monopoly was established for the production of textiles. Free lance weaving in the homes, at any hour and at any place, was, from then on, out of question. The savage rigor of Murad IV had delivered a fatal blow to this industry. The decline was further accelerated by the devaluation of the currency, which rapidly brought a huge rise in the price of raw wool.

New measures were also taken against the counterfeiting of tissues. Starting from 1650, under the reign of Mehmed IV, every tissue delivered was marked with a special sign. The Jewish commissary for quality control of textiles was carefully selected and worked under the supervision of a delegate from the Army, the *Tchaoush (Çavoush) Bashi.*

The author Haim Sabetay described in these words the distress of the Jews of Salonica:

"The City of Salonica, great in the sciences and sovereign in the Law, presently finds itself in a very unhappy situation because of the heavy taxes imposed by the State on the Jews and to which they are submitted by the threat of the sword... The city is struggling in the greatest distress, by the reason of the obligation it finds itself to pay the tax of the King's Clothes...Without the payment by Imperial Garments, this city, which always remains a true haven of rest and quietness, without par in all the Jewish world, would still deserve, as under preceding generations, the surname of small Jerusalem."

The *Midrash ha-Shir* (17), the poetic circle founded by Gedaliah was still in operation in Salonica almost throughout the full reign of Murad III, and reminded itself at least in spirit with Najara until the time of Murad IV. Najara, himself, was never in Salonica, but extensively corresponded with the circle. The effort attempted by the *Midrash ha-Shir* contributed to infuse the Salonician elite with the love of letters, which had become somewhat diminished in the generation of the Exile. The public regained affection for the things of art. The poetical works which had obtained favorable consideration at the Yahyia Academy, were loudly recited and even sung in the homes. For a few years life had been infused with poetry and songs. Parents, friends and correspondents in Constantinople, Adrianople and Damascus were contacted with requests for copies of odes, hymns, and epigrams circulating in the communities of Turkey, which when received were passed from hand to hand. With the death of Samuel-ha-Cohen Perahia in 1614, during the reign of Ahmed I (18, 19), however the Academy of Poetry created by Guedalia was almost forgotten.

The Academy of Yahyia inspired emulators in Venice. A century later the rich Jewish colonies of Livorno and Amsterdam, would revive with a new ardor the initiative of the pioneer Gedaliah, and would succeed to far beyond the Salonica model.

In Murad IV's time, there were persons in Salonica, who combined the qualities of rabbi, Torah doctor and physician. The most famous of them was Moses Amaraggi, physician of Murad IV, who then returned to Salonica, where he remained till his death (18). Among other famous physicians, one can include Moise ha-Cohen, a Calabrese Marrano, a fugitive of Catanzaro who returned to Judaism after many vicissitudes and died in 1638 during the reign of Murad IV. There also were distinguished physicians from the Perahia and Handali families.

From the early Seventeenth Century on, a sort of rabbinical "Mandarinism" prevailed in Salonica (18). The "Mandarins" honored for their scholarship, gained prestige and distinction. Every family's aspiration was to have at least one scholar son or son-in-law. In the hierarchy of education, the schoolmaster, the "*rubi*", as distinguished from the "*rabi*", was at the bottom of the ladder, together with the "*honadji*", who, an umbrella in hand, indicated to those coming for the *ziare* (*ziyaret*, visit to the dead), the locations of the tombs.

As to those at the top of the ladder, the Mandarins, no banquet or feast was held without them. They were high in demand, in the same way as today's celebrities. The Mandarins received no fee, because they were independently wealthy, their material needs being cared for by their family or that of the father-in-law. When a Mandarin took a walk on the street, he could be recognized as he moved on aware of his value, with an air of gravity, and pompously wrapped in his broad-sleeved robe. Passersby reached to kiss his hand and receive his blessing; then they lined up on the sides of the road, in respectful expectation. The Mandarin's displeasure was feared. His anger and maledictions could bring fire, sickness or death. Among the dynasties of Mandarins, one could cite the Amarillos, the Covos, the Molhos, the Nahmiases, the Perahias, and the Saportas.

A word of caution about this profusion of "Mandarins". They were not at all in the same class with the *Gaonim* (Leaders of Talmudic Academies). Despite their appearance of majesty, their scholarship was of a stagnant and dilatory nature. The Mandarins were entrapped within shrinking horizons. They continued moving in circles, endearing but rather sad figures caught in a perpetually rotating carousel from which they could not escape.

CHAPTER 15

IBRAHIM: THE NEW PHARAOH, HIS BEARD DECKED WITH JEWELS

Murad IV having died without progeny, he was succeeded by Ibrahim I (1640-1648), son of Ahmed I (1, 2). Ibrahim spent most of his time as a Sultan in the delights of the harem, largely oblivious of state affairs. Nevertheless he took enough time out from the company of his *djariyes* (*cariyes*, concubines, odalisques) to order the implementation of numerous death sentences; heads continued to roll during the full length of his reign. Modifying the rules of fratricide Murad IV had allowed his brothers to live until the age of twenty-five. Ibrahim's older brothers Bayezid, Süleyman and Kasim, had all succumbed... Luckily for Ibrahim, however awaiting his fate in terror, Murad IV died when his youngest brother was 24 years, 3 months and five days old. Murat IV in a strange spirit of dynastic suicide (1) had demanded Ibrahim's corpse in his final moments. The *Sultana Valide* (Queen Mother) Kösem Sultan averted the disaster. As Sultan Murad IV was being falsely assured that his brother had been executed, an infernal smile crept over his features. Moments later he was dead.

As Ibrahim ascended the throne, the baths of Istanbul were scoured on his orders to find beauties for his pleasure, Favored ladies were authorized to take what they pleased from the bazaars, without payment. At the request of a concubine, Ibrahim, a reincarnation of the Pharaohs, in the eyes of his Turkish subjects, appeared his beard decked with jevels. In the beginning of his reign, Ibrahim was advised by Kara Mustafa, an honest Grand Vizier who tried to set the Imperial finances in order and curb the influence peddling in the harem. The Grand Vizier's failure to flatter the Sultan and to follow one of his ladies' whims, led to his execution. He died fighting his stranglers with the sword.

While Ibrahim indulged in frivolities, the fate of Venetian rule in Candia (Crete) was to be sealed after a sensational act of piracy; the capture by corsairs of Malta in 1644 of a splendidly equipped Turkish galleon, travelling in convoy, with a valuable cargo to Egypt and carrying pilgrims to Mecca. On board there were very high personalities-- the *Cadi* of Mecca, the *Mullah* of Bursa, the *Kizlar Aghasi*

(Chief Eunuch of the **Seraglio**, a high lady of the court who was a favorite of the Sultan, with probably a foster-brother of Ibrahim's son the Crown Prince Mehmed. The Sultan, exploding in fury, first ordered the massacre of all the Christians in the Empire. Relenting at the urging of the Grand Vizier, he had all the Christian ambassadors placed under house arrest. The triumphant corsairs after their evil act of piracy, had docked in the safety of the Candia harbor. In 1645, a Turkish fleet, achieving surprise, besieged Canea, at the western end of the island as well. The siege of the capital Candia was to last twenty years, twice as long as the siege of Troy. Candia had from a distant past a Jewish community, which in the middle ages had gained fame by establishing a model of Jewish self-government in the diaspora. In the meantime the princely child captured in the galley by the Maltese corsairs had grown to become a Catholic priest, Père Osman. He was introduced as a possible Ottoman pretender. He aspired without success to rally all Ottoman subjects, whether Muslim or Christians, to the cause of a new Eastern State, a sort of hybrid Byzantino-Ottoman Empire.

The inner weaknesses of the Ottoman Empire ruled by an incompetent and mentally weak sovereign started to show. The Grand Vizier was dismissed. The Janissaries made three demands: the suppression of the sale of offices; the removal of the favorite Sultanas and the death of the dismissed Grand Vizier. A deputation from the army and the *Ulema* (hierarchy of theological scholars) approached the *Valide Hanim* (Queen Mother) who had been removed from the *Seraglio* through the intrigues of the favorites. The Queen Mother, Kösem Sultan, received the delegates arrayed in a black veil and turban, attended by two Black Eunuchs. The Judge heading the delegation disclosed their resolve to depose the Sultan and to enthrone in his place her seven year old grandson Mehmed. The *Sultana* asked how it was possible to put a child of seven on the throne. The Judge replied that, according to the verdict of the jurists (*ulema*) embodied in the *fetva*, a madman should not reign whatever his age. Under a child "a wise Vizier can restore order." The *Sultana* replied: "So be it."

Informed of his deposition by the grand judge of Rumelia, Ibrahim exclaimed: "Traitors! Am I not your *Padishah* (King, Emperor, Sovereign)? What does this mean?

The *Mufti* (High religious authority) replied:

"You are no longer *Padishah*, since you trample on justice and holiness and have ruined the world. You have wasted years in play and debauchery; you have squandered the treasures of the Empire on vanities; corruption and cruelty have governed the world in your place."

The Sultan was first led off into the prison of the *Seraglio*. The new Vizier and his followers sought a new *fetva* from the *Mufti*, to sanction Ibrahim's execution. The *Mufti* replied "Yes", based on a principle of Islamic Law "if there are two Caliphs, kill one of them." Two executioners were sent for, while the judges and the *Aghas* watched from the window. One of the two was the chief executioner who had often served Ibrahim. Thus, on the year 1648 took place the second act of regicide in Ottoman history.

Under Ibrahim, the tax evaders continued to affect the recurrent malaise of Salonica Jews. According to Galante (3-5) nothing is known about what happened to the Jewish community of Istanbul in Ibrahim's time. But Joseph Nehama and the Seventeenth Century spokesman of the Salonica Jews, Haim Sabetay are quite vocal about the ongoings in Salonica (6). The difficulties of the Salonica Jews were further compounded by the recurrent evasion of taxpayers in 1640, the year of Ibrahim's ascension to the throne. Many families expatriated themselves, abandoning those remaining to their ill fate. Those leaving often were the wealthiest. Soon nobody would be left but a mass of indigents requiring welfare support. In view of such a situation, a dual task confronted the leaders of the Salonica community; to recuperate from the tax evaders their due and to make sure that one could not simply leave Salonica to escape the payment of communal charges.

From a *mémoire* by the Salonica luminary Haim Sabetay:
"The fugitives are not carriers of letters of clearance from the community, as they are supposed to. This tax on textiles is not like the tax on residences and real estate. It is a collective tax, while the others are individual...The tax on textiles...is imposed on the universality of the Jews of the city, held responsible in collective solidarity, themselves and their descendants, in their personal properties and in their inheritances, till the end of the time. This, the Jews of Salonica have requested it themselves, in former times, by their own will. The Sultan acceeded to their expressed wish, and granted it as an authentic favor, in order to make it easy for them to pay their main taxes, which were replaced by this unique impost.If some of the people who are bound to contribute are exempted, then the others are obliged for them. Therefore, at no price can one of the contributors be freed from his obligation, because this would increase the share to be contributed by the others, and none has the right to do that. The Jews are for this tax of "brass" (i.e. bearing on them as hard as brass) like the true slaves of the King, whose command cannot be softened by anyone. The Jews must clip the wool to make it into thread, to weave it, and to manufacture the clothing of the military. The imperial command is that every individual must pay himself, and without delay, intensely, so that the required quantity of goods be ready in time. Everyone must even help his neighbor to accomplish his task. This tax cannot be replaced by a payment in money, because the clothes are required, year after year, in determined quantities."

Haim Sabetay then addressed words of exhortation to the Jewish leaders of Constantinople and to the fugitives themselves:
"I am writing to you these words, my eyes full of tears, faced with the unhappiness of Salonica."

Haim Sabetay's document was entrusted to the very influential Rabbi, Solomon ben Mohavar, who was sollicited to obtain the return to Salonica of the fugitives having settled in the capital. Ben Mohavar wrote:
"The Jewish officials of this city have come to see me, and have asked me to enlighten them on the obligations of the Jews who have left Salonica to escape the

impost. In the immense distress which here prevails, it cannot be a question of pure right, and absolute justice, and it is appropriate to discover at all costs a remedy to alleviate the suffering. We must ask the deserters to take their place in the city, or if it is impossible for them to return, a way must be found to make them pay their share to the impost. We are in our right to force them by having recourse to the State, and none could complain if we resorted to such procedure. But we prefer to abstain in so doing."

Despite the support of ben Mohavar, nothing concrete could be obtained. The Jewish officials from Salonica started to ask themselves if they should not request the help of the Turkish authority to force the recalcitrants to reintegrate their native city. This could have unpredictable and probably terrible consequences. In the meantime, Rabbi ben Mohavar had carefully researched the archives. He had found abundant documentation to the effect that the impost on textiles had been in former times spontaneously consented to by the Jews, its payment had been assumed to be collectively made in solidarity by all members of the Salonica community. By this fact, the members of the community were indeed in their right to ask their share of the quota from those leaving. Haim Sabetay wrote a sharp satire to a young rabbi who had interceded in favor of the recalcitrants. Sabetay also made an appeal to the expected higher qualities of the fugitives:

"If you allow Salonica to wither away, you will by the same stroke allow the withering away of the Talmud Tora which is is one of the pillars of the world...Do not try to evade your obligations by futile arguments, be generous and merciful."

The fugitives asked to be placed under the jurisdiction of the *Beth-dins* of their original synagogues. They hoped by so doing to entangle the litigation in an inextricable and protracted process. In the end the rabbinate of Constantinople rendered a judgment against the fugitives. The delegates from Salonica after hurculean efforts, settled the conflict by way of individual transactions.

During the whole reign of Ibrahim (1640-1648) Escapa was still the grand-rabbi of Izmir (5). He lived until the age of 93 and died in 1662, during the reign of Mehmed IV the Hunter (*Avci Mehmed*). Escapa was the teacher of Sabbatai Sevi, but later fought his doctrines.

The Ottoman-Venetian struggle for Crete brought new tribulations in Ancona. When the hostilities started in 1644, under Ibrahim, Venice went into a merciless hunt of Ottoman citizens, the majority of whom happened to be Salonician Jews engaged in trade. On November 13, 1644, all the Turkish vessels docked at Ancona and other ports were captured. Many Salonician Jews who were seized could not return home for nine months. In 1665, the Venetians rapidly advanced through the waters of the Thermaic Gulf, threatening Salonica. The energetic counterattack of the Grand Vizier Mohammed Köprülü repelled the agressors and tranquillized the Macedonian metropolis.

During Ibrahim's reign, and his successor Mehmet IV, the emergence of intellectual independence and free inquiry in Western Europe, contrasted with a stifling formalism and stagnation of Ottoman Judaism. Quite typically, it was

Spinoza vs Sabbatai Sevi. This was indeed about the time that Barouch Spinoza in Holland was revolutionizing human thought with his metaphysical theorems, the time that Ubriel da Costa (1591-1640) was rebelling against the stifling formalism of Orthodox Judaism, the time of Leon de Modena (1571-1649), Menasse ben Israel (1604-1647), Delmedigo (1591-1635), Sima Luzzato (1590-1673), all distinguished humanists, with total mastery in Greek, Latin and philosophy, nourished by mathematics and positive sciences, spreading the seeds of intellectual independence and free inquiry. Against the flowers of culture blooming all over Western Europe, the most that Turkish Judaism had to offer were the stagnating swamps of mysticism and cultural isolation.

Despite all, the love of melody and liturgical chants maintained the vibrancy of Turkish Judaism. The creativity of Najara, Longo, Abtalion and other members of Yahia's academy had resisted the corrosion permeating the life of Turkish Judaism. Popular chants flying from mouth to mouth in the plazas, ended up reaching the door of the oratory and gaining access to the repertories of the cantor in the synagogue. Some of the Jewish liturgical material was a reminiscence of the aragonese *jotas*, neapolitan *canzoni*, Turkish and Arabic *makams*.

In those circumstances, this people, so often martyrized and mortified in everyday matters on the Sabbath, became like another people escaping from past pain into an outburst of rejoicing intensified by the delights of liturgical music. The roster of great Jewish cantors in the seventeenth century included Meir Shimshon Ashkenazi (died in 1616), Juda Lebeth Hazan (died in 1652), Jacob Asher (died in 1661) and Vida Angel (died in 1682). They knew how to adapt in style the distress cries of the *rayas* (non-Moslems), how to cloak in a mystic mantle of acceptability the calls to pleasure by *beys* bent on enjoyment; how to mold the tunes from another world into the customary character of tradition. These cantors were the *paytanim* (liturgical poets).

Another lively musical culture which was perpetuated, was that of the *romanceros*, sung softly by the cradle, near the bed of the woman who had given birth, at the ceremonies of betrothals and weddings. They were melancholy, poignant melodies reflecting an incurable nostalgia and souvenirs rising from the depths of the unconscious, unforgettable memories from the Spanish past, mixed with new acquisitions from exposure to Turkish romances. The Spanish composer, Blasco Ibanez, saw in these delightfully antiquated chants, "a breath coming from distant ages, an inspired voice flying over the height of centuries, which has surmounted the ruin of all things."

The rewards of the time reveal that in Salonica, during the Seventeenth Century, the consumption of writing and printing paper was fifteen times smaller than that of wrapping paper used for sugar, which was a consumer product primarily accessible to the rich.

While the Empire of the Sultans was crumbling into inert anarchy, the Turkish Jews could not see beyond the minutiae of endless logical argument in their **Hiddushim** (Novellae, commentaries on the Talmud and later rabbinic works that attempted to derive new facts or principles from the implications in the text). The only flickers of light permeating the community were coming from the rare scholars who sometimes at the price of a simulated apostasy were able to initiate themselves in the texts of the Antiques in the Catholic College founded in Salonica at the initiative of Pope Gregory VII. Some elements of humanistic culture were also introduced through the passage of foreign adventurers, who while mainly engaged in profit-making ventures, had also penetrated at times the intellectual zones of Occidental cultures. Most of these people, opulent proconsuls, maintained rich libraries in their lavish homes. A feeble light could at times trickle out from their luxurious mansions to reach the culture-starved Jewish community of Salonica. In the enlightenment-deprived environment clouded by Lurianic vapors and the triumph of mystics, the only remaining sageguards against obscurantism were the Bible and the *Guide for the Perplexed* of Maimonides.

PART II: HISTORY OF THE SEPHARDIM AND TURKISH JEWS;
Memories of a Past Golden Age

NOTES AND REFERNCES

Chapter 1

1. There is no mention of Ertughrul by contemporary writers. First mention is in the *Iskendername* epic of late 14th-early 15th Century poet Ahmedi. The Chronicler Nashri Süleyman mentions the Aleddin Keykubat-Turcoman episode. Mentioned in the Ottoman Histories of Hammer, Hayrullah Efendi, Mehmed Ârif Bey, P. Wittek's *Deux Chapitres de L' Histoire des Turcs de Roum*, Fuad Köprülü's *Les Origines de L'Empire Ottoman*, cited in **MÜKRIMIN HALIL YINANÇ** *Islâm Ansiklopedisi* 4, 328-337.

2. Their new geopraphic location made Ertughrul's tribesmen the natural vanguard of Islam against the declining Byzantine Empire, **BARON, S.W.** (1983) *A Social and Religious History of the Jews*, Vol. XVIII, pp. 3-6. 11, 15-16.

3. **ARNAKIS, G.G.** (1951) Speculum XXVI, 104-118; **VRYONIS, S. Jr.** (1971) The Decline of Medieval Hellenism in Asia Minor and the Process of Islamization from the Eleventh through the Fifteenth Century, pp. 426, 427. University of California Press, Berkeley, California; **BOWMAN, S.** The Jews of Byzantium (1284-1453), pp. 69, 70. University of Alabama Press, Birmingham, Alabama; **NEHAMA, J.** (1935) Histoire des Juifs de Salonique, Tome I. Communauté Romaniote. Librairie Molho, Salonique, Greece.The origin of the name **Chiones** has led to many controversies. In 1337, Chionios, a high Byzantine dignitary, appointed to watch over Jewish interests was accused of judaization and brought to the high court of the Senate in Salonica. At the trial Chionios vehemently defended himself, changing from accused to accuser. A sentence of acquittal by the Holy Synod was ultimately obtained. The group of polemists which entered in disputation with Palamas may have acquired the name **Chiones** by analogy with Chionios, the judaizer.

4. *Hesychasts* are those that live in quietude or repose, attempting to reach intimate and total union with God by the **hesychia** or "silence". They had the support of Mount Athos. **VASILIEV, A.A.** (1932) *Histoire de l'Empire Byzantin*, pp. 362-369. Éditions de A. Picard, Paris.

5. According to Vryonis Orkhan's theologians, the Chiones, were a group of Jews who had apostazied to Islam. Meyendorff writes that the *Chiones* were Christian apostates who adopted Judaism to ally themselves to the Turks, seeking refuge in Judaism, of which the sacred books were venerated by both the Christians and the Moslems. According to Bowman classical Islam encouraged only conversion to the ruling religion, but in the syncretistic atmosphere of the Ottoman court, some individuals may have converted to Judaism or a Judaizing sect, but more probably the **Chiones** were indeed converts to Islam, as they themselves admitted to Palamas. George Arnakis suggested *Chiones* stands for the *Akhis* corporative groups (13th-14th centuries) which next to the dervishes, had strong influence on the guild organizations of the Greek and Armenian artisanate in Anatolia (13)12. **MEYENDORFF. J.** (1966) *Grecs, Turcs et Juifs en Asie Mineure au XIVme*

Siècle. POLYCHORDIA: FESTSCHRIFT FRANZ BULGER: Amsterdam, pp. 211-217, cited by Bowman, op. cited pp. 69-70. **VRYONIS** op. cited pp. 396-402; **WITTER, P.** (1954) *Byzantion XXVI*, 421-423.

6. The patriarch Philotheos Kokkinos who in his **Emcomion** presented a panegyric of Palamas was allegedly of Jewish origin. The use of the **Jew** label, was expedient tactics for Philotheus in further demeaning Palamas' unworthy opponents. **BALIVET, M.** (1982) *Byzantion LII*, 24-59; **BOWMAN**, op. cited 372; **BOWMAN**, op. cited 71; **TIHON. A.** (1981) *Byzantion LI*, 683-64.

7. Mara, originally Tamar, was the daughter of the Bulgarian Queen Theodora, who according to tradition was a converted Jewess. Mara, renowned for her beauty, was also the heroine of many folk poems however, recited for generations. She was not able in to save her brother, the last medieval Bulgarian tsar, Shishman II, who was ruthlessly slain when he became Murad I's enemy. **BARON**, op. cited p. 12-13, 17. **GALANTE, A.** (1948) *Appendice à l' Histoire des Juifs d'Anatolie*. Kâgit ve Basin Ishleri Anonim Shirketi, Istanbul, 17; **LEMERLE, P.** (1957) *L'Émirat d'Aydin, Byzance et l'Occident*. Presse Universitaire de France, Paris; **IBN BATUTA**, Vol. I, p. 333, Turkish translation, cited by Galante, op. cited p. 17; **ASHER, A.** *The Itinerary of Rabbi Benjamin de Tudela, Vol. I*. Hakesheth Publishing Co. New York, p. 56.

8. A group of Ashkenazim expelled from Hungary by the bigoted king Ludovic I (1342-1382) when they refused to be baptized (27) reached Thessalonika in 1375, joining themselves to the Hellenic Jews. **NEHAMA**, op. cited 102-116.

Chapter 2

1. The Dervish rebellion, prevented Sultan Mehmet I from achieving his goals. This was one of the most dangerous rebellions in Ottoman history. **HAMMER, J.** *Hammer'in Osmanli Devleti Tarihi* (translated by Mehmet Ata, summarized in Modern Turkish by Abdülkadir Karaman), pp. 67-68.
2. The fifteenth Century Byzantine historian Dukas, the author of *Historia Turco-Byzantina*, received a first hand account of Bürklüdje Mustafa (Perklizias)'s doings from a Cretan monk living in Samos. A fascinating Turkish sect was emerging which preached reconciliation between the rival faiths of Islam and Christianity. A simple-minded Turkish paesant, Bürklüdje Mustafa, was the prophet of a new movement who taught the Turks that they must own no property, everything must be shared in common. He gleefully sought to win the friendship of the Christians, expounding the doctrine that anyone among the Turks who contended that the Christians were not God-fearing is himself ungodly. The followers of this teaching, when meeting a Christian, would honor him as an angel of Zeus. This pseudo-monk (Bürklüdje Mustafa), dispatched two of his apostles, wearing only simple tunics, their uncovered heads shaved bald, and their feet without sandals to an old Cretan anchorite living in Samos on the mountain called Troulloti. Through them he, Mustafa, declared that he was a fellow ascetic who adores the same God that the

anchorite worshiped. That night he was going to walk barefoot over the sea to be with him. Taken in by the false monk, the true monk began to relate absurd stories on his behalf, and he related other marvelous deeds. Bürklüdje set forth the doctrine that one must not cover the head with a hat (**zerkulah**), and that one must go through life bareheaded, adhering to Christian beliefs rather than Turkish."
DOUKAS (1975) *Decline and Fall of Byzantium to the Ottoman Turks* (An annotated translation of "Historia Turco-Byzantina" by Harry Margoulias), pp. 28, 34 and section XXI, 11-14. Wayne State University Press, Detroit.
3. After the death of Musa (Pretender to the Ottoman Crown). the great judge of the army (**Kazasker**), Bedreddin, a magistrate with a high reputation of scholarship and sainthood among the Turks, was dreaming the revenge of the neglect in which his talents had been left. The intrigue, a vice quite rare among the Ottomans, was breeding inside Bedreddin, the more frightening that it was unsuspected. The dreamy imagination of the Turks which allows for a great deal of freedom in the terms of chimerical interpretation of the Koran, created a predisposition to become involved in all kinds of agitation. The utopia of communism was not a practical doctrine; the applicable doctrines have their limits, the chimerical doctrines have none. The utopia ran like a fire through the pastures of Ionia, and soon gained the villages and the towns. The Dervishes embraced the cause, which was that of their own sect: a general abnegation, renouncing of all property, an absolute communal ownership of all products of nature and work. The Jews and the Christians, flattered through a skilfull artifice by the Communists came to swell the ranks of the enthusiasts. In their favor the equality of the three cults was proclaimed. The Christian, Jewish, Greek and Mahomedan Communists desperately fought and fell as martyrs more ferociously attached to their illusions than to their lives. The Ottoman communism did not completely perish with its apostles. The mountains of the Balkans, between Servia and Thrace, rose in the name of the same principle. The old followers of Soliman, Isa and Musa (all brothers of Mahomed the First and all fallen pretenders to the Ottoman throne) skilfully flattered by Bedreddin, fused together in a huge proletarian faction in the service of the ambitious tribune, Bedredin. Vanquished and captured by Mahomed's son Murat, Bedreddin was hanged after a judgment rendered by the jurisconsults of the Empire. His title of chancellor of the House of Osman, his reputation as a scholar, his masterly written works, monuments of Ottoman legislation did not save him from execution. The oriental communism, a temporary delirium of ignorant people, became an unredeemable crime when taken up by a man too enlightened to have been sincere in these doctrines. It is the hypocrisy and the sedition that Mahomed aimed to punish in the person of Bedreddin rather than the doctrine itself. Communism, a sophism of justice and equality, moved from the Orient into Europe to remain latent with occasionnal exceptions: the *anabaptists* in Germany; in England after the revolution of Cromwell; the *niveleurs* (levellers) in France after the revolutions of 1789 and 1848; the socialists of Babeuf and the radical socialists. Everywhere communism failed. Property is the law of human society, charity its virtue, communism is its delirium. So says Lamartine!

LAMARTINE, A. de (1854) *Histoire de La Turquie*, Tome deuxième, Livre Neuvième, pp. 398-407. Librairie du Constitutionnel, Paris.
4. The family history of Badr al-Din (9, 10) is typical: his father, Israil (note the Biblical connotation) married the daughter of the Greek commander of a Thracian fort. She converted to Islam with 100 of her relatives, received the name of Meleke, and became the mother of Badr al-Din. Israil first settled in Samavna (Thrace) where he confiscated a Greek church and converted it into his residence. Badr al-Din himself married a Christian slave, Gazila in Egypt, who bore him a son, Ismail. The later in turn married the Christian Harmana (whose father was Armenian), the niece of a Christian priest from Ainus whom Badr al-Din had converted to Islam.
VRYONIS, S. (1971) *The decline of Medieval Hellenism in Asia Minor and the Process of Islamization from the Eleventh through the Fifteenth Century*, pp. 350=359. University of California Press, Berkeley, Los Angeles.
5. The Christian-Islamic symbiosis was apparent in the city of Bursa during the later half of the Fourteenth Century, when a Moslem preacher declared Christ no less a prophet than Muhammad. The sermon inspired the Ottoman poet Süleyman Çelebi to compose the *Mevlidi Sherif* on the birth of Muhammad. The Turkish syncretism was expressed by the belief in the three holy books, (Torah, Gospels, Koran) and the three prophets (Moses, Christ and Muhammad). Turkish syncretism must have originated within the **Mawlawi tariqa** (mystical religious group) founded by Mevlana Djalal al-Din Rumi (1207-1273). Both Rumi and his grandson Ulu Arif Çelebi were close friends with the learned abbot of the Greek monastery of Plato (St. Chariton) in the district of Konya. For a discussion between Rumi and a Christian on the divinity of Christ, Rumi always prostrated himself before those who greeted him (seven times before the Armenian butcher Tenik). He bowed his head thirty-three times in greeting a Christian monk from Constantinople. Rumi criticized a Moslem preacher who in one of his sermons praised God for not having created him and his congregation infidels. Rumi remarked that indeed the preacher was of greater worth than an infidel, by one-sixth of a **dram** (about one-fifth of a gram, a minimal weight). Rumi further said: "For some the road (to the Kaaba) is from Rum, for some from Syria, for some from Persia, for some from China, for some from India and Yemen...this man saying to that man, 'You are false, you are an infidel' and the other replying in kind...once they have arrived at the Kaaba, it is realized that warfare was concerning the road only, and that their goal was one."
The most eloquent testimonial to the great influence Rumi and his successors is Eflaki's account of his funeral, where the members of the different communities and nations were present, Christians, Jews, Greeks. Arabs, Turks, etc. They marched ahead, each holding aloft their sacred books, reading verses from the Psalms, Pentateuch. and Gospel. They said " We are like unto a flute which, which in a sole mode, is in accord with two hundred religions."
The Turkish sultans, while they fought seditious movements, ecumenically and philosophically shared in this syncretism. Bayezid the First named three of his sons (later day competitors for the Ottoman throne after monotheistic leaders: Musa, Isa and Mehmet. **VRYONIS** op. cited 381-391; **SÜLEYMAN ÇELEBI** (1943) *The*

Mevlidi Sherif by Süleyman Chelebi, Translated by F. Lyman, London in Vryonis op. cited 359;7. **ARBERRY, A.J.** (1961) *Discourses of Rumi*, pp. 134-136, London in Vryonis op. cited 387; **MEVLANA CELLALEDDIN** compiled, translated and interpreted by Gökpinarli, A. (1959) *FiHI MA-FIH* p. 70. Remzi Kitabevi, Istanbul; **BOWMAN, S.** (1985) *The Jews of Byzantium*, pp. 162-164. THe University of Alabama Press; **BABINGER, FR.** (1921) *Schejch Bedr el-Din, der Sohn des Richters von Simaw. Ein Beitrag zur Geschiche im altosmanischen Reich, Der Islam II*, 1-160, in Bowman op. cited 162-163.

6. As to the activist commander, the Trotsky of the Anatolian Red rebellion, Torlak Hu Kemal, a number of scholars have asserted that he was a Jew, as also mentioned in the Ottoman history of Hammer. Could the particle *Hu* be an abbreviated form of the Turkish word *Yahudi* for Jew? In Turkish the word *Torlak* means young and incapable, prodigal, vulgar and unscrupulous, vagabund and esoteric. Two references cited by Küçük for Torlak are Ziya Shakir's "Türkiye Yahudileri," *Millet Mecl.* October 9, 1947, No. 88 and Antonio Menavino's *Shehy Bedreddin ve dolayisile Torlaklar* (Sheikh Bedreddin and by his way the Torlaks), tr. Lütfü Yücer, Ankara 1971, 47. Sheikh Bedreddin Simavi and his caretaker Börlükce nedeed such a "Jew" for the propagation of the "religion" they had started. While Shakir consider Bedreddin's movement religious, for Galante it is rather a reformist social movement, started by Bedreddin in 1416, for the promotion of which, Torlak Kemal, a Jew from Manisa (Magnesia), converted to Islam, had been recruited. Torlak Mustafa mixed with the Greeks and played an important role in stirring Christian participation in the uprising. According to Professor I. H. Uzunçarshili, Bedreddin hired Torlak and had him named Torlak Hu Kemal in order to execute his plot of moving from *Sheikhdom* into *Shahdom* thus seizing the throne of the Ottoman Sultanate. Accordingly Torlak surrounded himself with an evil-motivated staff and took several actions directed against the *Sheriat*. His *taife* (sect, crew, group of men) was called *Kemaliler*. After having crushed Börlükdje, the army commanded by *Shehzade* (Crown Prince) Murat and Bayezid Pasha, moved against Torlak who had in the meantime forged an alliance with the Anatolian Shiites called *Alevi*. The Prince and the Pasha defeated the troublemaker Torlak and had him hanged, while at the same time suppressing the *Alevite* uprising. This is all recorded in Professor Uzunçarshili's *Ottoman History* I/363-364, which is itself based on Ashikpashazade's *History*, 90-94. According to the chronicle in verse, entitled *Menâkib-i Sheyh Bedreddin* written by the Sheikh's grandson Hafiz Halil, the mastermind of all, Bedreddin, was related by the way of Alaeddin Keykubad to the Seljuk royal dynasty. Professor Uzunçarshili reminds us that those with royal ambitions claim this kind of connection to legitimize their pretense. The Turkish historian I. H. Danishmend points to the fact that the region of Manisa in which Torlak had operated was in a region populated by *Alevites*. Danishmed looks at the uprising as a Communist rebellion and emphasizes that the simultaneous opperations in Asia Minor and the Balkan territories denote a masterly plan directed against the Ottoman Sultanate, when the state was barely recuperating from Tamerlane's onslaught and the ensuing civil war of the Ottoman princes, each

claiming Bayezid I's inheritance. The participation of a Jew such as Torlak in the sedition indicates that Bedreddin did not consider important religious differences. This was in disregard of the possibility that the Jews may have had ulterior motives, and once victory was attained would have no scruple in seizing the opportunity to further their own aims. Their targeting of the Alevites was to enable them to create a major disturbance in which they would thrive. Moshe Sevilla-Sharon in *Türkiye Yahudileri* (The Jews of Turkey), his work published in Turkish from Jerusalem writes that even though Torlak Kemal did play a significant role in Sheikh Bedreddin's uprising it is not easy to speak of an actual Jewish influence on the Socialist ideology or the rebellion itself. Moreover Torlak had abandoned his religion, not to alienate the Moslem populations, and he had adopted Islamism. On the other hand, it is worth recording that after the disabilities suffered under Byzantium's tyranny rule, in the early years of Ottoman rule, a Jew could have come to a position in which he was able to play -whether positive or negative- such a serious and significant role. This event is above all an indication that some of the Jews or the whole of the Ottoman Jewish community had been able to become "integrated" in a short time within the new culture. ABDURRAHMAN KÜÇÜK, *Dönmeler Tarihi*, 80-91, Rehber Yayinlari, Istanbul, 1990.

Chapter 3

1. According to an Ottoman legend, Murad II was asleep in his palace on the night when God came to him in a dream and gave him a beautiful, sweet-smelling rose to sniff. When Murad asked if he could keep it, God told him that the rose was Salonica and that he had decreed it should be his. **MAZOWER, M.** (2004) *SALONICA, City of Ghosts. Christians, Moslems and Jews 1430-1950*, 24-31. Afred A. Knopf, New York. **BARON S.W.** (1983) *A Social and Religious History of the Jews* Vol. XVIII, pp.14-17. Columbia University Press, New York, The Jewish Publication Societ of America, Philadelphia, USA; **DUCAS** in Baron op. cited, 17.

2. The **Gureba** were active in combat during the reign of Murad II and these Jewish janissaries seem to have excelled in martial arts. They distinguished themselves in the Transylvanian campaign against the nefarious Count Vlasd (Drakul). One can hardly visualize a certain Ribi Samuel Soncino splitting the skull of the fighting monk Capistrano (a fiery antisemite crusader) by a single stroke of his saber. **FRANCO, M.** (1897) *Essai sur l' Histoire des Israélites de l'Empire Ottoman depuis les Origines jusqu'à nos jours*, 31. Librairie A. Durlacher, Paris.

3. One hears of Rabbi Moses ha-Yevani (the Greek) and his teacher R. Shalom Neustedt in Vidin (5), an immigrant from the Ashkenazite community, perhaps from Hungary after the decree of expulsion by King Louis the Great in 1360. **BARON**, op. cited 21.

4. Sarfati's circular was addressed to the Jews of Swabia, the Rhineland, Styria, Moravia and Hungary:

"I have heard of the afflictions. more bitter than death, that have befallen our bethren in Germany--of the tyrannical laws, the compulsory baptisms and the banishments. And when they flee from one place, a yet harder fate befalls them in another...The clergy and the monks, false priests, rise up against the unhappy people of God and say: 'Let us pursue them even unto destruction; let the name of Israel be no more known among men.' Alas...How evilly are the people in Germany treated...The sword of the oppressor ever hangs over their head; they are flung into the devoring flames, into the swift flowing rivers and into foul swamps. Brothers and teachers, friends and acquaintances, I, Isaac Zarfati, from a French stock, born in Germany, where I sat at the feet of my teachers, I proclaim to you that Turkey is a land wherein nothing is lacking. If you will, all shall yet be well with you. The way to the Holy Land lies open to you through Turkey. Is it not better for you to live under Moslems than under Christians? Here every man dwells at peace under his own vine and his own fig-tree...And now, seeing all these things, O Israel, wherefore sleepest thou? Arise! and leave your accursed land for ever." **NEHAMA, J.** (1935) **Histoire des Israélites de Salonique**, Tome I, La Communauté Romaniote, pp. 115-118. Librairie Molho, Salonique.

Chapter 4

1. When Constantine IX Monomachus (1042-1055) was under suspicion of having secured the throne by murdering two Macedonian princesses, the last representatives of a dynasty which commanded great popular support, rioters had included Jews side by side with Greeks. Also Jew and non-Jew had united in the struggle for urban guilds. At Thebes and Thessalonika it was the guild of silk workers, with a substantial Jewish membership that led the way. There is, however, no evidence of a Jewish militia at the time of the ultimate peril in Constantinople. **DOUKAS** (1975) *Decline and Fall of Byzantium to the Ottoman Turks* (an annoted translation of *"Historia Turco-Byzantina"* by Harry J. Magoulias, p. 24, 205-210. Wayne State university Press, Detroit; **SHARF, A.** (1971) *Byzantine Jewry*, pp. 117-118) Shocken Books, New York.
2. Part of the Jews in Constantinople owed their allegiance to the Genoese. The Jewish fur and leather workers and the merchants were precious to the Republic of Venice. **STARR, J.** (1949) *Romania*, 20-33. Édition du Centre, Paris.
3. Jewish worker's taxes formed part of the revenues of the megaduke Doukas Notaras. **BOWMAN, S.B.** (1985) *The Jews of Byzantium (1204-1453)*, 83. University of Alabama Press, Birmingham, Alabama.
4. In his last speech before the fall of Constantinople, Constantine XI addressed in sequence his soldiers and nobles, then the Venetians standing on his right side, and then the Genoans, on his left. **SPHRANTZES, G.** (1988) *The Fall of the Byzantine Empire* (translated by Marios Philippides) pp. 123-124. The University of Massachusetts Press.
5. The Jews, were not residents in the imperial Old City of Constantinople, where stood Connstantine's Palace of the Blachernes, the churches of Santa Sophia, Saint

Irene and most of the fortifications. The administration of Galata, a town starting at the southern side of the bridge crossing the Golden Horn, had a separate charter, as an important commercial center, where elements from other nations, including Jews had been living. **GALANTE, A.** *Les Turcs et les Juifs (Türkler ve Yahudiler)*, Chapter IV.

6. The inhabitants of Galata sent a delegation to Mehmed II, with the message: "You are committing an injustice by trying to damage **our ships** and those of the Genoese, since we are your friends." They received in response: "These vessels are not manned by merchants but by pirates, who come here to aid the emperor. They should be thought a lesson, if possible, since they are my foes. You may depart in peace, since you claim friendship." **SPHRANTZES,** op. cited 3, 113.

7. In the messsage from Galata it is said **our ships** and those of the Genoese, thus pointing to an entity separate from the Genoese. Could there be Jews among the non-Genoese Galatiotes? **GALANTE, A.** (1948) *Les Juifs de Constantinople sous Byzance*, 64-67. Imprimerie Babok, Istanbul.

8. Mehmed III's **firman** said:

"At the reach of this imperial mark, you will be notified that the Jews, who inhabit this **Well Guarded** (Istanbul), have addressed to my Sublime Porte, a petition to let me know that the Jews present in this city, had taken a commitment, secretly towards one of my illustrious ancestors, the late Mehmed (Mahomed) Han, the father of conquests, may his soul lay in divine mercy (rest in Paradise), not to provide help and assistance to the Emperor of Istanbul (Byzantium)...(The Jews) should not be molested, their synagogues should remain as they were...nobody should dare to prevent them from reading the Torah and praying according to their rite..."

GALANTE, A. (1931) *Documents Officiels concernant les JUIFS DE TURQUIE,* Receuil de 114 Lois, Règlements, Firmans, Berats, Ordres et Décisions de Tribunaux, TRADUCTION FRANÇAISE avec résumés, annotations et un appendice avec sept autres documents, Première Partie, pp. 163-166. Établissements HAIM, REZIO & Co., Rue Çinar, Galata, Stamboul.

9. In the words of Nicolo Barbaro: "One squadron of that army (the Turkish) started its land operations through the Jewish quarter, in order to plunder the wealth and jewelry present in the houses of the Jews." **STARR,** op. cited 33,37.

10. **GALANTE, A.** (1941) *Histoire des Juifs d' Istanbul*, 1er Volume, pp. 111-112. Librairie Hüsnütabiat, Istanbul.

11. A Hebrew lament by R. Michael B. Shabbetai Kohen Balbo (16), on the fall of Constantinople, follows the arrival of the first news to Candia, Crete, on Friday June 20, 1453. There are allusions to over sixty verses of the Old Testament: "...For my people is captive (cf. Isaiah 52:2) in a great captivity along with my enemy (Edom, **i.e.** Byzantium) cf. Isaiah 34:5...And Bela (Constantine Dragoses, the last emperor) died (cf. 1 Chronicles 1;44). In the steep ravines (Cf. Isaiah 7:19) they lie upon ash heaps (cf. Lamentations of Jeremiah 4:5, literally those that were fed on purple are surrounded by trash). For this the earth shall mourn (Jeremiah 4:8); for utter destruction will be in the land (Isaiah 10:23)...

A second text (also dated 1453) from the *Seder Eliyahu Zuta* by Rabbi Eliyahu Kapsali (16), a descendant of the first Grand Rabbi under Ottoman rule R. Moses Kapsali, is an enthusiatic eulogy of Sultan Mehmed, the Conqueror: "In the first year of Sultan Mehmet, King of Turkey...the Lord ordered the spirit of the King, Sultan Mehmet...and his voice passed throughout the kingdom and also by proclamation saying: (Ezra 1:1-3) 'This is the word of Mehmed King of Turkey, the Lord of Heaven gave me a kingdom in the land and he commanded me to number his people, the seed of Abraham his servant, the sons of Jacob his chosen ones...and to provide a safe haven for them (based on verses in Ezra and Genesis). Let each one with his God come to Constantinople the seat of my kingdom and sit under his vine and under his fig tree with his gold and silver, property and cattle, settle in the land and trade and become part of it (Genesis 34:18).

The Jews gathered together from all the cities of Turkey both near and far...and the community gathered in the thousands and ten thousands and God assisted them from Heaven while the king gave them good properties and houses full of goods. The Jews dwelled there...and multiplied exceedingly (Exodus 1:7). **BOWMAN**, op. cited 340-345.

12. From George of Trebizond's letter: "Dear Emir and True Sultan, the entire race of man is divided into three parts, Jews, Christians and Muslims, of which the Jewish people is small and very diffuse, while the Christian is large and great, and has great power, wisdom, knowledge. If one unite these two races of men, Christians, and Muslims in one faith and dogma...the accomplisher of such union shall be elevated to the rank of angels." This no one except Mehmed could accomplish and compared to his greatness, Alexander the Great, and Caesar Augustus, and Constantine the Great themselves shall appear small. **GEANOKOPLOS, D.J.** (1984) *Byzantium*, 303-305. University of Chicago Press, Chicago and London.

12. **BOWMAN**, op. cited 186-189.

13. In Elijah Kapsali's account it is said that one day as the King passed through the camp of the Jews, he saw a large crowd. It was R. Kapsali rendering justice. The King was told that he was a scholar who interprets and delivers opinions every day of the year from its beginning to its end. The king commanded, and R. Kapsali was brought to stand before the king who called him *Rabbi*. Despite the fact that the *Rabbi* did not know Turkish, the King gave him honor and ordered that he be escorted home on his horse. The king disguised himself and went to the rabbi's house where Moses (Kapsali) sat to judge the people. The contestants were a rich man and a very poor man dressed in filthy rags. The verdict was in favor of the poor man. Kapsali ordered the rich man to return the stolen goods. The rich got angry, and raised his voice. Moses banished him from his presence, but not until he had returned the stolen property, The King knew that the wisdom of God was with Kapsali. One day there appeared at the Rabbi's door about twenty of the king's men, they brought Moses to the King. The King said: "Tell me the truth. What is your opinion of Ishmael b. Abraham; was he righteous?" Kapsali brought evidence from the Talmud regarding Ishmael and his importance. Exceedingly pleased, the

King commanded they bring him gold and silver clothes to dress Kapsali. Several times the King sent court cases involving Jews before his judgment. **ELIJAH KAPSALI**, *Seder Eliyahu Zuta*, ed. Shmuelewiz, 81-82, cited in Bowman op. cited 316-318.

14. **BOWMAN**, op. cited 186-188; **SANJIAN, A.K.** (1965) *The Armenian Communities in Syria under Ottoman Dominion*, 32-35. Harvard University Press; **HACKER, J.R.** (1990) *Zion*, Vol. LV, 1, pp. II-IV.

15. **FRANCO, M,** (1897) *Essai sur l'Histoire des Israélites de l'Empire Ottoman*, pp. 22-23. Librairie A. Durlacher, Paris, France.

16. From the imperial **firman**:

"The reason for writing this glorious firman on the subject of the Jewish physician Yakub, glorious among scholars and crown physicians, Galenus and Hippocrates of his time, is to exempt him, his male and female progeny and their descendants, for as long as God wills, from any kind of taxes and Government charges, be it the tax on capital, the taxes on vineyards and gardens, the taxes on the construction of fortresses and other compulsory labor, the yearly taxes or any other kind of impost levied by the Sultans or which will be levied by the Sultan who will be my successor...If anyone dares to ask to any of these persons, anything from what has been written above, may the curse of God, the angels and the men fell upon him...

Written and sealed at Bogaz-Kesen, in date of rebi ulahir, fourth month of the year 856 of the Hegira (corresponding to A.D. 1452)." **GALANTE, A.** *Documents Officiels concernant les Juifs de Turquie*, Vol. I, Section XXV, pp. 194-195. Établissements HAIM REZIO & Cie, Stamboul.

17. **BABINGER, F.** (1978) *Mehmed der Eroberer* (Mehmed the Conqueror) translated from German, pp. 290-293, 460.

18. **BARON, S.W.** (1983) *A Social and Religious History of the Jews*, Vol. XVIII, p. 35. Columbia University Press, New York. The Jewish Publication Society of America, Philadelphia.

19. It is believed that Mehmet the Conqueror had seven physicians, four Persians, one Turk, one Arab and one Jewish. Among them the Jewish physician "Hekim Yakub" had gained great fame in the practice of medicine. Ziya Shakir assumes that if it had not been for the watchful competition of the Persian doctor named "Lâri", Hekim Yakub might have played a more influential role over the life and welfare of *Mehmed-i Sâni* (Mehmed II) and as told by Hammer, he could have succeeded in threatening his *eyyâm-i hayat* (days of his life), cf. "Türkiye Yahudileri (the Jews of Turkey) *Millet Mecmuasi*, 1947, no. 91, p. 84.

Another source states that having been brought to our land of majestic benevolence after being expelled from Spain, Portugal and other countries of Europe and having reached happiness, fortune and comfort, the ungrateful Jews responded by committing the greatest act of treason and poisoned Sultan Mehmet [Cevat Rifat Atilhan, *Dünya Ihtilalcileri* (the World Revolutionaries) 1973. note in p. 48, Yelken Matbaasi].

Because Sultan Mehmet II died at a rather young age there has been an persistent suspicion that he might have been poisoned, a topic intensively elaborated by Franz

Babinger. He points out that after the Venetians lost one of their maritime possessions (the island of *Eghriboz*) to the Ottomans, they started to plot with the European Crusaders for the demise of the Conqueror. It is said that they attempted to poison him fourteen times, finally hiring *Maestro Iacopo* (Hekim Yakup) who had been for thirty years at the service of the Sultan and thus had his full trust. The incentive was a huge bribe in gold florins (*The Attempt by the Venetians to Poison the Conqueror*, trnns. Shevki Yazman, *Hayat Tarih Mecmuasi*, May 1979, I/17-20. Sh. Tekindagh wrote an article trying to invalidate Babinger's assertion and aimed to unravel the true causes of Mehmed II's death, in which he refers to Christian authors who have attempted to remain objective, rather than being driven by hatred against the Conqueror. Babinger was among those who believed *Fatih* (the Conqueror) to have been a man of evil ["Fatih'in Ölümü Meselesi (the Question of Fatih's Death)" I. Ü Edebiyat Fakültesi Tarih Dergisi, Istanbul 1966, 95-108].

There are both Eastern and Western sources which when discussing Fatih's death make no reference to the possibility that he might have been poisoned. Several Eastern authors, among Fatih's contemporaries, such as Neshri, Dursun Bey, Edirneli Rumi, do not mention poisoning. Only Baudrier writes that Fatih died after suffering with pain for four days and attributes such symptom to poisoning [St. Michel Baudrier, *Inventaire de l' Histoire Générale des Turcs* (Inventory of the General History of the Turcs) Paris 1620, p. 144 (cited by Tekindagh, p. 99].

According to Ashikpashazade Fatih had been suffering with discomfort in the foot (? of gout} which his physicians were unable to treat. His discomfort increased. The doctors convened in consultation and took blood from his foot. Fatih's condition worsened. As a last resort they administered him a potion (see below). Like many members of the Ottoman dynasty Mehmed II had been suffering from gout and with complications of the disease he ended up bedridden. His personal head-physician Lâri was called, and whe he failed they brought in Yakup Pasha. The latter did not agree with Lâri's medication. When after the medical consultation that resulted in bloodletting, Fatih worsened, the physicians as a last resort tried to reduce his torment by using Hekim Yakup's *sharab-i fârigh*. Fatih died. Yakup's potion has been considered by some authors as a possible poison! However Ashik Pashazade had been using the word **sharab** (wine, beverage) as equivalent with *shurup* (syrup), and this was what Hekim Yakup had been using as an emetic with his other patients to make them feel better (Tekindagh 98-107).

Tursun Bey, a historiograph who was in Fatih's intimacy, writes little about the circumstances of Fatih's death, but writes that towards the end, the Conqueror had been in consirable discomfort and pain, but kept his full mental vigor. He was prepared to abandon wordly possessions and sultanic powers to meet his Creator [*Fâtih'in Tarihi (Tarih-i Ebul Feth*, The History of Fatih) prepared by Ahmet Tezbashar, Tercüman 1001 Temel Eser, pp. 100-101].

A. de Lamartine writes that Mehmed was in the grips of a fulminating malady which had caught him as he had departed on an expedition with his army. When he died his entourage and doctors had hidden the news from the army and only said that a sudden malaise of the Sultan necessitated the return to Istanbul and his treatment at the *hamams* (bathhouses) there. Mehmed II had left two sons Bayezit and Cem. As the curtain-covered palanquin was reaching the capital, Mehmed Nishani Pasha who was devoted to the cause of Cem Sultan started to fear that Bayezid, reaching Constantinople first would agitate the Janissaries in his favor. He commanded a gathering of the local janissary garrison and stirred them to ask for an inspection of the curtained Imperial palanquin which was moving in direction of Üsküdar (Scutari), Istanbul, Asia. When the curtains were opened and the Janissaries saw that Fatih was dead, they entered in a fury and thought that an horrendous regicide had been committed. There was throughout their ranks a ferocious cry for avenging Fatih's death. The Janissaries first went to Istanbul, Europe and went on a rampage of the Jewish quarter. Then they assaulted the Imperial Palace and decapitated the *Vezir-i Azzam* (Grand Vizier) who was under suspicion of plotting against Cem [A. de Lamartine, *Histoire de la Turquie* (History of Turkey) *Cihan Hâkimiyeti* (Mastery of the World) trans. and prepared by M. R. Uzmen, Tercüman 1001, Temel Eser, III 567-569]. Lamartine by mentioning the suddenness of Fatih's death and the rampage of the Jewish quarter, does imply that there were grounds for ill intent.

There is also a poem by a Fatih contemporary lamenting that he had been a victim of his doctors:

The doctors gave the potion to the Khan (Sultan)

That Khan drank the potion to repletion

The potion cut into pieces the liver of this Khan Likewise instantly the wretched wailed

Why, why the doctors did me injury?

They tainted my liver and life in blood!

[*Ashikpâshâzâde Tarihi* (the History of Ashikpashazade) Istanbul 1332, p. 219].

According to Danishmed the poem could be interpreted in different ways, as the Sultan complains about his liver being cut into pieces, he may have alluded to inefficient treatment, but it also could mean ill intent [I.H. Danishmend, *Izahli Osmanli Tarihi Kronolojisi* (The Chronology of Ottoman History with Explanations) I/350-351].

Uzunçarshili writes that Fatih was poisoned by his physician, but it is not known whether the killer was Lâri or Hekim Yakup [*Osmanli Tarihi* (Ottoman History) III/144].

Tütüncü after refering to the allegations of Baudier and Babinger points out that Fatih had been poisoned by Hekim Yakup against a payment of 240 millions Turkish gold *liras* (pounds); but he also notes a similar enterprise by a Jew named Vlaco. He also alludes to the allegations by Hayrullah Efendi that Hekim Yakup had for a long time perpetrated a purposefully wrong treatment of the Sultan which culminated in his death by poisoning. Tütüncü concurs in the same opinion and writes that repeated attempts were made on the life of Fatih, the master plotter was the Republic of Venice and the perpetrator was the *Yahudi Dönmesi* (Converted Jew) Hekim Yakup who finally poisoned him (Ziya Tütüncü *Fâtih Sultan Mehmet*, Istanbul 1971, pp. 185, 199-202).

KÜÇÜK, A. (1990) *Dönmeler Tarihi*, pp. 99-107. Rehber Yayincilik, Ankara, Turkey

20. GALANTE, A. *Histoire des Juifs d'Istanbul*, Vol. 1, see ref. 15, op. cited, 111-114; 30. BOWMAN, S. (1990) *Cincinnati Judaica Review* 7-9; SATHAS, C. (1872-1894) *Bibliotheca graeca medii aevi III*, 102b. Venice, in Bowman, The Jews of Byzantium (ref. 6), p. 319; BARON, op. cited 29.

21. ANKORI, Z. (1959) *Karaites in Byzantium*, pp. 31, 233-237, 251, 282n, 280-282, 324, Columbia University Press, New York; NEHAMA, J. (1935) *Histoire des Israélites de Salonique* Tome I La Communauté Romaniote - Les Sefaradis et leur Dispersion, pp. 118-121. Librairie MOLHO, Salonique.

Chapter 5

1. BARON, S.W. (1983) *A Social and Religious History of the Jews*, Vol. XVIII, p. 35, 37. Columbia University Press, New York. The Jewish Publication Society of America, Philadelphia.

2. GALANTE, A. (1941) *Histoire des Juifs d'Istanbul*, Vol. I. p.112. Imprimerie Hüsnütabiat, Istanbul.

3. LAMARTINE, A. (1854) *Histoire de La Turquie*, Vol. IV, p. 10-33. Librairie du Constitutionnel, Paris.

4. CHAMORRO, K., RODERO, C.G., NUNEZ, F.O. and ORIOLA, M. Quinto Centenario (1492-1992) *Jewish Roots in Spain*, Introduction, Iberia Airlines of Spain.

5. REINACH, S. *Cultes, Mythes et Religions*, Tome III, pp. 475, 476 in Nehama, op. cited 129

6. NEHAMA, J. (1935) *Histoire des Israélites de Salonique* Tome I, LA COMMUNAUTÉ ROMANIOTE - Les Séfaradis et leur Dispersion, 124-142, Librairie MOLHO, Salonique.

7. NETANYAHU, B. (!972) *Don Isaac Abravanel Statesman and Philosopher*, 53-81. The Jewish Publication Society of America, Philadelphia.

8. NETANYAHU op. cited 218-257.

9. BARON op. cited 38-39.

10. NEHAMA, J. (1935) *Histoire des Israélites de Salonique* Tome I. op. cited 170.

11. NEHAMA, J. (1935) *Histoire des Israélites de Salonique* Tome II LA COMMUNAUTÉ SÉFARADITE Période D' Installation (1492-1536), p. 10-107, 142-148. Librairie Durlacher -Paris; Librairie MOLHO, Salonique. *Ordinamiento formado por procuradores de las aljemas hebreas pertenecientes al territorio de losestados de Castilla en la asemblea celebrada en Valladolid en el ano 1432--* published in Madrid in 1866 by J. Fernandez, in Nehama, Tome II. op. cited 46. NEHAMA, J. (1936) *Histoire des Israélites de Salonique* Tome III L'âge d'or du Sépharadisme Salonicien (1536-1593) Premier Fascicule, pp. 18-31. Librairie DURLACHER (Paris) - Librairie MOLHO (Salonique). CURIEL, R. and

COPERMAN, B,D. (1998) *The Venetian Ghetto.* Rizzoli International Publications Inc. GALANTE *Histoire des Juifs d' Istanbul* Vol. 1, 113-114.

12. MAX SCHWAB *Les incunables Orientaux.* Rapport sur une Mission Littéraire en Bavière et Wurtemberg, p. 37, 50-57. Reprint of the edition, Paris, L. Tehemer, 1883. FURST, *Bibliotheca Judaica II*, p. 84 in Schwab op. cited 37.

DE ROSSI *Annales I*, p. 68 in Schwab op. cited 37.

WOLFF, Biblioteca hebrea I, 637 in Schwab op. cited 37.

DE ROSSSI Disssertations critiques pour servir à l' Histoire des Juifs II, p. 293 in Schwab op. cited 45.

DE ROSSI *Annales I*, p. 186; *II*, p. 45 in Schwab op. cited 93. DE ROSSI *Annales hebreo-typographici ab anno MDI ad MDXL*, p. 6, no. 26 in Schwab op. cited 59. ROSSI op. cited p. 12 no. 59 in Schwab op. cited 59. BOD.I. no. 3453 and RAPH. N. RABBINOWICZ *Kurze Übersicht.* pp. 131-132 in Schwap op. cited 59.

13. BARON op. cited 74. SAGREDO, G. (1673) *Memoria istoriche de monarchi ottomani*, Venice and in later editions, in Baron op. cited 478.

14. JOSEPH b. MEIR GARSON *Porath Yosef* [Joseph's Winepress: holilies), quoted from a Gaster manuscript (now in the British Museum)] by H. Gross in "La Famille Juive de Hamon", *Revue des Études Juives* LVI, 8ff; and by H.H. Ben Sasson in "The Generations of Spanish Exiles" (Hebrew) *Zion XXVI*, 27 f. f. 21, in Baron op. cited 478.

BARON op. cited 462. BENAYAHU, M. The Sermons of R. Yosef b. Meir Garson as a Source for the History of the Expulsion from Spain and the Sephardic Diaspora (Hebrew), Michael VII, 42-205. based on Gaster MS no. 762 (now in the British Museum) in Baron op. cited 462. HEYD, U. Oriens, XVI, 155 f. in Baron op. cited 478.

15. SHMUELEVITZ, A. (1978) Capsali as a source for Ottoman History, 1458-1523. *J. Middle East Stud.* 9, 339-344. HEYD, U. (1967) *Osmanli Tarihi için Ibranice Kaynaklar* (Sources in Hebrew for Ottoman History) in *VI Türk Tarih Kongresi* (VIth Congress of Turkish History) Ankara 1967, pp. 295-303 in Shmuelevitz.

Chapter 6

1. FRANCO, J. (1897) *L'Histoire des Israélites de L'Empire Ottoman* depuis les origines jusqu'á nos jours, p. 46. LIBRAIRIE A. DURLACHER, 83 *bis* Rue Lafayette, Paris.

2. GALANTE, A. *Médecins Juifs au service de La Turquie HISTOIRE DES JUIFS DE TURQUIE* Tome IX, p. 85. Isis. Éditions ISIS, Isis Yayicilik Ltd., Kuyumcu Irfan Sokak, 22/2, Nisantasi, Istanbul, Turkey.

3. GALANTE, A. Histoire des Juifs d' Istanbul depuis lla pride cette ville en 1453 par Fatih Mehmed II jusqu'á nos jours (1er volume) HISTOIRE DES JUIFS DE LA TURQUIE Tome I, pp. 119-150. ISIS Yayincilik Ltd.

4. GALANTE, A., *Histoire des Juifs de Turquie*, Vols 1-9, Isis, Istanbul.

5. The Abbasid Caliph al-Mutavakkil 'ala' ilah who had his siege in Cairo, next to the Mameluk Sultan Tomanbay, had taken part in the fateful battle of Mercidabik (Mere Dabik) and fallen captive. Selim treated him with great honor and tried to use him for negociations with the Mameluk Sultan, which led nowhere. The assertion in d'Obsson's book that al-Mutavakkil had formally transfered the Caliphate to Selim finds no independent confirmation, but has been purposefully accepted by Ottoman historians to legitimize the succession of Ottoman Sultans to the Abbasid Caliphate. Selim I ascended to the Supreme Caliphate when he brought back from Egypt the **Sancaki Sherif** (the Holy Standard of the Prophet Mohammed) and **Hirkai Sherif** (the Holy Tunic of the Prophet). Their ascent to the highly coveted title of Caliph, **Emir-ül-Müminin** (Commander of the Believers) was, however, a mixed blessing for the Ottoman Sultans, leading to political adventurism associated with Panislamic dreams. **D' OHSSON** (1788, 1791) *Tableau général de l' Empire Ottoman* I, 232-270, in *ISLAM ANSIKLOPEDISI* Vol. 10, pp. 430-431, 433 (1980) Milli Eghitim Bakanligi.

6. **LAMARTINE, A. de** (1854) *Histoire de La Turquie* Vol. IV. Librairie du Constitutionnel, Paris.5.

7. When he was in Jerusalem, Sultan Selim watched from the window of his site of residence there, an old Christian woman bring a sack of garbage and dropping it a spot near his office. She was brought to his presence for questioning and revealed that it was imposed by the Christian leadership that daily deposits of garbage should be made at such location. The Sultan then had silver and gold coins scattered at the place, as an incentive to the poor for picking these and thus clearing the garbage. Ten thousand people took part in the clearing until it revealed the Western Wall and its foundations. The tale comes from the 17th Century author Eliezer Nahman Poa. There is a similar story, with the hero being Selim's son Süleyman I,(Soliman the Magnificent). **BEN-DOV M., NAOR, M, and ANER Z.**, tr. Raphael Posner, pp. 108-110. Adama Books, NewYork.

8. The people living there (in Jerusalem) consisted of 4,000 families and of the Jews there had only remained 70 impoverished families. There was practically no individual who was making a living and, if he was lucky to do so for one year, he was called a rich man. There were also many widows, old and lonely; seven women for one man. **YAARI, A.** (1946) *Travellers's Tales from Eretz Israel*, p. 127, Tel Aviv, in **BENSASSON, H. H.** (1969) Dvir Publishing House, Tel Aviv, first Eng tr George Weidenfeld and Nicolson Ltd, Third Printing 1976, 572-573, 1112, Harvard University Press, Cambridge, Massacusttes.

9. **NEHAMA, J.** *Histoire des Israélites de Saloniquel,* Tome II *LA COMMUNAUTÉ SÉFARADITE* Période d' Instalation (1492-1536). Librarie DURLACHER, Paris, Librairie MOLHO, Salonique.

10. **BARON, S. W.** (1983) *A Social and Religious History of the Jews* Vol. XVIII. Columbia University Press, New York. The Jewish Publication Society of America, Philadelphia.

Chapter 7

1. **BARON, S. W.** (1983) *A Social and Religious History of the Jews* Vol. XVIII, p. 49, 50-54. Columbia University Press, The Jewish Publication Society of America.
ALADAR BALLAGI, in Baron. According to the contemporary historian Joseph b. Joshua ha-Kohen "the heads of their community came out of the city, prostrated themselves before the Sultan and surrendered to him." It is assumed that as most of the Christians had fled from Buda before the siege, the Jews were the only organized group left behind to negociate a surrender.
2. In recognition of the Jews' collaboration, Süleyman granted a perpetual tax exemption to their leader, Joseph ben Solomon. His descendants, established in Turkey, were later known as the Salto and Israel families. The privilege (renewed by several successive sultans) specified that they should be exempt from the poll tax and other taxes, not be forced to billet soldiers, and be permitted to acquire ten male and five female non-Muslim slaves from among the new captives. Even in 1865, the sixty-five families of Salto and Israel, then living in Istanbul and its vicinity, secured from Sultan Abdül Mecid, *noblesse oblige*, another confirmation of their tax-exempt status. **GALANTE, A.** (1931) *Documents Officiels Turcs concernant les JUIFS DE TURQUIE*, Recueil de 114 Lois, Réglements, Firmans, Berats, Ordres et Décisions des Tribunaux. Traduction française avec résumés historiques, annotations et un appendice avec sept autres documents, pp. 166-169. Établissements HAIM, ROZIO et Cie. 28 rue Çinar, Galata, Stamboul.
3. The firman was in contradiction to the spirit of the reformist **Gülhane Charter** which had already abrogated the disabilities of the **reaya** (non-Moslems). It was an anachronism, if the Gülhane Charter was to be respected. Nonetheless, the author of the **firman**, Abd-ül-Medjid edicted that the will of his ancestor Süleyman I should be respected. The **firman** was destined to remain largely symbolic. Its challenge in an Ottoman court did not lead to a reaffirmation of descendants' rights. **GALANTE, A.** (1931) *Documents Officiels Turcs concernant Les JUIFS DE TURQUIE* Deuxième Partie Titre XXVIII Divers, p. 213, Établissements HAIM, ROZIO & Cie, Galata, Stamboul.
4.**NEHAMA, J.** (1935) Histoire des Israélites de Salonique, Tome II, pp. 122-168. Librairie Durlacher, Paris - Librairie Molho, Salonique.
5.**AESCOLY, A. Z.** (1937) *David Reubeni in the Light of History*, reprinted from Jewish. Quart. Rev. New Series XXVIII. The Dropsie College for Hebrew and Higher Learning, Philadelphia; **BIBERFELD** (1892) *Der Reisebericht des David Reubeni*, in Aescoly op. cited 3; **NEUBAUER** (1895) *Medieval Jewish Chronicles, Anecdote Oxoniensia*, Oxford, Vol. II. pp. 133-223 in Aescoly op. cited; **ROTH, C. and WIGODER, G.** (1977) *The New Standard Jewish Encyclopedia* p. 606, 1622, Doubleday, N.Y.
6.**NEHAMA** Tome II op. cited 149-169.
7.**NEHAMA, J.** (1936) *Histoire des Israélites de Salonique* Tome III. *L'ÂGE D'OR DU SÉFARADISME SALONICIEN (1536-1593)* Premier Fascicule, pp. 10-

51. Librairie DURLACHER, 142, Rue du Faubourg Saint-Denis, Paris -- Librairie MOLHO, Salonique.

8.ANKORI, Z. (1959) *Karaites in Byzantium*, Columbia University Press, New York.

9.NEHAMA Tome III 52-57.

10. NEHAMA Tome III 68-70.

11. NEHAMA Tome III 173.

12.NEHAMA Tome III 71-89.

13.NEHAMA Tome III 92-124

14.GALANTE, A. (1937) *HISTOIRE DES JUIFS d'ANATOLIE* Les Juifs d' Izmir (Smyrne) 1er Volume, pp. 8-12, 37-38, 207, imprimerie M. BABOK, Saint-Pierre Han, Galata, Istanbul; REINACH, S. *Revue des Études Juives* 11, 235-238 in ibid.

9.76. GALANTE, A. (1939) *HISTOIRE DES JUIS D'ANATOLIE* 2me Volume, p. 21. Imprimerie BABOK, Saint-Pierre Han, Galata, Istanbul.

15.BARON op. cited 74-79. *Histoire des Médecins Juifs*, pp. 160-164. In Bibliothèque de Communauté Juive de Genève. 83. GALANTE, A. (1941) *Histoire des Juifs d' Istanbul* Vol. I, pp. 9-10. Imprimerie Hüsnütabiat, Istanbul.

16. NEHAMA, J, (1936) *Histoire des Israélites de Salonique* Tome IV *L'AGE D'OR DU SÉFARADISME SALONICIEN* Deuxième Fascicule, p. 154-178. Librairie DURLACHER, 142 Rue du Faubourg Saint-Denis, Paris -- Librairie MOLHO, Salonique. FLAVIO JACOBO in Nehama Tome IV op. cited p. 157. NICOLAS DE NICOLAY (15676) *Navigations et Pérégrinations faites en Turquie*, Anvers in Nehama Tome IV op. cited 160.

17. ROTH, C. (1948) *The House of Nasi The Duke of Naxos*, p. 176-178. The Jewish Publication Society, Philadelphia.

18. NEHAMA Tome III op. cited 126-177.

19. NEHAMA op. Vol IV op. cited 96-121.

20. BARON op. cited 72-73.

21. GALANTE, A. (1928) *Les Turcs et les Juifs*, Chapitre 3, Istanbul.

22. ROZANES II, p. 52 in Galante, Les Turcs et les Juifs, Chapitre 3.

23. BARON op. cited 55-67, 73-74, 83, see also FRANCO op. cited.

24. GALANTE, A. *Histoire des Juifs d' Istanbul* Vol. I, 117-119.

25. GALANTE Hist. Juifs Ist. Vol. I op. cited 11.

26. GOLDMAN, I. M. (1978) *The Life and Times of Rabbi David Ibn Zimra*, pp. 1-137. The Jewish Theological Seminary of America, New York.

27. HAMMER, J. von *Hammer'in Osmanli Devleti Tarihi* (Hammer's History of the Otttoman State) pp. 297-308. Translated into Contemporary Turkish by Abdülkadir Karahan, Istanbul.

28. NEHAMA Tome IV op. cited 25-28.

Chapter 8

1. GALANTE, A. (1941) *Histoire des Juifs d'Istanbul* Vol. I, pp. 11-12. Imprimerie Hüsnütabiat, Istanbul.

2. **BARON, S.W.** (1983) *A Social and Religious History of the Jews* Vol. XVIII, pp. 84-118.Columbia University Press. The Jewish Publication Society of America, Philadelphia.

3. **ROTH, C.** (Hebrew Calendar 5748--CE 1948) **The House of Nasi The Duke of Naxos**, pp. 7-19. The Jewish Publication Society of America, Philadelphia.

4. **LAMARTINE, A. de** (1854) *Histoire de la Turquie* Tome Cinquième, pp. 34-39. Librairie du Constitutionel, 10 Rue de Valois, Paris.

5. **ROTH** op. cited 07-133.

6. **ROTH** op. cited 178-183, 182-186.

7. **NEHAMA, J.** (1936) *Histoire des Israélites de Salonique* Tome III. *L'ÂGE d'OR DU SÉPHARADISME SALONICIEN (1536-1593)* Premier fascicule, pp. 90-92. Librairie DURLACHER, Paris, Librairie MOLHO, Salonique. **GALANTE, A.** op. cited Vol. I, p. 120.

8. **NEHAMA** op. cited 175-209. **FÉLIX-BEAUJOUR** (1800) *Tableau du Commerce de la Grèce* Tome I, p. 9 et suivantes, Paris in Nehama op. cited 207.

9. **ROTH** op. cited 165-173.

10. **NEHAMA, J.** (1936) *Histoire des Israélites de Salonique* Tome IV *L'AGE D'OR DU SÉPHARADISME SALONICIEN (1536-1593)* Deuxième fascicule, pp. 12-22. Librairie DURLACHER, Paris, 142, Rue du Faubourg Saint-Denis--Librairie MOLHO, Salonique.

11. **BARZILAY, E.I.** (1967) *Between Reason and Faith*, 216-222. Mouton, The Hague, Paris.

12. **NEHAMA** Vol. IV op. cited 31-58.

13. **PIERRE BELON du MANS** (1550) Observations de plusieurs singularités et choses mémorables trouvées en Grèce, Asie, Judée, Égypte, Arabie et autres pays étrangers Livre I, Chapitre I, pages 41 et suivantes, Paris in Nehama IV op. cited 56.

14. **NEHAMA** op. cited 61-75.

15. **NEHAMA** op. cited 85.

16. **NEHAMA** op. cited 89.

17. **NEHAMA** op. cited 93-94.

32. **NEHAMA** op. cited 124-128.

Chapter 9

1. **MA'OZ, M.** (1975) *Studies in Palestine during the Ottoman Period*, pp. 107-109. The Magnes Press, The Hebrew University Institute of Asian and African Studies Yad Itzhak Ben-Zvi, Jerusalem.

2. **SCHECHTER, S.** (Hebrew Calendar 5786-C.E. 1945) *Studies in Judaism, Second Series*, p. 203-228. The Jewish Publication Society of America, Philadelphia.

3. **KRAVITZ, M.** (1973) HEBREW LITERATURE from the earliest time through the 20th century, pp. 233=237.

4. **SCHECHTER** op. cited 233=237.

5. DENBURG, C. M. (1954) Code of Hebrew Law, Shulhan 'Aruk Yoreh Deah, Vol. I, p. XI. The Jurisprudence Press, Montreal.

6. WERBLOWSKY, R. J. Z. (1977) *Joseph Karo, Lawyer and Mystic*, p.3. The Jewish Publication Society, Philadelphia.

7. WERBLOWSKY ibid. p. 292.

8. DENBURG ibid. pp. XIII-XIV.

9. DENBURG op. cited IX-X.

10. WERBLOWSKY op. cited 2-5.

11. ROTH, C. and WIGODER, G. (1977) *The New Standard Jewish Encyclopedia*, p. 403. Doubleday & Co. Inc,. Garden City, New York.

12. DENBURG op. cited XV, 2-11.

13. WERBLOWSKY op. cited 24-37.

14. WERBLOWSKY op. cited 9-23.

15. WRRBLOWSKY op. cited 279-292.

16. GORDON, H. L. in Werblowsky op. cited IX; WERBLOWSKY op. cited 13-18.

17. WERBLOWSKY op. cited 88-112.

18. SCHECHTER op. cited 237-251.

19. KRAVITZ op. cited 363-368.

20. WINEMAN, A. (1988) *Beyond Appearances*, pp. 8-11. The Jewish Publication Society, Philadelphia.

21. SCHECHTER op. cited 230-284.

22. WAITE, A. E. *The Holy Kabbalah*, Eighth Printing, pp. 196-199, 412-420. University Books. Citadel Park, Secacus, N.J.23; FRANCK, A. (1843) *La Kabbale*, Paris in Waite op. cited, pp. 413, 418. ZOHAR 2:89b-99b.

23. KRAVITZ op. cited 364-367.

24. WINEMAN op. cited 14, 18-23.

56. Ma'OZ op. cited 111-118.

Chapter 10

1. **GALANTE, A.** (1936) *Don Aben Yaéche, Duc de Mételin*. Istanbul. Incorporated in **GALANTE, A.**, *Histoire des Juifs de Turquie*, Vol. 9, pp. 18-40, Isis, Istanbul. The French agent in Constantinople, M. Berthier wrote that a certain Portuguese named Alvaro Mendes, would arrive in Salonica, with the intention of accomplishing his conversion to Judaism as soon as possible. Those from his nation had sent a guarded escort to bring him here, and he had with him valuables in the amount of eight hundred thousand to a million gold pieces (Galante 26)--The Ambassador Lancosme was writing on April 2, 1586 to Henri III that Alvaro Mendes (Solomon) twice had come to see him. His effects responded to his promises and words; he would be able to help in various subjects and His Majesty has in him a good servant, to which Henri III answered: "I have seen that you have written me about the affection of Alvaro Mendes, from which I am sure you will know how to prevail" (Galante 27)--Juda Sarfatim, aide of Solomon wrote in

March 1594 to the privy Council of the kingdom of England, that Solomon farmed the Ottoman customs-revenue which was supposed to secure 1,000 ducats daily and 40,000 nobles quarterly for the payment of the Janissaries. Sarfatim wrote that the duchy of Metelin (Mittilli) which the Sultan had bestowed to Monsignor (Solomon) was a good country, large and fertile, calculated to bring an income between 16,000 and 18,000 ducats (though the greater part had to be made over to the imperial treasury). Its subjects were Greeks and Hebrews with few Turks. The son of Monsignor had a town and 7 or 8 villages around a place called Tiberias, near Safed. He had built many lodgings and a beautiful castle in the said Tiberias; he was much loved by the Arabs. Galante 36-37. **ROTH** (ref. 10).--In a letter addressed to the privy Council of England, Sarfatim informed their excellencies that on the last 10th of April, the Grand Signor being in his garden with the Pasha captain of the sea, Tchagal Oglou, sent for Don Solomon, High Commissioner to the Court to join them to discuss foreign policy, bringing together the *mapamundi* or Atlas, which to the envy of the savants of Constantinople (only the French Ambassador had one) he had brought with him when he arrived from overseas" Galante 38.--Queen Elizabeth's letter bearing the date of March 1592 started by the words *Augustissime and Potentissime Imperatore*. The Queen wrote that His Majesty's subject, Solomon Abenyaerx, Knight, had sent a letter stating that since some time, he was unjustly and falsely importuned by several slanders. The Queen would like graciously to help him with her testimony. She had found him to be an important man. She could certify that not only she, but several other Christian princes, had desired he resides and remains in their kingdoms because of his virtues. But, he had chosen rather to establish residence in Constantinople, in the Sultan's domains, rather than anywhere else in the world. However, the artifices and lies of the ministers of the King of Spain, were preventing him to remain in safety even there. The Queen was of the opinion that these slanders have been brought falsely against him. If, similarly the Queen's agent resident in Constantinople had said or done anything against his reputation or interest, this was done by the machinations and artifices of Paulo Mariani, the Italian, who being there a spy in the service of the King of Spain, had persuaded himself, that by so doing, he would gain the favor of the agent resident.--Solomon wrote on July 26, 1592 to thank Her *Sacra Royal Majesty*. He had realized with what clemency Her Majesty had remembered and acknowledged his infinitesimal services and he certainly was placing himself under the most safe shadow of her high and sacred wings, being infinitely thankful for the gracious Mercy of the letter addressed by Her Majesty to the Grand Signor.--On May 23, 1587 Bernardino Mendoza, Spanish Ambassador in Paris wrote to the king of Spain that he had a letter of Alvaro Mendes, who came to Constantinople as a Jew, stating that Spain's truce with the Turk, must be contracted only through his intermediary. To the purported truce supposed to include the Pope, the Duke of Florence and other Italian Princes, Alvaro Mendes, in accordance with Luch Ali (the Turkish Admiral Kilitch Ali Pasha) was using his influence, to request from the side of the Turk, the inclusion of the Queen of England...Mendes was on bad terms with the ambassador of France in Turkey, who was treating him with disdain, having known him a practicing Christian, while he was actually a Jew. Galante 33-34.

2. **ROTH, C.** (Heb. Cal. 5708, A.D. 1948) *THE HOUSE OF NASI The Duke of Naxos*, pp. 205-216. The Jewish Society of America, Philadelphia.

2a. **KÜÇÜK, A.** (1990) *Dönmeler Tarihi*, Rehber Yayinlari, Ankara, Turkey, p. 125, citing Ziya Shakir, "Türkiye Yahudileri, *Millet Mecmuasi*, no. 92; Sharon, *Türkiye Yahudileri* (The Jews of Turkey) 30. According to Avraham Galante, the first Jewish-Turkish encounter in the early Fourteenth Century, much before the arrival of the Iberian Jews starting 1492, meant for the Jews that they went from tyranny to light, from slavery to freedom. The Jews looked at the Turks like brothers, professing a religion close to theirs. The Turks also had trust for the Jews and confidence in them. They felt proximity to the Jews in terms of similar practices regarding circumcision, fasting, and simplicity of their places of cult, Galante, *Türkler ve Yahudiler*, p. 10 in Küçük 78. Küçük has his doubts that the massive introduction of Jews within the Turkish realm was in the overall primarily beneficial, as Galante would like us to believe. The Jews who sought refuge in the Ottoman Empire, he says, rapidly gained control of Turkish possessions and fortunes. As money came into the hands of the Jews, not only they prospered in their businesses, but they took over and changed not for the better the administrative pattern of the Ottoman State and its functioning in an orderly way. Just for a few Jews to enrich themselves they altered and weakened the fabric of the Ottoman State leading even to bloodshed (Küçük 117). The author Küçük continues to elaborate on his doubts over Galante's assertions of a beneficial role by refering to several authors. Shahap Tan cites the comments of German Emperor Frederic II, regarding the welcome extended by Bajazet II to the Iberian Jews, calling it a a thoughtles, heedless action (*Yahudileri Taniyalim*, Let us know the Jews, p. 50 cited in Küçük 125). Küçük also refers in p. 125, note ** of his book to Théodor Fritsch: The Jews interpret the word freedom as meaning domination. Where they do not dominate they complain of tyranny (*The Jewish Question Throughout History*, p. 45). In *Le Drame Juif* (Paris, 1930, p. 30) the author Robert de Beauplan says: "The Jews of the Ottoman Empire took excessive advantage of their freedom there...Yet, the Jews still considered themselves foreigners and admitted that there remained an abyss between themselves and the nation with whom they lived together" (Küçük 126). More from Fritsch: "The Jews were quite skillful in adapting themselves to the times and to use to their advantage the currents of the times...The Jews using their money power were increasingly able to influence public opinion. It is not for nothing that the Italian Jew Montefiore had alerted his people: 'It is useless for you to bankrupt the states and to then give them loans. To deceive and confuse the nations, as long as you do not take over all the newspapers of the world, our world mastery is condemned to remain a fancy.' In reality the successes of the Jews in this area are remarkable." (*The Jewish Question Throughout History*, p. 108, cited in Küçük 126-127). Küçük mentions that there have been assertions regarding the exact application of the Monteforie plan to take over the press in Turkey, and Jews have tried to gain control of some newspapers (p. 127).

3. **WOLF, L.** Jews in Elizabethean England, Transactions of the Jewish Historical Society of England, cited in Roth, Note 33 to Chapter VIII, p. 248.

4. **FRANCO, M.** (1897) *Essai sur L'HISTOIRE DES ISRAÉLITES DE l'EMPIRE OOTOMAN*, pp. 66-73. Librairie A, Durlacher, Paris.

5. **LAMARTINE, A.** (1854) *Histoire de la Turquie*, Tome V, Livre Vingt-Deuxième, pp. 95-101, 104-108, 151-173, 195-199, 213-219. Librairie du Constitutionnel, 10, Rue de Valois, Paris.

5. **LAMARTINE** op. cited 145.

6. **DANISHMEND, ISMAIL HAMI** (1972) *Izahli OSMANLI TARIHI Kronolojisi*, Cilt:3, M. 1574 H. 987 - M. 1703 H. 1115, pp. 1-4, 71-72. Türkiye Yayinevi, Istanbul.

7. **ROTH** op. cited 216-221.

8. **LEVI, A.** (1992) *The Sephardim of the Ottoman Empire*, pp. 13-41. Darwin Press, Inc., Princeton, N.J.

9. **GÜLERYÜZ, N.** (1993) *TÜRK YAHUDILERI TARIHI*, pp. 102- 105. Gözlem Gazetecilik ve Yayin Anonim Sirketi, Istanbul.

10. **ROTH** op. cited 133-135.

11. **ROTH** op. cited 196-205.

12. **ROTH** op. cited 212-213.

13. **LAMARTINE** op. cited 199.

14. **DANISHMEND** op. cited 58-60.

15. **LAMARTINE** op. cited 207.

16. The occasion was the festivities to be held (for 57 days) around the circumcision of the son of Murad III and his Beloved Safiye Sultan in the summer of 1582. Murad III had intended these celebrations to be the marking event of his reign. On June 1st, for the inauguration, Murad III ceremoniously moved from the Imperial **Seraglio** to the Palace of Ibrahim Pasha with a view on the hippodrome. The Sultan was escorted by attendants in gold embroidered purple satin, his turban surmounted by two black heron feathers, a priceless ruby hanging from his right ear, and a huge emerald shining in his right hand. The Sultana followed three days later with a full armamentarium of pastries, including an architectural bakery wonder made of nine elephants in sugar-works, and likewise seventeen lions, nineteen leopards, twenty-one horses, twenty-two camels, four giraffes, nine-sirenes, twenty-two falcons, nine herons, eight ducks, and several other objects. It took fifteen horses to drive this gigantic masterpiece of sweets and pastries. Entertainers and acrobats exhibited their skills. At night there were marvelous fireworks, and part of the daytime entertainment consisted of Moorish dances and farces played by Jewish comedians. There were **mattesina** (burlesk dances) executed by Moors and Jews. Daily processions took place organized by the different corporations, many of which were affiliated with guilds of Dervishes. These processions were inaugurated by the guilds of shoemakers and

saddlemakers; the former passed by the imperial stand equipped with foliage-wrapped thyrsi (staffs tipped with a pine cone); on one of the thyrsi was figured the seal of Solomon. The members of the guild donated to the Sultan a monstruous boot in **maroquin** and a kind of yellow oriental shoes (**babouches** in Lamartine's words). LAMARTINE op. cited 151-177.

17. **ROTH** op. cited 189, 198-199. Murad III, fanatic and somewhat unbalanced needed little incitement to turn into a persecutor. The ostentatious display of the Jewish woman procured the opportunity.

LAMARTINE op. cited 112.

19. **GALANTE, A.,** *Histoire des Juifs de Turquie,* Vol. 1 128, 129-132; Vol. 2 46-47; Vol. 8 63; Vol. 9 23, 87-88.

20. In the colophon in one of Joseph Caro's works published in Venice it is written: "...there was here the Lord and Prince, the expert physician, Solomon son of Nathan Ashkenazi of Udine, an envoy sent from Constantinople...to the honorable government of Venice (and) to the Doge (may his might increase!). Our own eyes have seen what our fathers have known not since the day that Judah separated from Ephraim, the verity of glory and honor done to him by the princes here among us. Such has never been done to any Jew since the destruction of the Holy Temple." **ROTH,** op. cited 151-160.

21. The Jewish physician Solomon Ashkenzi (*Alamanoghlu*) played an important part in the Polish succession, when in 1572 his previous employer King Sigismond Augustus died childless. Polish kings at that time were chosen by election. At the national Polish Convention held in Varsaw five candidates were considered, among them Henri, Duke of Anjou (future Henri III, son of Catherine de Médicis, the French Queen-Mother). Poland had a long border with the Ottoman Empire. Therefore, Ashkenazi, at the Service of Murad III, must have looked for a King of Poland friendly to the Ottomans. Henri, Duke of Anjou, was the right person, but there were critical considerations, because a French king of Poland might disturb the balance of power in Europe. Ashkenazi persuaded Grand Vizier Sokullu to throw the weight of Turkish influence on the side of the French prince. Henri was elected.--Another intervention of Ashkenazi in international politics took place when in 1578, the grand-duke of Tuscany wished to resume diplomatic and commercial relations with the Ottoman Empire. The Jewish physician did his best to smooth out the difficulties. He sent to the grand-duke a personal letter sealed with the Shield of David, surrounded by a garland, advising the Tusacan ruler on the procedure. The imperial dragoman, Hurrem wrote about Ahskenazi: "Rabbi Salamone, because of his good conduct, takes part in most of the negociations of this Porte."

ROTH, op. cited 197-199.

22. **ROTH,** op. cited 199.

23. **ROTH,** op. cited 200-204, 212-213.

24. With no less verve, Lamartine writes: "The money of the empire, this gage of sincerity in transactions, was altered by the Jews, inspectors of coins and alloys. The Jewish fabricant of the mint, presented the treasurer of the sultan, says Ali, the

historian of the reign with ten pieces of gold "as thin as the leaf of an almond-tree, and not weighing more than a drop of dew." LAMARTINE, op. cited 195-199.

25. DANISHMEND op. cited 111-113.

26. ROTH, op. cited 204.

27. TUCKER BROOKE, C. F. (1922) *Times Literary Supplement* of July 6, 1922 in Roth, op. cited 247.

28. ROTH, op. cited 247, note 22 to Chapter VII.

29. NEHAMA, J. (1936) *Histoire des Israélites de Salonique* Tome IV *L'AGE D'OR DU SÉPHARADISME SALONICIEN (1536-1593)* Deuxième fascicule, pp. 163-167. LIbrairie DURLACHER, Paris--Librairie MOLHO, Salonique.

39. NEHAMA Tome IV op. cited 167-171.

40. NEHAMA Tome IV op. cited 174-178.

41. NEHAMA Tome IV op. cited 178-180.

42. NEHAMA Tome IV op. cited 181-185.

43. NEHAMA Tome IV op. cited 185-188.

18. ROTH op. cited 200, 204-295, 209-212, 215.

26. CHARRIÈRE *Négociations du Levant* III, p. 883 in Roth op. cited 247.

27. ROZANES III, pp. 274-275 in note 21 Roth op. cited 247.

28. TESTA *Recueil de Traités* 129-30 in note 21 Roth op. cited 247.

37. MARLOWE, CHRISTOPHER (1592) *The Jew of Malta*, London, cited in Roth, ref. 36.

Chapter 11

1. KINROSS, Lord (1977) *The Ottoman Centuries*, p. 291. Marrow Hill Paperbacks, N.Y.

2. Ferhad Pasha, who had become an old man in the wars of Persia was appointed Grand-Vizier in place of Sinan Pasha. The latter returned for the third time to sumptuous exile in Malghara. Ferhad had married a daughter of Safiye. From the recesses of the harem, Murad III's wife, now Queen Mother, held greater authority under Mehmet III, than she ever had under his father. Ferhad called the Army to war on the banks of the Danube, in order to avenge the incursions of the Germans and Hungarians in Valachia. The Spahis refused to march until they got the certain gratifications and privileges they demanded. Ferhad called on the Janissaries to disperse the rebellious Spahis. Cicala Pasha and Siyavush Pasha, two other son-in-law of the Sultana Safiye were sent into exile. These two viziers were under suspicion of having provoked the Spahi turmoil aimed at discrediting Ferhad.

A ferocious masssacre by the Valachs of the Ottoman garrison in Giurgewo hastened the march of Ferhad's army towards Valachia. But there was still Spahi discontent which bode an ill omen for the expedition; in the course of the night the Spahis removed the horse tails flying in front of the Grand-Vizier's tent and also the gold **Bulla** (Sphere) from the top of the pole standing at the center of the Pasha's pavilion. Ibrahim Pasha, an ex-favorite of Murad III, and also a son-in-law of the *Valide Sultan* (Queen Mother) had been appointed *Kaymakam* (Lieutenant-

General of the Empire) to cover for the absence of the Grand Vizier from the capital. Ibrahim had now the full of authority of the Grand-Vizier and generalisimo. He used his temporary powers to harm Ferhad as much as possible. As Ferhad was in the process of positioning his army on the Valachian shore of the Danube, Ibrahim was obtaining from the young Sultan Mehmed III, Ferhad's death sentence. The Grand-Vizier's reported crime was to have told the recalcitrant Spahis, that "if they did not return to the fold of discipline, their wives would remain barren forever." By the mores of the time, this was an unforgivable outrage. Since the origin of the Empire it was the first time that a disgraced Grand Vizier had not resigned himself to get ready for the slaughter by the dagger or strangling by horsehair, at his Master's word. He decided not the wait for the executioner to reach Valachia. He ran away from his encampment taking with him three thousand horsemen from his household, on a march towards Constantinople. On his side the reappointed Grand Vizier Sinan Pasha advanced with twenty thousand Janissaries to take command of the troups abandoned in Valachia with no leader at their head. The two enemies Ferhad and Sinan advancing in opposite diections met by coincidence in the neighbourhood of Ostranidja. Sinan had already exhorted his Janissaries: "the head of the rebel is mine, his treasures are yours!" Ferhad, intimidated by the enormity of his disobedience, having defied the sentence of the Sultan, watched from a hill, surrounded by his cavaliers, the pillage of his treasures and of his tents by Sinan's Janissaries. Then losing heart, he precipitated himself towards the forest of Bulgaria, and succeeded to reach with no one in pursuit of him, a farm he owned near the capital of Bulgaria. The intercession of the *Valide Sultan* plus the presents of his Jewish banker Solomon (see the preceding Chapter, Solomon Ashkenzi), got a pardon for Ferhad. The Sultan sent him a *Hatti Sherif* (Imperial Order superceding all other Government Orders) allowing him to live in peace at his farm in Litrof. But the hatred of Ibrahim had not stopped. At the very moment Ferhad was starting to feel safe in Litrof, receiving his friends coming to congratulate him, the *bostandji-pasha* arrived there to take him away and carry him to the castle of *Yedi Kule* (Seven Towers), the antechamber of death! Three days later he was duly strangled in a way juridically sanctioned by an order of the *Kaymakam* Ibrahim which had been ratified by Mehmed III. By an unfortunate circumstance Ferhad had managed to offend Mehmed III, always jealous of his power. The Valide's son-in-law, Cicala Pasha, having received the order to join his army in Hungary, had wished to buy Ferhad's horses, while the latter was disgraced and exiled to his farm in Litrof. The Sultana summoned Cicala and forbade him to buy Ferhad's stables. Cicala interpreted this prohibition as a sign that the Sultana was preparing to restore his favorite Ferhad to power. Cicala revealed his suspicions to Mehmed III. The Sultan was indignant that his mother was undermining whatever he loudly commanded. Ferhad's head was delivered to his enemies. **LAMARTINE, A.** (1854) *Histoire de la Turquie*, 213-218. Librairie du Constitutionnel, Paris.

3. **BARON, S. W.** (1973) *A Social and Religious History of the Jews* Vol. XVIII p. 156, Columbia University Press, New York. The Jewish Publication Society of America, Philadelphia.

4. **KINROS** op. cited 292-294.

5. **KINROS** op. cited 299-300.

6. **GALANTE, A.** (1941) *Histoire des Juifs d'Istanbul* Vol. I p. 16. Imprimerie Hüsnütabiat, Istanbul.

7. **GALANTE, A.** (1937) *Histoire des Juifs d'Anatolie Les Juifs d' Izmir (Smyrne)* 1er Volume, pp. 49-50. Imprimerie M. BABOK, Saint-Pierre Han, Galata.

8. **NEHAMA, J.** (1959) *Histoire des Israélites de Salonique* TOME V *PÉRIODE DE STAGNATION LA TOURMENTE SABBATÉENNE (1593-1669)* pp. 170-173. Publication de la Fédération Sépharadite Mondiale Département Culturel Imprimerie EMMANUEL STEFANIAKIS Rue Franquini 2, Salonique.

9. **ibid** 172-183.

10. **Nehama** op. cited 48.

Chapter 12

1. **BARON, S.W.** (1983) *A Social and Religious History of the Jews* Vol. XVIII, pp. 129-131. Columbia University Press, New York. Jewish Publication Society, Philadelphia.

2. **GALANTE, A.** (1941) *Histoire des Juifs d'Istanbul* Vol I, p. 16. Imprimerie Hüsnütabiat, Istanbul.

3. **GALANTE, A.** (1937) *Histoire des Juifs d'Anatolie. Les Juifs d'Izmir (Smyrne)*, Ier Volum, p. 49. Imprimerie M. BABOK, Saint Pierre Han, Galata, Istanbul.

4. **LAMARTINE, A.** (1854) *Histoire de la Turquie,* Tome cinquième, p. 315.

5. **NEHAMA, J.** (1936) *Histoire des Israélites de Salonique* Tome IV *L'AGE D'OR DU SÉFARADISME SALONICIEN (1536-1593)* Deuxième fascicule, pp. 185=188. Librairie DURLACHER, 142 Rue du Faubourg Saint-Denis, Paris--Librairie MOLHO, Salonique.

6. **GRAVES, R.** in Idries Shah, *The Sufis*, Introduction, p. Introduction p. X, 7, back cover. Anchor Books, Doubleday & Co. Inc., Garden City, New York.

7. **WAITE, A. E.** *The Holy Kabbalah* (Eighth printing) pp. 75-80. University Books, Secaucus, N.J.

8. **Jewish Encyclopedia**, Vol. Xi, p. 579, in Idries Shah, *The Sufis*, p. 307. Anchor Books, Doubleday & Co. Inc, Garden City, New York.

9. **Roth, C. and WIGODER, G.** (1977) *The New Standard Jewish Encyclopedia*, p. 2003, Doubleday & Company, Garden City, New York.

10. **ANKORI, Z.** (1959) *Karaites in Byzantium*, pp. 8, 16, 214, 367. Weizmann Science Press, Jerusalem, Israel and Oxford University Press, London, Toronto, Bombay and Karachi; First ed. (1957) Columbia University Press, New York.

11. **IDRIES SHAH** (1971) *The Sufis*, p. 385-309, also 306n. Anchor Books, Doubleday & Co, Garden City, New York.

12. **IDRIES SHAH** op. cited 133.

13. **IDRIES SHAH** *Tales of the Dervishes*. Dutton Paperbacks.

14. **IDRIES SHAH** *Wisdom of the Dervishes*. Dutton Paperbacks.

15. **NEHAMA, J.** (1959) *Histoire des Israélites de Salonique* Tome V *PÉRIODE DE STAGNATION LA TOURMENTE SABBATIENNE (1593-1669)*, pp. 18-23. Publication de la Fédération Sépharadite Mondiale, Département Culturel. Imprimerie EMMANUEL STEFANIAKIS, Rue Franguini, Z - Salonique.

16. **NEHAMA**, op. cited 56-64.

17. ibid 164-165.

18. ibid 215-216.

Chapter 13

1. **KINROSS, Lord** (1977) *The Ottoman Centuries*, pp. 287-289. Morrow Quill Paperbacks, New York.

2. Among the victims was Prince Mustafa, endowed with all the attributes of a good nature, genious and education, a handsome figure reminiscent of Süleyman, the Magnificent. On the night before the execution he made his farewell to life writing an elegy bathed in the tears of his waning existence, reminiscent of the Constantinople-born poet André Chénier's elegy, the night before facing the guillotine during the French Revolution. **LAMARTINE, A. de** (1854) *Histoire de La Turquie*, Vol. Cinquième, pp. 211-213. Librairie du Constitutionel, 10 rue de Valois, 10, Paris, France.

3. **DANISHMEND, I.H.** *Izahli OSMANLI TARIHI KRONOLOJISI*, Cilt:3. pp. 147-156 p. 201. Türkiye Yayinevi, Istanbul.

4. **ROTH, C.** (1948) *The House of Nasi The Duke of Naxos*, p. 203-204. The Jewish Publication Society of America, Philadelphia, Penna.

5. **LAMARTINE** op. cited 213-219.

6. **BARRON, S.W.** *A Social and Religious History of the Jews* Vo. XVIII, pp. 131-134. Columbia University Press, New York. The Jewish Publication Society of America, Philadelphia.

7. **ROTH, C.** (Heb. Cal. 5708-C.E. 1948) *The House of Nasi The Duke of Naxos*, pp. 200-202. THe Jewish Publication Society of America, Philadlphia.

8. **GALANTE, A.** (1926) Esther Kyra, Société Anonyme Papéterie et d' Imprimere (Fratelli Haim) Istanbul. See also rep. Galante, *Histoire des Juifs de Turquie*, Vol. 9, pp. 3-18.

9. **ROZANES, S.** *Divre Yeme Israel Betogarna* Vol. III, in Galante op. cited Vol. 9, 3.

10. **MEHMED MURAD,** referred to in Galante op. cited Vol. 9, 4-5

11. **MUSTAFA EFFENDI SELANIKI ZADE,** referred to in Galante op. cited Vol. 9, 9-13.

12. **MEHMED BEHMEDMI EFFENDI,** referred to in Galante op. cited 13-14.

13. **GALANTE** op. cited Vol. 9, 16-18.

14. **LAMARTINE** op. cited 237.

15. **ROTH** op. cited 213.

16. **NEHAMA, J.** (1936) *Histoire des Israélites de Salonique* Tome IV *L'ÂGE d'OR DU SÉFARADISME SALONICIEN (1536-1595)* Deuxième fascicule pp. 151, 183-166. LIBRAIRIE DURLACHER, 142 Rue du Faubourg Saint-Denis, Paris--LIBRAIRIE MOLHO, Salonique.

17. **GALANTE, A.** (1939) *Histoire des Juifs d'Anatolie* Vol. II pp. 25-26. Imprimerie BABOk, Saint Pierre Han, Galata, Istanbul.

Chapter 14

1. **KINROSS, Lord** (1977) *The Ottoman Centuries*, pp. 308-313. Morrow Quill Paperbacks, New York.

2. **LAMARTINE, A. de** (1855) *Histoire de la Turquie* Tome VI, Livre vingt-cinquième, Chapitre XXIX, pp. 87-91. Librairie du Constitutionel 10, rue de Valois,Typographie Morris et Cie, 64 rue Amelot, Paris.

3. **RACINE** *Théâtre Complet*, Notices et annotations par Henri Clouard, Tome II, p. 129. Bibliothèque Larousse, 13-17, Rie Montparnasse, Paris.

4. ibid 140.

5. **NEHAMA, J.** (!936) *Histoire des Israélites de Salonique* Tome IV *L'AGE D'OR DU SÉFARADISME SALONICIEN (1536-1593)* Deuxième fascicule, pp. 76-77. Librairie DURLCHER, 142, Rue du Faubourg Saint-Denis, Paris--Librairie MOLHO, SAlonique.

6. ibid 71.

7. **GALANTE, A.** (1941) *Histoire des Juifs d' Istanbul* Vol. I, pp. 17-18. Imprimerie Hüsnütabiat, Istanbul.

8. **Revue des Études Juives** XVIII, 40, in Galante op. cited 17.

9. **GALANTE, A.** *Histoire des Juifs d'Istnbul* Vol. II, pp. 125-126, Istanbul.

10. **LAMARTINE** op. cited 119-120.

11. **BARON, S.W.** (1983) *A Social and Religious History of the Jews* Vol. XVIII, pp. 156-157. Columbia University Press, New York. The Jewish Publication Society of America, Philadelphia.

12. ibid 161-162.

13. **BARON** op. cited 102, 149-159.

14. **GALANTE** Vol. I op. cited 121-122.

15. **GALANTE, A.** (1937) *Histoire des Juifs d' Anatolie* Les Juifs d'Izmir (Smyrna) Ier Volume, pp. 50-51. Imprimerie M. BABOK, SAint Pierre Han, Galata, Istanbul.

16. **NEHAMA, J.** (1959) *Histoire des Israélites de Salonique* Tome V *PÉRIODE DE STAGNATION - LA TOURMENTE SABBATÉÉnne (1593-1669)* pp. 71-90. Publication de la Séphardite Mondiale Département Culturel. Imprimerie EMMANUEL STEFANAKIS, Rue Franguini, 2 - Salonique.

17. ibid 187-188.

18. ibid 219-221.
19. ibid 223-245.

Chapter 15

1. **KINROSS, Lord** (1977) *Ottoman Centuries*, pp. 313-318. Marrow Quill Paperbacks. New York.
2. **DANISHMEND, I.H.** (1972) *Izahli Osmanli Tarihi*, pp. 387-411. Türkiye Yayinevi, Istanbul.
3. **GALANTE, A.** (1941) *Histoire des Juifs d' Istanbul*, Vol. 1, p. 18. Imprimerie Hüsnütabiat, Istanbul.
4. **GALANTE** op. cited 122-133.
5. **GALANTE, A.** (1937) *Histoire des Juifs d' Anatolie* Les Juifs d'izmir (Smyrne) 1er Volume. pp. 50-51.
6. **NEHAMA, J.** (1959) *Histoire des Israélites de Salonique* Tome V *PÉRIODE DE STAGNATION LA TOURMENTE SABBATÉÉNN (1593-1669)* pp. 179-183. Publication de la Fédération Séphardite Mondiale Département Culturel. Imprimerie EMMANUEL SFAKIANAKIS, Rue Franguini 2 - Salonique.

APPENDIX 1

THE CHIONES

The *Chione* polemists could be identified as "judaizing" in a derogatory sense by their opponent, the archbishop, who fell into the hands of the Osmanli Turks while crossing the Dardanelles. Palamas was the leader of the **Hesycasts** (4), The captivity of Palamas provides an insight into the life of the Ottomans when this pastoral group started to spill over the remaining Byzantine dominions. The Osmanli lifestyle reveals a mixture of intellectual curiosity, culture and civilization in the person of Emir Orhan's grandson, the young prince Ismail, hosting Palamas. In a landscape beautified by thick shaded trees, delightful meadows, valleys surrounded by mountains, the Archbishop met prince Ismail. They had lunch on the grass and the prelate digressed on the martyrdom of Christ. the worship of the Cross, the supernatural birth of the Christ. The prince never showed an hostile attitude finally a heavy rain ended the discussion.

At that time, the Emir Orkhan was under treatment by the Greek physician Taronites, who interceded in favor of Palamas. Orkhan straightaway sent to call the *Chiones*. Palamas wrote of the *Chiones*, in his epistle that they were men who have thought of nothing, and have been taught by Satan nothing, except blasphemy and shamelessness towards our Lord Jesus Christ. The **Chiones** came accompanied by *archontes* (dignitaries) and they all took seats out of doors, with presiding the session Palapenis (Balaban, or Balabangik), a semi-legendary veteran warrior. The minutes of the meeting (*dialexis*) were taken by the physician Taronites and they appear right after Palamas' epistle to the Thessalonians. The Ottoman court appears to have believed in the practicability of religious syncretism (compromise) as a basis for the **rapprochement** of the Greek and Turkish people. Balaban put the question very succintly: "We believe in your prophet, why don't you believe in ours?" As the Chione theologians attempted to challenge Palamas by drawing on Old Testament practices, they reinforced the archbishop's perception that his interlocutors were Jews or Judaizers. Palamas retorted: "Why don't you Turks keep all the precepts of the Mosaic law---the Sabbath, the Passover, sacrifices by Priests, the altar and so forth?" Orkhan's erudites then went on: "Why do you have images in your churches though it is written 'Thou shall not make any likeness whatsoever...'?" At last, after a sublime apology by Palamas, the Turkish dignitaries rose and bade the Archbishop farewell with respect. It seemed at first, that this meeting of erudite theologians, even if it did not lead to a syncretic view, would at least have ended in an ecumenical tone. Then, at the last minute, one of the departing *Chiones* lagged behind and struck the archbishop in the eye. Reprimanded by the others, the assailant was immediately taken to the Emir.

As to the etymology of *Chiones*, Arnakis (3, 5) thought that Palamas in his pastoral epistle formed the word from *Al-Akhiyan*. The *akhis* were guild members, merchants and craftsmen. Through their affiliation with the *Mawlawis* (Dancing Dervishes), they obviously had mystical and theological interests. Witter also suggests a connection with the Persian and Turkish *Khoja* (master, teacher, clergyman). Perhaps they were Christian or semipagan mountain folk who, finally came down to join the Ottomans in Bythinia, where they converted to Islam.

Byzantine Jewish history connects competence in occult sciences to sacerdotal functions which are in the realm of the *Kohen*, a word which may share a common root with *Chiones*. The origin of his alchemic quest was the discovery of the work of a Jew, maybe a native of Byzantium, who was "priest, levite and astrologer." The *Chiones* of Bursa could have been the official astrologers (arabic *Kahin*) at the court of Orkhan. Fascination with Judaism leads Balivet to draw a line of continuity between Melchidekians, Athingonians and Chiones (6).

(see Chapter 1 refs 4-6)

APPENDIX 2

Who Were The Iberian Sephardim?

If one would believe an antique legend (4) popular at the court of King Alphonso (Eleventh Century), the Sephardim were the elite of Palestine, from the seed of King David, a sacerdotal caste, members of the tribe of Juda, who in the sharing of the spoils after the conquest of Jerusalem (587 B.C.) by the Babylonians, had been the lot of Hispanos, on the staff of Nabuchodozor II the Great. They had been carried as captives to Spain, in the sixth century before the Christian era, spreading to Provence under the Romans. After the destruction of the second Temple (C.E. 78) a new contingent of refugees had come to swell the Jewish colonies. When the Council of Elvira was held (4th Century CE), the Jewish population of the Iberian peninsula was considerable. Under the Visigoths the Sephardi Jews, most intrepid and vigilant guardians of the Northern marshes, were masters of the martial arts and engaged in harmonious cohabitation with the Christians. Christian cultivators would bring their wines to be blessed by rabbis and the accession to titles of nobillity was not barred to the Jews.

Under the Andalusian Arabs the scepter of the Jewish academies of Soura and Poumbedita in Mesopotamia was carried to the banks of the Guadalquivir (C.E. 948) by Rebi Moche and Rebi Hanoch Yaen. Till the dawn of the Fifteenth Century Jewish culture in Moorish Spain embraced religious sciences, astronomy, medicine, philosophy, grammar and mathematics. The *Mekor Haim* (the Spring of Life) of Solomon ibn Gabirol (C.E. 1021-1078), poet and philosopher, introduced into Europe the Greek way of thinking. Juda Halevy (C.E. 1086-1141) gained authority as a philosopher by his book *Khouzari* on fictional discussions with the King of the Khazars. Andalusian caliphs had in their entourage prominent Jewish statesmen such as Hasday Ibn Chaprut of Cordova. Samuel Ibn Nagrela, XIth Century's military commander, was a rabbinical scholar and renowned writer.

When the Caliphate of Andalusia fell to the North African Almohades, the Jews found refuge in Christian Aragon and Castilla, reaching the peak of prosperity under Alphonso X the Wise (1252-1284) who ruled from Toledo. This city called *Corona de España I Luz de todo el Mundo* (Crown of Spain and Light of all the World) became the most flourishing center of Judaism, with at its peak a Jewish population of seventy thousand (4). The Jewish quarters of Cordoba and Toledo retain even today their unmistakable Hebrew flavor with the narrow streets that surround their ancient synagogues.

When during the 12th to 14th centuries the kings conquered a city, they used to grant the Jews a fortress (or part of one), vineyards, fields and everything necessary to settle the place. Maritime and geographical enterprises in the Christian kingdoms were under the guidance of Jewish astronomers and mathematicians. Jews also exerted a quasi-monopoly in the fields of medicine and philosophy. They had become the charterers of ideas in medieval Spain. Most of the members of the Spanish cultural elite were trilingual with fluency in Spanish, Arabic and Hebrew, and they used Latin to introduce in Europe the gnostic and didactic literature in favor among the Arabs. In Toledo, under Alphonso the Wise, a School of

Translation was set up. The Sephardim had become an important bridge between cultures, whether medieval Arab, Greek, Latin, Egyptian or Syrian.

The Castillan had become the main language of the Sephardim, as the popular masses were no longer knowledgeable in Hebrew. Physicians and even rabbis used Castillan in their writings. Multimillionaire Jewish magnates like Abraham Senor, financier of the Catholic Kings had his own armory, and walked with a sword at his side, like members of the Spanish nobility. In 1086, 40,000 Jews followed the standards of Alphonse VI at the battle of Zaleca. In 1100 at the battle of Ucles between Moors and Spaniards, they almost composed the whole left wing of the Castillian army (5).

In the Fourteenth Century the situation began to deteriorate (6) with massacres and plundering in Navarre (C.E. 1329) and Castille also engulfed in the torment (1388). The flames of hatred were fanned under the impulsion of the Church, the monks and a jealous "bourgeoisie". The populace joined in, hoping to profit from the wealth of the tormented Jews. In the year 1391 a fanatical priest, Fernand Martinez, was preaching the destruction of Israel. On January 6, 1391 it was the assault on the Jewish quarter of Sevilla. Identical scenes were soon to take place in the *Juderias* of Cordoba, Toledo and Mallorca. In 1412 the Dominican Vincent Ferrer preached the Holy War and the Gospel of Hatred against the Jews. Rabinical scholars were dragged to disputations in the presence of the Court, Church dignitaries and high functionaries, tragic comedies ending with the conversion of the Jewish scholars carrying with them thousands of their faithful.

The odious ordinance of Valladolid (C.E. 1412) confined the Jews to the ghettos. They were prohibited to cut their hair and shave their beards and had to wear the despised insignia of their cult. The number of synagogues was restricted to one per city. The reading of the Talmud was prohibited, and Jews were then expected to attend sermons destined to bring them into the fold of Christianity. Despite all these tribulations, in Southern France and in Balear Islands the Jews were the foremost geographers and cosmographers, the only cartographers and nautical instrument manufacturers in all of Spain. Isaac Nafrier had built an "Astrolab" for the king of Aragon. Abraham Jaffuda Cresques constructed a "mapemunda" for Charles VI, King of France. Jaime the Jew was put in charge of training the Portuguese captains for long-range navigation. Abraham Zacuto, professor of mathematics and astronomy at the University of Salamanca, assembled the astronomical tables which made possible Christopher Columbus' travels. According to Nehama, Columbus' second expedition was paid for by money confiscated from the Jews. The first man to have touched land in the New World was the Jew Luis de Torres.

The existence of the Marranos (Jews converted to Christianty), in the beginning gave to the Jews an apparent increase of infiltrating power. Marrano professors and students abounded at the University of Salamanca; Marranos had also penetrated the hierarchy of the church and magistrature.

The role of the Jews in medicine was so crucial, that there was a strong popular uproar each time an attempt was made to stop the physicians of Jewish descent from applying their art. Medical treatises included the *Pandectes* of medicine, a

Seventh Century collection in Syriac of excerpts from Galenus, translated into Arabic by a Jew from Bassorah (C.E. 685).

In 1474 Ferdinand and Isabella sollicited from Pope Sixtus IV, a Borgia, the authorization to create a Court of Inquisition. The bull signed by the Borgia Pope was ready in 1478. None was immune, if guilty of heresy, from prosecution by the Court of the Holy Office, even the Grand Inquisitor himself. The thirty seven signs characterizing the "crime" of Judaism were proclaimed in all public places and churches. The auto-da-fes consumed 4,000 "heretics" in Sevilla, 2,000 within the archdiocese of Cadix. Those donating wood for the **quemadero** (burning pyre) were granted an **indulgence** (remission of the temporal and especially purgatorial punishment).

From 1482 to 1490 the Inquisition was run by the fiery and sinister Torquemada. Himself, he perpetually lived in terror of being murdered. Two hundred and fifty guards, fifty of them mounted, maintained an uninterrupted watch on his security.

For Ferdinand, any means were good to fill the royal treasury. Queen Isabella was fanatical, passionate and tormented by the idea that the faith of her subjects could be tainted by the "leprosy of the unbelievers". The Edict of Expulsion signed at the Alhambra of Granada on March 31, 1492, came like a thunderbolt (7).

(see Chapter 5 refs 4-7)

APPENDIX 3

Don Isaac Abravanel

The chief spokesmen of the Jews was Don Isaac Abravanel (The Moses of the Sephardi Exodus). Abravanel offered the Crown the maximum sum of gold the Jews could muster, possibly 300,000 ducats. Ferdinand indicated that the expulsion was also a decision of the Queen of Castilla. Abravanel who was the financial agent of the Queen, confronted her like a scion of the House of David and the representative of an unconquered and unconquerable people. He pointed out to Isabella that the Jews had outlived all who had attempted to destroy them, and that those who tried to do so only invited upon themselves divine punishment and disaster. Isabella who had a mystical vein in her invoked the very opposite. "The Lord", she said, "hath put this thing into the heart of the king." Abravanel knew that the verdict against the Jews was sealed.

As a friendly gesture from the Spanish Crown, Abravanel obtained a special permit for himself and his son-in-law to take out two thousand ducats each in gold and other valuables. The only Italian realm which offered hope was the kingdom of Naples. Ferrante, the king of Naples and his son Alfonso, were absolutist rulers, free to accept the Jews. The Ottoman realm, however, was a much preferable long-term option.

Don Isaac and his family, arrived in Naples a month later. Ferrante was friendly, and he offered Abravanel a position in his service. Abravanel called the King and his son "princes of mercy and righteousness". Actually these princes were "ruthless and unscrupulous in their dealings with their opponents; but they were also capable of paying generously for loyal services.

On January 26, 1494, King Ferrante died. In August of that year Charles VIII of France invaded Italy. The new king Alfonso, seized with panic, resolved to abdicate the throne and retire to Sicily. According to Guicciardini, "he communicated his intention only to his mother-in-law, keeping it even from his brother and his son." Nevertheless, he also revealed his secret to Don Isaac. On January 21, 1495, Abravanel accompanying King Alfonso left Naples for Mazzara, a coastal town of Northern Sicily, and a gift to Alfonso from Ferdinand of Spain. One month later, on February 22, Charles VIII entered Naples, with reports of a pogrom loosened against the Jews. Among the homes sacked was that of Abravanel. Much of his precious library as well as the manuscript of *Eternal Justice* were lost. Abravanel's son Judah, settled in Genoa as a physician. His youngest son was studying in Salonica under Turkish rule.

In the middle of June 1495, Abravanel left for the island of Corfu which was under Venetian rule. Abravanel waited for the arrival of his family so that together they might finally proceed to Salonica. The prosperous Jewish community of Corfu could absorb a considerable number of exiles from Spain.

Among the Jewish notables met by Abravanel in Corfu, was David ibn Yahya, the Lisbon preacher and the nephew of the Yahyas, Alfonso V's courtiers, who was now on his way to Turkey. He was dismayed to note the great change the misfortunes of exile had wrought in many an admired personality, "as if they had departed and then intellectual giants were turned into broken pots of clay." In Corfu, Abravanel did not rush to emigrate to Turkish-controlled territory. He did not know, how he would culturally fare in a Moslem-ruled country. He felt fully European. A window of opportunity opened when the town of Monopoli, a seaport on the Adriatic, nominally under the king of Naples, was seized from the French on June 29, by the Venetian navy under Antonio Grimany. In Monopoli, a Venetian possession outside the territory of the Republic proper, Abravanel could count on freedom from the disabilities imposed on Jews.

The completion of Abravanel's commentary on the Deuteronomy is dated February 6, 1496, from Monopoli. He was then 58 years of age, attacked by the malaise that grips strangers in a foreign land. Nonetheless he embarked on a new philosophical work called *Days of the World*. Abravanel was asking himself "How long could the Jews continue to take such punishment?" Then, at the request of his son Samuel, Abravanel began writing the *Inheritance of the Father*, a commentary on *Abot* (Ethics of the Fathers). The only real value the Jews still possessed, the only asset which gave meaning to their suffering, was the moral heritage which they had guarded through the ages. Don Isaac utters the oath: "If you forget the law of God, let my right hand forget its cunning."

Abravanel became engaged in Messianic speculations. He is the author of a Messianic trilogy: *Wells of Salvation, The Salvation of the Anointed* and *The Announcer*. In the Wells (C.E. 1496) Abravanel suggested 1503 as the most likely date of redemption, based on the puzzling indication in Daniel (8) that redemption would come after "a time (*i.e.* period of First Commonwealth, 410 years) and times (*i.e.* a duplication of this number) and half a time (*i.e.* half of 410). At the end of the Middle Ages, the line of demarcation in the human mind between the possible and the miraculous was very thin. Abravanel predicted a gigantic war between Islam and Christendom. In 1486, Turkey and Mamlukide Egypt planned to attack Sicily. In 1406 the Turks resumed their attacks on Hungary, Moldavia and Poland. In 1497, they captured Lepanto, the last important Venetian port in the Gulf of Corinth. Yet Abravanel had no high regard for the military of the Turks. Tremendously impressed by the Spanish victory over the Moslems in Granada, he conceived Christian Rome as made of "Iron" and the Moslem power as made of "Clay". He believed that in the Era of Redemption, Christendom would be defeated not on its own ground, but in East, in Palestine, far from its source of power.

"Quo vadis, Israel? was the question of the time. And Abravanel answered: 'toward the era of great blessedness, toward the kingdom of Heaven" (9).

(see Chapter 5 refs 7-9)

APPENDIX 4

The Reubeni Episode

David Reubeni, the "Annunciator of the Messiah to come, **i.e.** the Son of Joseph" seemingly emerged from the depths of Arabia; his success in Lisbon gained him a new convert, the young Portuguese Marrano Diego Pierez, a splendid scholar occupying high functions at the court of Portugal under King John III (5). Diego Pierez declared himself for Reubeni, underwent circumcision and adopted the Hebrew name of Solomen Molho. Molho went about to announce to the Jewish world the advent of the Messiah. In 1526, his peregrinations brought him to Salonica where he became the pupil of Joseph Taitacek.

From Pope to Emperor, Reubeni created a furor in the world. By the greatest number of historians, Biberfeld, Graetz and Dubnow, he was declared to be an Oriental Jew. *The book of Reubeni's Travels* exists in the manuscript form. It was written in ungrammatical Hebrew by Reubeni or a contemporary. Fragments of the diary were plubished by Biberfeld. In the archives of the Doge's palace in Venice, in the *Diarii Sanuto alla Marciana* a notice dated November 1530, under the heading *David Judaeus* states:

"David claimed to be a son of King Solomon of Tabor and a brother of King Joseph. He traveled through the whole of Europe to persuade the princes to liberate the Jews and he also visited the Emperor Charles Vth."

By Reubeni's words his brother was the king of the Tribe of Ruben. His diary describes his journey from the time he left his brother Joseph and the Kingdom of Habor (Tabor, **Mons Thabor**, in the desert of Arabia, see the epistle of Pope Clement VII). He moved through a mountainous road to the Red Sea shore, then Nubia, south Ethiopia, and the kingdom of Sheba (the dwelling place of King Amra, king of the province **Amhara**). Reubeni mentions Lamoule as the metropolis of the Kingdom of Sheba-Shoa, near the Nile. Reubeni traveled throughout Ethiopia the land of the Gallas, and the edge of the Sudan on the border of Ethiopia. Reubeni visited Prince 'Abd-al-Wahab's palace in Dongola on the way to Egypt, proceeding to Egypt through Alhabor (Kaibar on the right bank of the Nile). According to Aescoli, Reubeni's journey from Habor to Egypt seems the roundabout way of a wanderer. A man whose purpose is to go to Europe via Egypt and Palestine, and who travels on a diplomatic mission, such as being sent by King Joseph of Habor to announce the good tidings, would undoubtedly have gone from Gidda to Massawa and sailed to Egypt. It is strange that Reubeni, although his journey led him through Semien, was completely unaware of the existence of the Ethiopian Jews or Falashas. Reubeni was unaware that the King of Ethiopia and its inhabitants were Christians, that his so-called arrival in Ethiopia coincided with a period of warfare between the Christian Ethiopians and the Mohammedan Gallas under Ahmed Gran. Reubeni recounts sums paid to him in Italian florins, while numismatists are unanimous to agree the florin never gained currency in Arabia, Ethiopia and Sudan.

In the letter written by Raphael Tarboto of Jerusalem to Rabbi Abraham Tarbato of Perona we read"...there came to us a youth from the Ten Tribes. His father, he says is from the tribe of Reuben, while his mother is from the tribe of Dan. He brought us good tidings and proclaimed great and wonderful things about the redemption...this week a dispatch arrived from Damascus stating that one of the messengers sent by the King of Reuben had arrived thither to Saloniki, bearing a letter signed by the King and his twelve councilors, urging the Jews to be of good spirit."

Reubeni surfaced in Venice in 1524 asserting that he had been sent by his brother, the King of the tribe of Reuben, to obtain help of the Christian powers. His brother, King Joseph, disposed of three hundred thousand men--six hundred thousand according to other allegations. He claimed also that King Joseph needs guns and canons to operate the junction of the Ten Tribes of Israel and move towards the septentrion to liberate the Holy Land, which is languishing under Moslem domination. Going to Rome he had come to sollicit the support of the Pope Clement VII, who received him with great favor. Reubeni succeeded in making a great impression on the Pope. Perhaps Reubeni's intentions were really of a nationalistic character aimed at the alleviation of the terrible sufferings of his people, as Max Brod depicts in an interesting novel. Reubeni may have genuinely believed that he had found the panacea to stop the Inquisition in the form of romanticized messianism involving the retrieval of the Ten Lost Tribes, a topic bound to fascinate not only Jews, but Christian princes, kings and even the Pope. In a letter written from Venice we read: "Rumors about the coming of the Jews and about the river Sabbation are current in Venice to such an extent that many Gentiles give credence to them." From Rome embarked on a ship flying the pavilion of the Jewish nation, Reubeni went to Portugal where John III (1521-1557), at first complacently listened to him. Reubeni's success brought Lisbon to a frenzy. Aescoly indicates (6) that one cannot be too sure of whether Pope Clement VII deep inside himself really believed in Reubeni, or whether he might have wanted to use him as a political scapegoat in his relations with the Emperor Carlos Quintus and the King of Portugal.

Reubeni, in his lifetime, while initially successful in gaining some recognition, impressed neither the Eastern nor the Western Jews, who looked upon him as an impostor or as one mentally deranged. Only the ever-credulous Solomon Molho, *alias* Diego Pierez, and the Marranos, with their great hope for redemption, were the only ones to cling to him.

As to Reubeni's prophet, Solomon Molho, he remained for some time in Salonica, surrounded, by these who admired for his irresistible manners, his romantic past, and his deep and varied knowledge. He was a charmer. In Salonica, he divided his time between studies beside to his friend and tutor Joseph Taitacek and messianic predictions at the synagogue. A bundle of his collected speeches was published in 1528 by his disciples under the dithyrambic title of *Sefer Amefoer* (the Splendid Book).

The passage of Solomon Molho through Salonica brought to a climax the Messianic enthusiasm in this city. The stress of the times had become overbearing unless one could escape into the marvelous and the miraculous. With Molho they were getting a full dosage of both. Marranos were also having recourse to *gematria*, a method to penetrate the future based on the interpretation of words according to the numerical value of their letters. In Salonica the Taitacek team was most instrumental in expressing the Kabbala's supremacy.

Molho left with great expectations, to resume his life and adventures in Palestine, but he met there a vigorous opponent. The Grand Rabbi of Jerusalem Levi ben Habip had initiated a merciless war against the deleterious influences of mysticism as propounded by the cabbalist Joseph Berab and the visionary Solomon Molho. Ben Habip obliged Molho to leave Palestine. The year 1525 was to turn into a fateful one for Molho and his inspiration Reubeni. Both attended an important diet in Ratisbone in the hope of enlisting the support of Charles V but were arrested. Molho's adversary Jacob ben Mantin, the famous physician and translator in Italy, through his intrigues succeeded in having Molho condemned by the Inquisition. Molho underwent martyrdom on the pyre in Mantua. As to Reubeni he was taken to Spain and imprisoned in Badajoz. He first languished for a time in the Spanish jails, and he ultimately perished at an auto-da-fe.

Neubauer remarks that the Hebrew style of Reubeni's diary is that of a German Jew. Aescoly writes "however, it is least plausible to accept that Reubeni's native country was Egypt, for it is not likely that he would have tried to accomplish his affairs where he could have easily been proven to be an impostor. If we regard Arabic as his native tongue, it is more proper to consider him a Yemenite Jew, as fits the descriprtion left by Abraham Farissol: small posture, shriveled face, dark complexioned, and his pronunciation of Hebrew jarring to the ears of the European Jews. Nonetless the language of Reubeni's memoirs contains the idiosyncrasies of an European Jew, possibly those of an Ashkenazic Jew!"

As to Molho's host in Salonica, Joseph Taitacek, at his death his wife was to reveal that during 40 years he had slept in a wooden chest, refusing to lay in his bed more than one night out of seven. His most resolute and systematic adversary was David ha-Cohen, the leader of the Greek ritual. It is unfortunate that a scholar of Taitacek's intellect had to fall under the spell of the mystico-messianic duo of Reubeni and Molho. Nehama writes (6) "that under the influence of the negro David Reubeni and his prophet Salomon Molho, the speculations of the mystique initially confined to the neo-platonician philosophy, moved to ascetism and salvational utopia, announcing the subterranean work which will lead in the following century to the collective psychosis of sabbatianism." Israel never ceases to be oscillating betwee the reality and the dream, between the narrow utilitarianism and the chimera.

(see Chapter 6 refs 5, 6)

APPENDIX 5

The Luminaries Of Safed

Among the Safed luminaries Solomon Alkabez (2, 3) is a prominent figure. A disciple of Joseph Taitacek, Rabbi of Salonica, he later became a brother-in-law of the Cabbalist Moses Cordovero. Alkabez was a scholar and a poet. A story says that he offered his book **Manoth ha-Levim** (Gifts of a Levite, a homilitical commentary about Esther), as present to his fiancée, on the occasion of a **Pourim** festival. Alkabez's fame mainly rests upon his poem of poems, known as **Lekah Dodi** (Come my friend), used to receive Queen Sabbath, as part of Sabbath eve's liturgy all over the world. It has been translated by Herder and by Heine into German. The poem soon became the Song of a People, sort of a national anthem:

Come, my friend

Come my friend, to meet the bride,

Let us welcome the presence of Sabbath.

"Observe" and "Remember" the Sabbath day,

The only God caused us to hear in a single utterance;

The Lord is One, and his name is One,

In His reknown and His glory and His praise

Come my friend...

Another Safed luminary Ra. Jacob Berab (4), had a Megalo Idea: the Restoration of Rabbinical Ordination (*Semichah*) and the Restoration of the Sanhedrin. He was the most prominent of Caro's Associates (4). He was recognized head of the Jewish community in Safed, around 1535. Caro himself called him "our great master". Ordination, is "the mere ceremonious laying on of hands in connection with a candidate for Rabbinical office with some solemn speech attendant thereon". Berab and his friends decided to aim at the re-establishment of the Sanhedrin, a body which could be established only in Palestine, and which would wield supreme authority over the whole of Israel, thus forming a new Jewish spiritual center. During the days of the Patriarch Hillel II (5) the seats of Jewish learning in Tiberias, Sephhoria and Lod, the last strongholds of Judaism in the Land of Israel, were destroyed and the long uninterrupted chain of Ordination beginning with Moses had come to an end. The grand design of restoring Ordination, gave rise to a feud between Safed and Jerusalem. Together with Jacob Berab, twenty-five scholars of Safed signed the epistle sent to the sages of Jerusalem, that contained the resolution to reintroduce the Ordination. Four elders of Safed, including Caro, were ordained by Berab. Through his Mentor-Angel, Caro received the heavenly promise that he would be the instrument through which Ordination should be restored. The excitement faded away with Berab's death (1540).

Everybody in Safed knew that R. Joseph Caro (1488-1575) was *Doctor Synagogae*, the Lawyer, the Codifier of Judaism and also a *Doctor Mysticus*, a Kabbalist (6, 7), the Mystagogue of the Maggid. Caro wrote a Code that would be acceptable as the central authority in Jewish life (i.e. *Beth Yosef*, later presented in concise form in the digest *Shulkhan' Aruk* (8, 9). He also experienced an intense mystical yearning when he fell under the spell of the messianic dreamer Shelomo Molho (5).

R. Joseph b. Ephraim b. Joseph, called Caro, was born in Spain or Portugal; his parents moved to Nicopolis in the Balkans under Turkish rule. In Nicopolis (9) two events profoundly and decisively affected Caro's life; the death in martyrdom of Solomon Molho and his meeting with Solomon Alkabez. The encounter between Caro and Molho took place in Adrianople, and induced Caro to move to the Holy Land, where he settled *ca.* 1505.

The standard code for Jews up to time of the *Shulhan 'Aruk* was the *Tur*, produced by R. Jacob Asher. In Caro's time "The Torah had become like many Torahs." Caro began to write *Beth Joseph* in Adrianople (9), thus striving to have "one Torah and one law". Joseph Caro's magnum opus traced each *halakah* (rabbinical code) to its source in the Bible, Mishnah, Talmud, *halakic Midrashim*, or rabbinical *Responsa* literature of the *Gaonim*.

Graetz thought that Caro in his turn fell into the same kabbalistic enthusiasm as Molho. In his Kabbalistic mystical book *Maggid Mesherim*, Caro invoked his dream-prompter *Maggid* (*i.e.* Mentor Angel) who disclosed to him the most *geshmactlose* (tasteless) mystical interpretations and revealed the future." This *Maggid*, *drollig* (amusingly) enough, personified *Mishnah* who descended on Caro generally at night and whispered revelations. For more than thirty years the activity of Caro's mind was divided between dry rabbinical learning and the fantastic ideas of the Kabbalah.

Caro's *Beth Yosef* was the book for the scholar, and *Shulkhan 'Arukh* (The Prepared Table) a simplified version of codified Judaism for the layman. Graetz concludes about *Shulkhan 'Arukh* that "religious promptings, Kabbalistic enthusiasm, and personal ambition equally contributed to the making of this book". As it becomes more obvious in the *Maggid Mesherim*, narcissism and a search for power may have been among the driving motives which brought Caro to the ambition of being the master Codifier of Judaism. However the Judaism reflected in the *Shulkhan 'Aruh* was different from that revealed on Sinai and that taught by Maimonides (10). Nevertheless the "Prepared Table" of Joseph Caro became the authoritative code (11).

A contemporary was R. Moses Isserless born in Cracow about 1620 (12), a pupil of the Lublin scholar R. Shalom Shakna. He was a great admirer of Caro. Yet, he takes Caro to task for omitting the opinions, customs and decisions of the German and Polish authorities. Isserles' book *Darke Moshe* (the ways of Moses) is a commentary on *Tur* (Jewish Code antecedent to Caro), also including Caro's *Beth Yosef*. Iserless contented himself by preparing a *Mappah* (Table Cloth) for Caro's "Prepared Table". The "Table Cloth" was a striking success, it made *Shulkhan 'Aruh* acceptable for the Ashkenazim, thus providing a unified code of Jewish law for the two great branches of Judaism.

More than seventy years after Caro's death, *ca.* 1616, a certain Isaac Dingo of Jerusalem (13) brought to a Lublin printer by the name of Kalonymos (Kalman) Yaffe, a precious manuscript. Yaffe published the book which the title page describes as the "the book *Maggid Mesherim*", in which there are explanations of the luminous, exalted and great mysteries that were revealed to the (perfect) man and prince in the Law, Rabbi Joseph Caro. In his introduction Dingo somewhat cryptically writes that Holy scriptures were revealed by the holy *Maggid* to the aforementioned holy and scholarly rabbi, who was being fed from the table of the King of Kings, and entering into the innermost sanctuary of the King of the universe. The genuineness of the diary has, however, been challenged over the centuries (14).

A number of scholars regret that the serious and respected jurist Caro should have felt it necessary to move into the field of Kabbalism (15). The daylight personality of Caro was that of a scholar and canonist. His nocturnal personality was kabbalistic, unleashed from the depths of the unconscious and overpowering.

Caro probably was not part of the Safed mystics. The story (16, 17) is that Caro fell asleep whenever Safed greatest mystic Luria began to discourse on the mysteries, a sign that his soul was not prepared to receive them. Caro's widow had told of a banquet at Luria's house in celebration of the engagement of their son to Luria's daughter. On returning home Caro went into raptures over Luria's absolute eminence, had said: "Oh my dear wife, Even an angel hardly possesses the knowledge he has. There is no doubt that his soul is of the early prophets, for even a *Tanna* (Jewish Sage) could not teach as he does..."

We are told of Caro that every time he recited the *Mishnah*, the Maggid appeared to him and people could hear the voice saying: "Peace upon thee, Rabi Joseph Caro. I am the *Maggid* which thou hast studied. I came forth to teach thee understanding. I the *Mishnah* have seen thy place that is prepared for thee in Paradise and now I have come to reveal the following Kabbalistic mystery. And all the revelations of the *Maggid*, (Joseph Caro) collected in a book entitled The book of *Maggid*...but ARI (Luria) refused to teach Caro, saying that Caro's soul was unfit to receive higher wisdom than that of Cordovero's system.

According to Werblowsky (15) who carries out a psychoanalysis of Caro's *Maggid*, whatever else, the *Maggid* may be, he certainly also represents Caro's conscience or, in the current psychoanalytical jargon, his super-ego. Freud described the redirection of part of our libido to the 'self' (narcissistic libido)...The speeches of the *Maggid*, with their untiring reprimands as well as their excessive confirmations of his unparalled greatness are a most instructive example of this redirection or displacement of narcissism.

It was discovered that there existed in Turkey gradually crystallizing or, fully organized even devout brotherhoods on the pattern of Safed, sharing common ascetic practices (cf. Alkabez's *Shabu'ot Epistle*, 18, 19). The *Shabu'oth* vigil in Caro's house was accomplished in keen awareness by the participants that they were in full spiritual communion with their brothers in Salonica, engaged in the same liturgical and mystical devotion.

R. Moses Cordovero (1522-1570) (18, 19), known by his abbrevated name Remak, was a disciple of Caro. As a mystic, it is said that at the age of twenty "the Voice warned him to heal the altar of the Lord which is broken down." At the age of twenty-seven he is found in the company of the *Choverim* (Associates). This was a society consisting of mystically-inclined students of Safed, apparently presided over by Solomon Halevi Alkabez. The members of the society occasionally used to hold staff meetings near by the graves of the ancient Rabbis supposed to be buried in the neighborhood of Safed. A manuscript listing moral precepts drawn by Cordovero may have constituted a sort of handbook for all the Associates.

Key precepts were:

--not to divert thoughts from the words of the Torah and things holy, so that their hearts become the abode of the *Shekhinah;*

--not to be betrayed by anger, as anger delivers man into the power of sin:

--not to speak evil of any creature, including animals;

--never to curse any being, but to accustom oneself to bless even in moments of anger;

--never to take an oath, even on truth;

--to be careful not to be included among the four classes excluded from the Divine Presence; *i.e.* the hypocrites, the liars. the scoffers and the tale-bearers;

--not to indulge in banquets except on religious occasions;

--to behave in a kindly spirit toward their fellow-men, even though they may be transgressors;

--to meet with one of the Associates for one or two hours every day to discuss matters spiritual;

--to use the sacred languages when speaking with Associates, and to let this always be the language of conversation on Sabbath with other scholars as well.

Cordovero's *magnum opus* is the *Pardes Rimonim* (the Orchard of Pomegranates), the clearest and most rational exposé of the Kabbala in existence.

To the question as to God's knowledge and man's knowledge, Cordovero answered as follows:

"God's knowledge is different from that of His creatures, since in the case of the latter, knowledge and the thing are distinct, thus leading to subjects that are again quite separate from Him. This is described by the three expressions:--the cogitation, the cogitator, and the subject of cogitation. Now the Creator is Himself Knowledge, the Knower, and the object known. His knowledge does not consist in the fact that He directs his thoughts to things outside Him, since in comprehending and knowing Himself He comprehends and knows every thing that exists. There is nothing which is not united to Him, and which He does not find in His own substance. He is the archetype of all existing things, and all things are in Him in their purest and most pefect form."

By holding such views Cordovero is not very far from Spinoza's Pantheism, and seems to have been a Spinoza before his time. When, in a letter to his friend Oldenberg, Spinoza wrote that he owes his theory to an old Jewish philosopher, some scholars think that he meant it was Cordovero.

There were also in the same period mystical excesses and exuberances (19). R. Abraham Halevi Beruchim, would rise in the middle of the night and walk through the Jewish quarter, addressing in tears "His brethren of the House of Israel!", asking isn't it known to them that their Strength, its very Divine Presence, is in exile because of their sins; that Israel is subjected to the most bitter persecutions, saintly men and women being martyred by sword and fire...? And yet the brethren, allow themselves to enjoy their sleep on their beds in quiet and rest!.

R. Abraham Halevi's assistants in his missionary work possibly were members of the *Succath Shalom* (Tent of Israel) about which R. Eliezer Askari wrote his devotional treatise, *Sepher Charedim*. Citing *Ezra* 18:3 "those that tremble at the commandments of our God".

The thought absorbing the "Tremblers" was the delay of the advent of the Messiah, and the sins responsible for his delay. A systematic program was therefore carried out, with weekly sessions of auto-critique in which each of them would give a full and detailed account of his actions during the preceding days.

In this attempt to create a "sin-free" Jewish world, another group that excelled was the Society of Penitents. Its members refrained from food and drink during the day (*i.e.* a perpetual *Rhamadhan*), performed their afternoon devotions in tears, and put on sackclothes and ashes.

There were also occasional outbursts of demonology. Thus, the Jewish Faust of Safed, Joseph de la Reina, in his passion for salvation, did not hesitate to employ exorcisms and conjurations of a very daring nature. It is said that he succeeded in bringing the Evil One into his power, whose destruction is a preliminary condition to the advent of the Messiah, but in an unfortunate moment, he fell victim to the same pitfall which had made King Saul feel pity for the vainquised King Agag. Reina was persuaded to show compassion for the fallen angel, allowing him to smell of the frankincense. The Evil One then regained his former strength, and achieved full mastery over his captor, who after realizing his fall, abandoned himself to the most revolting immoralities, and ended his life by suicide.

Safed held many joys for the Torah scholars. The Safed of the Sixteenth Century must have been a veritable Paradise on earth to any man with a tendency toward intellectual pursuit. If more rationally inclined he could attend lectures by the giants of the time such as Caro, Trani, Sagis. If mystically inclined he would attach himself to Alkabetz or Cordovero. A taste of homiletics would carry him to to the Biblical expositions of Alsheich. He also might have stopped to listen to R. Samuel of Useda lecture on the Chapters of the Fathers (*Pirke Aboth*). A visit to the ancient R. David ben Zimra, would not be out of question, and an occasional walk with Vidal might have held its own attraction, as the conversation would wind from mysticism into alchemy, astronomy or astrology. The mystical bard, R. Israel ben Moses Najara (19) author of the hymn book, **Zemiroth israel**, might have provided the entertainment. The hymns were somewhat "vividly erotic" in metaphors, but it is that Najara counted angels among his audience.

Najara himself picked up some Turkish and Arabic melodies and subsequently composed poems to the music. He also wrote love poems using a synthesis of Turkish, Spanish, and Greek metric forms. As it goes in one of his famous poems:
Loved of my soul

Loved of my soul! Father of Grace!

Lead on Thy servant to Thy favoring sight; He, fleetly as the hart (the male of the red deer); shall spend his pace...

Central to the mystical literature is the Ari (The Lion) (20, 21) Rabbi Isaac ben Solomon Ashkenazi Luria (1534-1572), the *Eagle of Safed*. His birth in Jerusalem took place under miraculous conditions. It was heralded to his father by Elijah: "...The Holy One, blessed be he, sent me to bring thee the good message that thy wife will bear thee a son. Thou shall name him Isaac; he will deliver Israel from the power of the Husks (powers of evil) and through him shall be revealed the teaching of the Cabbala to the world." At the tender age of eight, none of the Jerusalem Scholars could compete with him in Talmudical discussions" (21).

After his father prematurely died. Luria and his mother sought refuge next to his maternal uncle, Mordecai Frencis, a wealthy tax-farmer in Cairo. The tradition goes that Luria was introduced to the Cabbala by a Marrano who read his prayers at the synagogue from a manuscript. Luria recognized by a single glance that the manuscript embodied great mysteries. The book proved to be **Sepher ha-Zohar** (the Book of Splendor). Through strict solitude, meditation and prayer, Luria managed mastering the mysteries of the Cabbala. He reached in the end communion with the prophet Elijah, and "became worthy of the gift of the Holy Spirit'" He undertok his exodus (21), in obedience to a distinct command from Heaven, which ordered him to leave the polluted land (Egypt) and go up to Safed in Upper Galilee.

The whole ministry of Luria in Safed lasted six years (21), from the year 1570 on, when he succeded Cordovero as the head of the mystical school. Luria was regarded as one of those superhuman beings who, by a special act of Providence, are permitted to visit mortals for the special purpose of their salvation. Every night Luria's soul, released from all earthly ties, would ascend to heaven in the company of the "ministering angels" who watched over him until he reached the abode of the Celestials. There he would have the choice of attending any of the supra-mundane academies, in which the souls of the departed saints and great sages continue the occupations which formed their moments of bliss in the course of their earthly careers. In hagiology Luria's name appears as ARI (LION), the anagram of the Hebrew words "the Divine Rabbi Isaac". His disciples were called "the Lion-Welps".

Luria's priority care was for the young "Lions" (21), apparently in the need of gentle taming and discipline. He attempted to create for them an ideal setting by creating an "enclosure". This was a square-shaped block of buildings, also providing chambers for their wives and children. Isolation from the world, though living in the world, forms part of the program of every mystic. The "enclosure" was designed as a Utopia for the mystics.

Luria (21) was not very communicative in the revelation of "the mystery of the mysteries". He grudgingly gave the permission to take down notes in his lectures, and subsequently withdrew it. He was known in Safed as the "Holy Man" or the "Divine Cabbalist". His devoted Associates watched how he rose from his bed, how he washed his hands, how he cut his nails, how he read his prayers, how and when he fasted, how he said Grace after his meals, how he prepared for Sabbath, how many garments he wore in one day, what songs he intoned during the meal, how he cut his bread...Every action of the blessed Superman, surrounded by the Divine halo was worthy of Attention, as if a whole universe was in a Cabbalistic view made sensitive to all his motions. There is a whole literature of Attentions or Devotions, bearing upon Luria's intepretation of the contents of the ritual and mystical meaning which he divined in the performance of evey commandment.

Luria was a master of physiognomy (the reading of faces), and chiromancy (palmistry); he understood the conversation of the trees, the language of the birds and the speech of the angels. He could discern the souls of the wicked which as a punishment had taken abode through transmigration in woods and in stone quarries, in the beasts of the field, in insects and unclean birds. He was able to tell men their past and future, and to prescribe the rules of conduct on how to make amends for shortcomings in a previous existence.

Prayers were Luria's life. In prayer, by reason of his close communion with God, man becomes a receptacle of Divine Light and an outflow of Divine Mercy. Every word of the ritual, every letter in it, had, besides its literal meaning, its mysteries.

Luria was charitable, with the same disregard for possessions as in the tradition of Moslem Dervish mystics. He considered his Associates, as one body in the fullest sense of the world, each of the Associates being a member or a joint of the body. Luria's ideology was one of 'Love' in the richest meaning of the word. He recommanded the Associates to constantly pray one for the others, so that each may pray for Israel, in Israel and with Israel. In reading the Confession prescribed for *Yom Kippur*, one should atone even for sins he had not committed, because he felt himself to be a member of the great body of Israel. Further broadening the concept of One Organism, one could conceive the Organism as encompassing the whole of Humanity, includig non-Jews.

In a walk around Safed, Luria would at almost every step encounter persons harboring the souls of ancient historical figures. He believed that all souls were evolved from the "original soul" of Adam, derived from various parts of his body, and they suffered by his Fall. A certain neighbor of Luria was for him harboring the soul of the Biblical Korah, who rose against Moses and Aaron in the desert. Because of the Jeremiah-like vision he held, R.Abraham Halevi of Safed was identified in carrying in himself a spark of Jeremiah's soul. R. Moses Alscheich of Safed was pregnant with the soul of the Fourth Century Agadist R. Samuel ben Nachmani. Luria and his Associates themselves were the reincarnation of the heroes of the *Zohar*, headed by R. Simon ben Yochai and his son R. Eleazar.

Luria was in a sense a Freud-like personality. Freud used the analysis of dreams and visions to unravel the mysteries of the unconscious; Luria used a similar approach to unravel the transmigrated souls harbored by the persons he encountered. Luria saw in himself a spark of the soul of Moses. Freud in his controversial study of Moses and Monotheism, did not discover a spark of Moses in himself, he rather discovered in Moses a spark of the monotheistic Pharaoh Ikhnaton.

After his death in 1572 (20), Luria became the hero of many legends, which portray Ari as possessing infinite and wondrous knowledge.. The Lurianic Kabbalah became the predominant ideology of the Jewish world for almost two centuries. In bringing forth what holds together the whole of Israel. Ari acts as a precursor of Jung who was to tell us about "the collective unconscious".

To obtain Messianic fulfillment through Ari's theosophic teachings, the unknown must be made accessible to mending by the principle of *tikkun* (kabbalistic practice first spread in circles close to Luria, of reading on certain occasions Biblical, Mishnaic and Kabbalistic passages). The togetherness in lamenting and mourning, accelerates the advent of redemption, shutters both the historical exile of Israel and the greater cosmic exile expressed in the estrangement of the Divine itself. It was believed by the Safed mystics that the Jews' intense empathy with the *Shekhinah* (Divine Presence in the midst of its people, Divine Immanence), sharing Israel's suffering and exile, can serve to destroy the very force of exile itself. To further the process of redemption, the study of the Kabbalah is to be made accessible to a large number of Jews. The crux of Lurianic teaching is in the disclosure of that which is hidden, unknown, unknowable. The Sabbatianic Messianic movement, even in its heresy, shared the pietistic and ascetic mood of the Lurianic Kabbalah. The Lurianic mysticism gained a new vitality and expression in the Hassidic movement. Luria' doctrines have primarily come to us through his scribe, disciple, follower and spiritual heir, the mystically inebriated Hayyim Vital. Baron Von Rosenroth, author of the *Kabbala Denudata* (The Kabbalah Unveiled) calls Luria the Eagle of the Kabbalists. The thesaurus of Luria's doctrines, as collected by Vidal and printed in the *Kabbala Denudata* includes:

1. Book of Dissertations
2. A commentary on the Book of Concealment
3. The Book of The Revolutions of The Souls.

(see refs 2-21, Chapter 9)

APPENDIX 6

The Sufis and the Kabbala
The affinities between Jewish mystics and the Dervishes go far back to the origins of Sufism and that of the Kabbalah. As stated by Robert Graves (7) the sufis are an ancient spiritual freemasonry whose origins have never been traced or dated and the Sufis are at home in all religions. If they call Islam the "shell" of Sufism, this is because they believe Sufism to be the secret teaching within all religions. Yet according to Ali el-Hujwizi, an early authoritative Sufi writer, the Prophet Mohammed himself said: "he who hears the voice of the Sufi people and does not say **Aamin** (Amen) is recorded in God's presence as one of the heedless. It was in Sufi style that the Prophet ordered to respect all people of the Book. The natural Sufi may be as common in the West as in the East, and may come clothed as a general, a merchant, a lawyer, a school master, a housewife, anything. To be in the world, but not of it, free from ambition, greed, intellectual pride, blind obedience to custom, or awe of persons in higher ranks; that is the Sufi ideal.

Idries Shah refers to the Jewish Encyclopedia for some answers on the origins of Sufism (8). The spread of Sufism in the Eight Century was probably due to the revival of Jewish mysticism in Mahommedan countries of that period. Under the direct influence of the Sufi arose the Jewish sect called **Yughanites**. Yughan (9, 10), the founder of the sect called **Yughanites**, lived in Hamadan (Persia) and was a disciple of Abu Issa Al-Isfahani founder of the **Issawite** sect. Influenced by the doctrine of Moslem Sufism, he advocated a mystical or spiritual interpretation of the Torah. The sect he founded was short-lived, however.

Idries Shah (11) makes reference to a characteristic of Jewish scholarship that honesty and detachment are wedded to the search for truth. The Jewish Encyclopedia stresses the determining role of the Brethren of Sincerity on the production of the mighty Kabbalah system. The Kabbalah as the inner, secrete doctrine is generally thought to be anchored in the very essence of ancient Hebraic doctrine, with a most intriguing link between the Sufi stream and the Kabbalah (11). The poem **Salomon and Absal** in the famous work entitled the **Seven Thrones** of the Sufi poet Nuruddin Abdurrahman Jami of Herat (1450), is a mystical story of earthly and heavenly love, which looks like an adaptation of the **Sephirotic** Doctrine of the Kabbalah. A form of composition which occurs almost verbatim in the Kabbalah is found in **"The Life of Hai Ebn Yokdan"**, the philosophical romance of Abu Bakr Al-Tabali (1100 Guadix, Spain--1186 Morocco), a noted Arabian physician, poet, mathematician: "The Divine Essence is like the rays of the material sun, which expand over opaque bodies and appear to proceed from these, though they are only reflected from their surface".

(see Chapter 12, refs 7-11)

APPENDIX 7

The Kabbala as Viewed and Understood By a Privat-Docent Associate Director at the Faculty of Divinity of Ankara

In the Fifteenth Century Picus de la Mirandola purchased from a certain Jew certain strange codices in manuscript. The treasure of Picus was the *Zohar* (the Book of Splendor, XXVII). The authenticity of the *Zohar* manuscript has been questioned, as well as the authorship of the *Zohar* by Moses de Leon (Waite XXVII) in late 13th Century. The true *Zohar* may be impossible to determine respect to age and value. The text of **Sepher ha Zohar** was translated by the French bibliographer Gaffarel in 1651 (Waite XXVIII). The second component of the Kabbala, *Sepher Yetzirah* (the Book of Creation) written in the Ninth Century was translated in Latin by William Postel (Waite XXIX). *Sepher Yetzirah* is supposed to embody a tradition handed down from the time of Abraham. Tradition has ascribed its formal authorship to Rabbi Akiba (Second century Christian era, Waite 42). There is also a tradition that *Sepher Yetzirah* was written by Joseph bern Uzziel towards the end of the Fifth Century (Waite 45).

As to the *Zohar*, Solomon Munk did not consider that it was anterior to the Seventh Century, but rather that the Kabbalistic developments it represents took place in the Thirtheenth Century and had also been influenced by Solomon ibn Gebirol [1021-1070 (Waite 50-51). There is an account by Isaac de Acco of Valladolid, an acquaintance of Moses de Leon, which breaks off abruptly in the middle of a sentence describing some testimony he received at Toledo as to an ancient Rabbi, named Jacob, who had "testified on heaven an earth that the book of *Zohar* of which Simeon R. Simeon ben Yohai is the author..." (Waite 53-54).

The Turkish Privat-Docent Abdurrahman Küçük who writes on the Kabbala, had done his doctoral thesis on

A Research on Sabbatai Sevi and his Community. He states that the Jews have carried wherever they went their mystical views and the Kabbala. In one of the two books forming the Kabbala, the Zohar, which is assumed to have been written in the Thirteenth Century, there is mention of the prophecy that the time for the deliverance and the coming of the Messiah is close. With some mystical ideas, the Kabbala also includes computations about the actual date of the Messiah's advent (Küçük 135). In the end the computations lead to the dates of 1648 or 1666 (coincident with Sabbatai Sevi's time). As the Jews have the Messiah (*Meshiha* in Arabic or Aramaic, *Ha-Mashiah* in Hebrew, *Mesîh* in Ethiopian), the Shiites have their *Mehdi* (*Mahdi*) Küçük 137-138.

Moses was the first Messiah. Freud finds in *Hosea's* text irrefutable proof that Moses was killed by his own tribe. Only at the end of their Babylonian captivity the hope took life that Moses would ressuscitate and come back as Messiah to liberate his people (Freud, *Moses and Monotheism*, 41, 90, 98-99, 129, cited by Küçük 151-152).

Starting from the Thirteenth Century we witness the rise of the Kabbalist Messiahs: Abraham Abulafia (thirteenth century), followed in the Fourteenth Century by

Asher Lemmlein, Niseim ben Abraham, and in the Sixteenth Century David Reubeni, Samuel Molho and Isaac Luria. The last in the line is the Jew from Izmir Sabbatai Sevi (Küçük 165-166.

The meaning of tradition is to take, to understand, to grasp, also meaning knowledge that is inspired, encompassing or traditional knowledge. Kabbala is also named *hokhmah nishtara* (hidden knowledge, wisdom). As a term, Kabbala embodies the Jewish mystical tradition to predict the future based on numerology and the letters of the Hebrew alphabet. The Kabbala is Jewish mysticism and gnosticism (the science of perception, discernment). It contains the hidden mystical doctrines on God, man and the universe. The Jewish kabbalists have advanced the opinion that the Kabbala is "ancient" knowledge and was transmitted from generation to generation; they have made it into a science which can expose the hidden things (Küçük 166, 167).

There are differing opinions on the origin of the Kabbala. For some it is *vahiy mahsulü* (the product of divine revelation) and its origin goes as far back as Adam. For others it is connected to Persian, Babylonian, Neo-Platonic or Hellenistic influences. While its origin is often brought back to very ancient times, actually it is not possible to date it from a time earlier than the Twelfth or Thirteenth Century (Küçük 167). The first source of the Kabbala, which may be considered the beginning of the *Mishnah* and the *Talmud*, is to be found in the *Tanah* (Old Testament) in Daniel V and XII, having also drawn information from Isaiah VI and Ezechiel I, XI. The writing of the Kabbala in its most ancient expression is attributed to Rabbi Akiba. In the Kabbala it is asserted that there exists a universe other than that described in the Talmud and the rabbinical texts. All the ideas and thoughts contained in the Kabbala will help the establishment of another world while all of this revolves around the bringing forth of the Messiah. According to the Kabbalists, the Kabbala contains a grandiose world order which human intelligence and reason cannot comprehend; it tackles the invisible, hidden world, and deals with a sacred doctrine on the Universe and God (Küçük 167-168).

H. Ziya Ülken describes the Kabbalistic movement and its influence on the Islamic world in the following way: "Kabbalism was within Judaism a current which did not content itself with the external meaning of the *Tevrat* (Pentateuch) Torah (Old Testament) and *Zebur* (Psalms) and derived from the letters of these books secret meanings, in accordance with its desires. In the Moslem world the first such tendency is encountered in Hakim Tirmizi from the Sufis. Hallaci Mansur, took advantage of the view that certain letters in the beginning of some *suras* of the Koran have an unknown (hidden) meaning, the Book of T and Ss [*Kitab-i at Tavasin* (the 26th, 27th and 28th suras of the Koran)]. Ibn-al-Arabî also joined this view. Various interpretrations were given of the letters E L M in the beginning of the Koran. The Batinites (school attributing special importance to the hidden meaning of the Koran) used these interpretations, and extending this theme to the infinity, tried to introduce within the Islamic doctrine all the ideas they wished. In the following centuries a new form of their doctrines, expounded in Fazlullah Esterbadî's book *Cavidan-i Kebir* (the Great, the Sublime Eternity), led to the Islamic *Hurufî* sect (mystics, who to understand matters yet concealed in the mystery of the Divine Purpose, draw conclusions from combinations of letters). In the *Ashk-name* (Epic of Love) of Ibn Firishte the doctrine was carried to the point of *noktavîlik* (interpretations of punctuations?). Such excessive interpretations penetrated the sect of the *Bektashis* at time Sultan Yildirim Bayezid (Bayezid I). Despite Sultan Selim I's efforts to purge such excesses, the Bektashi literature remained permeated by *Hurufî* influences untill recent times." (Küçük 168-169).

Kutluay advances the view that Kabbalism was a movement against Talmudic rabbanism, and as it could not escape the influence of the Islamic world it became an imitator of *Ihvanu's-Safa* [Brotherhood of the Dervish (Mevlevi?) Order]. In this form Kabbalism perpetuated itself through the Middle Ages. Sabbatai Sevi belonged to the Kabbalistic movement. In the Nineteenth Century Kabbalism took on a new life in Russia and Eastern Europe in the form of the *Hasidut* movement (Küçük 169). There is a view that Kabalism, by influencing the Sufis, the Batinites and the sect of the *Vahdet-i Vücut-cu* led to the birth of new various currents within Islam.

Abdülkadir pretends that one has to look for the origin of the amulets and charms which are prohibited by Islam and even considered *shirk* (idolatry), in the Jewish Kabbala mysticism. In the Thirteenth Century these were tabulated in the form of a book and were transmitted to the Islamic world by the way of Spain (Küçük 169-170).

The Kabbala was greatly influenced by the Jewish philosophers who were against materialism and considered that there are two principles: matter and spirit. In this dualism the two principles complete each other. It is a kind of Zoroastrianism with the Evil deified as well as the Good. A theory was created to confront the problem. Creation is a step by step process which proceeds from God's emanation (radiation). As the creatures arising from God's Emanation distance themselves from God they plunge into darkness. Matter is identified as the object of creationn most distanced from God and therefore the source of Evil. This doctrine was born in Alexandria spreading from there East and West, and the Kabbala has been accepted as being one of its branches. According to the Kabbala no substance has come out of nothingness. Everything that exists has come from a light, from God; God can only be comprehended by what comes from God, by what is visible. God which has not come out as an Emanation, God which is invisible cannot be known and is abstract. In that meaning God is the Hidden of the Hidden. In that sense it can be considered as Absolute Blindness. Thus the Universe has been created from Infinite Light and is Infinite Unity, which cannot be limited. It is everything and nothing is outside of it. The primary cause is the cause of the causes. The first actualization that has come out of the non-actualized dark Being is the beginning of appearance, of becoming , manifest, the Great Universe, the First Man, *Adam Kadmon*. From there came out the lower worlds, and man, who is the "small world" (Küçük 170-171).

According to the Kabbala, God has exteriorized Himself and everything in the universe has resulted from this exteriorization. This happening has come about by the ranking of thirty two circumferences which are called the *Sefiroth* and point to the thirty-two roads leading to Wisdom. The purpose of it is to describe how the existence (creation) has developed by itself, and how the infinite abstract being has given rise to the limited real being. Each one of these circumferences has one of the names given to God by the Old Testament and the last one takes the name of *Adonai*. The sum of the circumferences makes *Adam Kadmon* (Perfect Man). These *Sefiroth* are God's Kabbalistic conceptions. The first ten *Sephiroth* are the creative Verb (*Kelâm*) and they make up God's inner world. The twenty-two *Sefiroth* which come after correspond to the twenty-two letters of the Hebrew alphabet which make up the creative Verb. Every letter is at the same time a number. The divine mystery is hidden by these letters and numbers, and opens only to those who know how to read them. It has been advanced that the secret cannot be comprehended by reason or imagination, it can only be comprehended through a mystical conception of the structure of the creatures which can yield their symbolic character. Everything comes from Him and returns to Him. Everything comes from the Creator and returns to Him. The Kabbalist reaches the word of the *Sephiroth* via a shortcut. Here ascent is explained not in the physical, corporal sense but rather as a spiritual ascent towards God. (Küçük 171-172).

The first ten *Sephirot* are: 1. *Kether* (the Supreme Crown); 2. *Chokhmah* (Wisdom); 3. *Binah* (Intelligence or Understanding); 4. *Hesed* (Mercy), otherwise *Gedulah* (Magnificence, or Benignity and Greatness; 5. *Geburah* (Severity, Judgment, Awe, Power); 6. *Tiphereth* (Beauty); 7. *Netzach* (Victory); 8. *Hod* (Glory); 9. *Yesod* (the Foundation); 10. *Malkuth* (the Kingdom).

The other twenty-two *Sephiroth* are 11. Essence; 12. Quantity; 13. Quality; 14. Relation; 15. Influence 16. Doing; 17. Time; 18. Space; 19. Possession; 20. Correspondence (the position and shape of existence); 21. Infinity; 22. Intelligence; 23. Perspicacity (the first of the sacred triad, which establishes the world of the Spirit); 24. Gift; 25. Justice; 26. Beauty (second of the sacred triad, which establishing the world of Ethics; 27. Might; 28. Covering of space; 29. Measure (the triad, establishes the material world); 30. Spiritual world; 31. Ethical world; 32. Material world (This supreme triad which emanates from the other three triads establishes the Kingdom of God). (Küçül 171, Waite 195).

In the Thirteenth Century under the influence of different philosophies and pantheistic views the Kabbala was rewritten and it incorporated the thoughts of Ibn Gabirol as expressed in his book *Yenbuul'Hayat* (the Source of Life). It also utilized Maimonides' thoughts as expressed in the Thirteen Articles of Faith which make the basis of Judaism. The twelth article of faith is the belief in the coming of the Messiah, which was entered in the Kabbala. Maimonides (1135-1204) declared that whatever may be, the Messiah **will** come, **will establish** a new world order, and the Jews **will found** their own states. The Messianic concept became the foundation of Judaism and the Kabbalists took upon themselves to use the knowledge of the Kabbala to create the circumstances leading to the coming of the Messiah and accelerate his coming.

The Kabbala is a hidden doctrine and is divided in two parts: theoretical and practical. The practical Kabbala remains unwritten, transmitted from immemorial times by tradition. It has recourse to Magics and uses symbolism. The theoretical

Kabbala is the written Kabbala and basically consists of *Sefer Yetzira* and *Sefer Zohar*. **Yetzira** (Creation) was born in the Tenth Century and *Zohar* (Radiation, Splendor) was completed between the Eleventh and Thirteenth Centuries, incorporating medieval philosophies. In the *Sefer Yetzira* numbers, and letters are viewed as the elements of God's words, and their symbols as they exist in the world. The doctrine of letters as manifestations of the hidden universe has been incorporated and extended in the Zohar. There is also the view that the Zohar consists of commentaries expounding the *Pentateuch, i.e.* the first five books of the Old Testament (Küçük 172-173).

There are in the Zohar three systems to calculate and predict the coming of the Messaiah:

1. *Themurah* (Exchange) transposition of a letters in a given word (or sentence) thus using the word in another meaning;

2. **Gematria** (Numerology) assigning a number to each letter of a word, and summation of these numbers to get the arithmetical value of the word. This value was used to explain its internal sense.

3. *Notarikon,* described as a system of shorthand, in which each letter of a word was taken as the intial of another word, or conversely, the initial letters of each word of a sentence were combined to form a new word, which helped to throw light on the sentence (Küçük 174, Waite 36).

For the Turkish authors probably the concerns arise on how the actions taken by the Jewish Kabbalists, whether open or covert (???), in order to accelerate the coming of the Messiah, might affect the destinies of the Turks. There would not be much concern if these actions remained only in the domain of theory, whether theological or philosophical.

Bash, a Jewish Professor at the Sorbonne University in Paris, wrote on April 23 1916 (when the battles of World War were at their peak) in Gustave Hervé's newspaper an article entitled Appeal to the Jews, in which he says: "Friends, the day is near, everything comes togeter to announce it. From the tumult of the gigantic cannons and the lightnings of the machine-guns, the Messiah, your Messiah will come forth." (Küçük 218, cited from C. Rifat Atilhan's *Gizli Devlet ve Fesat Programi* (The Program of the Secret State and Agitation), p. 48.

ABDURRAHMAN KÜÇÜK, *Dönmeler Tarihi* [The History of the Dönme (Moslem Crypto-Jews, the folloewers of Sabbatai Sevi who converted to Islamism). Rehber Yayincilik, Ankara, Turkey. March 1990.

For extensive sources and notes on the Kabbalah, see **A. E. WAITE,** *The Holy Kabbalah,* A Study of the Secret Tradition of Israel as unfolded by Sons of the Doctrine for the Benefit of the Consolation of the Elect dispersed through the Lands and Ages of the Greater Exile. University Books, Citadel Press, Eighth printing, Secaucus, N.J.

APPENDIX 8

A Sephardi Luminary's Five Versions of Osman Ii's Death
He was Abraham Danon (1857-1925), member of the Asiatic Society of France, the Ernest Renan Society, the Royal Academy of Madrid, also Director of the Rabbinical Seminary of Constantinople, and Professor at the École Normale Israélite Orientale. His known oldest ancestor was Rabbi Saadia ben Maimon ben Danon who flourished towards 1485, at the time of Ferdinand and Aragon and Isabelle of Castille. He was knowlegeable in French, Turkish, Hebrew, Arabic, Aramaic, Latin, Greek and German and a brilliant Talmudist. The voluminous bibliography of Danon includes works on Jewish general history, Turkish Jewish History, Jewish folklore, Hebrew poems, Jewish romances and proverbs, Judeo-Spanish linguistics, Greco-Karaite literature, unpublished sources of Ottoman and Tatar history, Moslem heretics, origin and religion of Falashas (Ethiopian Jews), Karaites and reminiscences on Joseph Halevy, known for his studies on the Falashas and travels among them.
An interesting booklet by Danon offers five versions on the drama of Sultan Osman II [*Genç Osman* (1618-1622)]'s murder by the Janissaries and the return to the Ottoman throne of Mustafa I after the regicide. Danon superbly tackles the tragedy of the regicide, in a blend, of Shakespearian *Macbeth* and Alphonse de Lamartines *Histoire de la Turquie*. Considering the considerable alienation of his contemporary Sephardic Jews from Turkish language, culture and history, Danon is remarkable for his penetration of Turkish things and history at the level of great Ottoman scholars. A magnificent ease of style and loving care characterizes Danon's piece of work on a crucial event of Turkish history refering to the *Janissary malaise* which would end up in shaking the foundations of the Ottoman Empire. Danon emerges as a superior scholar, equally at home whether he deals with *Genç Osman*'s typically Turkish dynastic drama, Constantinople's Karaites, Halevy's Falashas, Sabbatean mysteries or the teachings of the *Tannaim* (teachers in the period beginning with the death of Hillel and Shammai and ending in the generation after Judah ha Nassi) and the *Amoraim* (Jewish scholars in Palestine and Babylonia in the IIIrd to VIth centuries).

Tarihi Sultan Osman (Version I of the Osman II drama). This is a five-page text in Ottoman Turkish with occasional Arabic and persian words.
The Tuesday, the 7th of the month of Receb, year 1031 of the Hegira, Janissaries, Spahis, *Sipahi-Oghlanis* (Spahi recruits), *Topçus* (Artillery men), *Cebecis* (Armorers) and the rest of the pretorian corps all rose up, rioted in the meat market and sent messengers to His Majesty the *Padishah*, Sultan Osman to tell him that he should cancel his holy pilgrimage to Mecca since it was being said that he planned to liquidate all the old *kuls* (soldiers, slaves, serves), enrolling in their place the *kuls* of Aleppo and Damascus, with idea of moving the imperial throne to Damascus. The rioting militia were suspicious about the Sultan's intentions, seeing the announced pilgrimage as a smokescreen to hide moving the capital from European Constantinople deep into the Asian provinces.

208

The Imperial communication returned: "We the Sultan, are not abandoning our trip to the Holy Pilgrimage!"

As their calls were being rejected, the *Kuls* became furious; they left the meat market where they had ran to the house of the *Hoca*, Ömer Efendi, preceptor and counselor of Osman II. Finding that His Sainthood was not home, the militia completely ransacked his property, not leaving stone upon stone. From there they went to the house of Dilaver Pasha, the Grand Vizier. There, they destroyed all his goods and furnitures.

On Wednesday, the body of the *Kuls* gathered at the mosque of Sultan Mohammed shouting that their cause was supported by the Muslem Religion and that they were not doing anything against the *Sheriat* (Sacred Law). The troop of the *Kuls* posted five hundred men at the door of each *Ulema* (personage of the legal corps of counsellors of Islam, doctor of Moslem theology), catching them by force, and dragging them to the mosque of Sultan Mohammed.

Equipped with arms they reached the gate of the Seraglio, and the Sultan was told that he must surrender the *Kizlar Aghasi* (Chief Eunuch, Master of the Seraglio) and the Grand Vizier. Otherwise they would proclaim Sultan Mustafa Osman's II's brother as Padishah (instead of Sultan Osman). No response came from the interior of the Seraglio. The troop of the *Kuls* erupted into the interior where they found out that His Highness Sultan Mustafa, Osman's brother, was hiding in a well covered with lead; the door was broken with axes; men descended with ropes to remove Sultan Mustafa and two girls in his company; the Prince was set on the throne.

While all this was happening, Sultan Osman had been sitting in an interior kiosque when they brought him the news that Sultan Mustafa had been acclaimed Padishah. The *ulemas* told him: "Sire! Deliver the *Kizlar-Aga* and the Grand-Vizier! Otherwise the throne will slip away from your hands!" Upon this counsel, Osman had the *Kizlar-Agha* and the Grand Vizier brought to the Imperial Palace gate. The soldiery brandishing knives and axes hacked them to pieces.

In the aftermath, the now Majesty Mustafa was escorted from the New-Seraglio to the Old-Seraglio, and then in the evening he was again moved, this time to the Mosque of Orta Cami.

Ali Aga. made Aga of the Janissaries by Osman, said: "I can stop the sedition of the *Kuls*" and with this purpose he came to the Mosque. The soldiery gave him no quarter and cut him to pieces.

The Friday, Sultan Osman himself was caught and sent to *Yedi-Kule* (the Castle of the Seven Towers). As to Sultan Mustafa, he was set on the throne, and the *ulemas*, the viziers, the sheikhs, all came and presented the Sultan their homage. Towards the evening, a maleficent man called Daud Pasha, went with ten accomplices and caused His Majesty Osman to perish with the fatal noose. Oh! God of the two worlds! The reign of Sultan Osman had lasted four years, four months and eight days.

**

*

Version II (in Turkish) authored by Hüseyin bin Sefer, a retired *Solak* (guard standing on the left side, one of the sixty men, who on the days of ceremony, walked beside the Sultan's horse). The style is reminiscent of the chroniclers. The author is partial to Mustafa I, whom he surrounds with an aura of sanctity. Hüseyin bin Sefer's pen name was *New'y*.

In the name of Allah, clement and merciful. The extraordinary events which took place in the city of Constantinopler in the year 1031 of the Hegira, led to the deliverance of the Sultan of Islam, shadow of God on earth, His Majesty the Sultan son of Sultan, Sultan Mustafa Khan, son of Sultan Muhammad Khan.

On the venerated Receb of 1031, the Janissaries and the Spahis gathered in the early morning near the Süleymaniye mosque, and from there proceeded towards the military barracks and the bazars closed. The soldiery gathered at the meat market for deliberations. The object was to obtain from the Padishah (Sultan) the execution of those who had inculcated in his mind the passage to Anatolia under the pretext of pilgrimage to the Ka'aba (to go thereafter to Egypt to establish there the capital of the Empire). The Spahis and the Janissaries wanted the sovereign to renounce this voyage.

Those were the persons, who were seeding dissent between the troops of the *Kuls* and the Padishah: Süleyman Aga, Palace Aga of the Imperial Harem, who was praising the Egyptian horsemen (mercenaries) and maligning the *Kuls*, saying it is better to have Anatolian (*Seghban* and Türkmen) and Arab horsemen"; Koca Ömer efendi who was in agreement with the Palace Aga; the *Bostandji* (Governor of all the seraglios and pleasure cottages of the Grand Sinior) Mohammed Aga, the enemy of Yussuf Aga, Aga of the Janissaries. Mohammed Aga had caused the Sultan to disguise himself and frequent in nocturnal rounds the taverns which were the hangouts of Spahis and Janissaries, catching them by surprise to reprimand them or dispatch them to the galleys.

A year before during Osman II's campaign against Poland, when the Sultan had come to Ishagti, most of the war booty had gone to the Imperial Guard and the *Kuls* were deprived of these munificences. They assumed a lazy attitude at the war, arguing "Let those who were rewarded do the fighting!". As a result, the "vile infidels" could not be vainquished and peace had to be concluded.

Back from the Imperial expedition, with the advice of Süleyman Aga and Koca Ömer Efendi, Osman II was persuaded to break the Janissary and Spahi Corps and to recruit the Turks as *Seghbans* (literally guard of dogs, actually regiments of soldiers attached to the special service of the Sultan). That is what caused the *Kuls* to surge from *Karaman* (Armenian quarter of Constantinople) and move to the meat market.

A number of old Janissaries and Spahis went to his Beatitude the *Sheikh-ül-Islam* [Highest Moslem authority in the Ottoman Empire with powers to depose even the Sultan-Caliph, if he violates the *Sheriat* (Moslem Law)] asking a *Fetwa* (decision) on the question: "What is recommended by the Law with regard to persons who excite the Padishah of the Universe, cause the Public Treasury of the Muslim to be dilapidated and are at the origin of so many intrigues and acts of cowardness?" His

Beatitude answered: "They should be killed." In possession of the fetwa the crowd of *Kuls* returned to the Hippodrom.

The soldiers agreed among themselves that Hoca Ömer Effendi should be delegated to the Sultan to dissuade him from going to Anatolia and to have the Aga of the Harem, Süleyman Aga decapitated. The Hoca (preceptor) of the Sultan was sitting in the balcony and had his doors heavily bared. Seeing the multitude the Hoca escapated through a door connecting two contiguous houses. The soldiers ransacked Ömer Hoca's house...From there they went to the Grand Vizier Dilaver Pasha's palace to ask his mediation. At the arrival of the troops at the palace of the Grand Vizier, those in his following shot arrrows on the mutitude of *Kuls* who had come unarmed. The Janissaries and Spahis thereupon returned to the Meat Bazar for discussions.

The Sheikh-ül-Islam addressed to Sultan Osman a respectful *fetwa* in these words: "The pilgrimage of the Sultan to the Ka'aba is inopportune." It is said that the Sultan tore the *fetwa* into pieces. The *ulemas* and viziers having been unable to restrain the Sultan, the troops revolted. At that point, Sultan Osman convoked the *ulemas* and told them: "I have renounced my departure." The next day, Thursday, 8th of Receb, the venerated, the Janissaries and Spahis went in large numbers to the sacred enclosure of the mosque of His Majesty the Conqueror Gazi Sultan Mohammed where they made their devotions and after pronouncing three times the formula *Allahü-Ekber* (Allah is Greater) they went to the Hippodrome.

The Scholars of the Sheriat, the Sheikh-ül-Islam Essad Effendi, Zakarya-Zade Yahya Effendi, *Kethüda* (Intendant) Mustafa-Effendi, Bostanzade Mehmed Effendi, Azmi Zade Effendi and other ulemas rode on horses and they dismounted before the mosque of Ahmediye. As some thoughtful men among the soldiers of Islam, entered the mosque and invoked the ulemas, they asked for the blood of six persons: Hoca Ömer Efendi, the Aga of the Imperial Harem Süleyman Aga, the *Kaymakam* (Governor of Constantinople), the *Defterdar* (Finance Minister) Baki Pasha, the Grand Vizier Dilaver Pasha and the *Seghban Bashi* Nasuh Aga.

The ulemas mounted their horses and went to the Seraglio, where they informed H. M. Sultan Osman of the impressive military gathering taking place. The Sultan categorically refused to deliver the persons of whom the heads were being asked. The ulemas insisted: "Sire! Otherwise it is the ruin of the State!"

The Janissaries and Spahis had someone climb to the minaret of Santa-Sophia and look for a build-up of the *bostancis* (Sultan's guards) on the Seraglio ground. From up in the minaret no returning ulemas were seen and no bostancis. With the cries of Allahu Ekber. the soldiers of Islam rushed from the Hippodrom to the Seraglio. They found the gates of the Seraglio open. The concierges warned: "Beware of the bostancis who are prepared." The soldiers of Islam penetrated through the first gate of the Seraglio and filled the courtyard. They fired their guns, shouting: "Legally we claim the Aga of the Harem, by the Law of we want the Hoca, in the name of the Sheriat we ask the head of Dilaver Pasha. Like a torrent the crowd reached the second gate, the third gate!

Some white eunuchs, the *Kapu-Oghlans* run to the interior. A clamor rose, the source of which is unknown: "In the name of the Law, we wish to have Sultan Mustafa Khan! By the Sheriat, we claim Sultan Mustafa Khan!"

They reached the compartment of the *iç-Oghlans* (page trainees or pages in the interior of the Seraglio), inquiring about the place where Sultan Mustafa Khan was imprisoned. One Iç-Oghlan from the special chambers indicated the side of the harem. Rushing, the Spahis climbed over the coupolas and marching over the domes, screamed: "By order of the religion, we claim Sultan Mustafa Khan!" Then, from under a vault, a sad voice made itself heard it was the imprisoned sultan. The soldiers with axes started to break the lead and pierce the dome. By order of Sultan Osman, bostancis (imperial guards) were dispatched to seize Dilaver Pasha from his hideout in Scutari (on the Asian side of the southern mouth of the Bosphorus); the Pasha was placed on a boat.

The coupola having been pierced, with ropes taken from the curtains of the hall where the viziers held their sessions, three audacious men descended to the bottom of the dungeon and put their heads at the feet of the just sovereign: "With a common accord, Sire, our word is unique! The *taht* (throne) is yours! Be our Lord, we are your subjects, ready to execute your *firman*. Sire, the soldiers of Islam wait for you outside, O just king!" At these words, the incomparable Padishah, of noble character and beautiful like Yussuf (Joseph), Sultan Mustafa, asked for water. He had not drank water for three days. A few valiant men went to the Old seraglio to carry the good news to the *Valide* (Queen-Mother), mother of Sultan Mustafa Khan. His Majesty Sultan Mustafa Khan, was brought on top of the coupola, with the two odalisks who were imprisoned together with him, to serve him.

One of the doors of the harem was opened to let out Dilaver Pasha and Süleyman Aga of the Harem, and then the door was barred. Both were hacked to pieces. The Sheikh-ül-Islam Essad Effendi and the Kethüda Mustafa Effendi said: "Comrades, let us go! Sultan Osman has delivered to you those you wanted. If you want other ones, we will obtain them from the Padishah." The Janissaries and Spahis answered: "Sirs, we have found the One we wanted. In the past, our Padishah was Sultan Mustafa Khan and he is still our sovereign."

The Janissaries and the Spahis forced by the sword the reluctant ulemas to present the homages due to the Sultan. The great Sheikhs presented without resistance their homages to the Pole of Happiness, at the center of perfection, the One beautiful like Yuseuf, His majesty Sultan Mustafa Khan.

Sultan Mustafa, too weak to be placed on a horse, was placed on a chariot together with the odalisks who were serving him. He was brought to the Old Seraglio.

Kurd Ali was appointed the new Aga of the Janissaries by Sultan Osman.

The soldiers of Islam drew the chariot and brought H.M. to Orta Cami.

Sultan Osman, Hüseyin Pasha (second vizier) and the Bostanci-Bashi Sufi Mahmud Aga, escaped by horse at midnight, they arrived at the house of Ali Aga (not Kurd Ali Aga, Osman's new appointee, but the Aga before the riots, reconfirmed in his position by Sultan Mustafa). An agreement was reached promising 50 ducats and a purple drapery to each Janissary, with the aim that they renounce their allegiance to Sultan Mustafa Khan. Ali Agha was sent back to Orta-

Cami. Meanwhile it did not remain unnoticed to the Brothers (the *Khuls*), that while Sultan Mustafa had taken shelter in the house of God, Sultan Osman had taken refuge in the house of a servant...

Friday, the 9th of Receb, the venerated, Ali Aga came to Orta Cami and presented himself to H.M. Sultan Mustafa Khan. To the Janissaries and Spahis, Ali Aga said: "Comrades! May God bless our Padishah! Sultan Osman also is at the Gate. He orders to gratify each of you with 50 ducats and a purple drape. Agree then that Sultan Osman still remains the king!" As soon as spoken, the soldiers hacked Ali Aga into pieces.

H.M. the Sultan Mustafa Khan bestowed the Grand-Vizierate upon Daud Pasha. Those in charge of bringing Sultan Osman went and placed Sultan Osman on a horse. They made Sultan Osman pass in front of the cadaver of his Grand Vizier Hüseyin Pasha. Sultan Osman gasped and cried: "This poor servant was innocent, he was always speaking well about the Spahis and the Janissaries. At times, I neglected his counsel. If I had always taken the advice of Hüseyin Pasha, this misfortune would not have taken place. It is Khoca Ömer Effendi and the Aga of the Harem, Süleyman Aga, who exhorting me day and night have created the hostility between yourselves and me...it is me who is careless, I thought to have properly acted in following the advice of these plotters, while the world was becoming hostile to me."

The soldiery brought Sultan Osman to Orta Cami. Sultan Mustafa Khan appeared at the window. The soldiers of Islam shouted: "Allahu Ekber". Then Sultan Osman, from the place where he was, showed his beautiful face and said: "My Agas of Spahis and Janissaries! Don't you want me?" At these words, many of the Spahis and Janissaries loudly answered: "Anyone who wants of you, may God not want of him!"

That Friday there was no prayer at the Mosque of Orta Cami!

Daud Pasha came to Orta-Cami, placed Sultan Osman on a chariot taken from the bazar, and he was brought, followed by crows, to *Yedi-Kule* (the Castle of Seven Towers).

How extraordinary are the vicissitudes which took place in Constantinople. A crowned monarch, commander of seven regions, was dethroned, and the servants who previously had been praying for Him became hostile. At the same time, on a simple pretext, and at a moment that nobody was thinking of it, God freed his servant who, son of Sultan and innocent, had remained 19 years in captivity, and made him sovereign of the habitable earth. When the soldiery dispersed itself far away from Yedi-Kule, they had Sultan Osman meet his fate. May the divine mercy and broad misericord be upon him!

**

*

Version 3, is an Arab elegy of 444 verses authored by Miri-Liwa Emir Osman Bey. It betrays a deep feeling of pain for the young martyr Sultan.

Osman II sat on the Throne of Felicity, and the Siege of the Kingdom and the Principality, the 17th of Sefer in the year 1031.

As soon as he came back from his victory over the ignoble infidels, he projected a pilgrimage towards the sacred house of God and a visit to the tomb of the Prophet. The pilgrimage was not easy for any of his ancestors, the Sultans, because of the need to safegaurd the country and the Moslems. Nonetheless, by his supreme effort and his constant vigor Osman insisted on what no other had tried before him and no other lion had reached.In hexameta:

Man does not reach all that he wishes
the winds run where the vessels do not wish.

And events took place which revealed that Osman's sublime project was misinterpreted. One thought of seeing evil in that where Osman was innocent of evil. Malevolent talk spread and it was not possible for Osman either to resolve the situation, nor to transform the absurd ideas. Troubles arose and opinions diverged between scholars, viziers, dignitaries of the state and leaders, some of whom marched with the troops and soldiers. And the Sultan did not find anybody among his auxiliaries who would defend the Sultan, who took pity of his youth, and of whom he could invole the assistance. And they rushed on him, denied his beneficient actions, betrayed the pact and the duty, and did not observe any respect for his ancestors and for Himself.

They were not afraid of the vengeance of Allah, they forged lies against him. They humiliated the Honorable Sultan, cruelly and tyranically they killed him, a fact which, eternally, had been predetermined by the omnipotent judge. In his case, the pen ran on the Table of Destiny, "We belong to God and return to Him."

And those who have practiced this tyranny, let them know what deserts they will undergo. And it is transmitted by the traditions from the side of the doctors and the scholars that the doctor 'Omar Molla told in the name of Ibn-Abbas who says: "the angel Gabriel has informed me that GOD (be He honored and exalted) killed to avenge the blood of Yahia ben Zakarya (Hebrew prophet) 70,000 and for the blood of Hüseyin, he massacred 70,000 and 70.000. And the Imam 'Abderezak has said that 'Abd'Allah ben Salam entered besides the besiegers of the Caliph Othman and said "Do not kill him and by God! none of you will assassinate him without encountering God! The sword of Allah does not remain hidden, and by God, if you kill him, God will hold you responsible, then he will not hide from you his anger." And no prophet was killed without 70,000 who were massacred because of him, and no Caliph was killed without, for this reason, 35,000 being immolated.

And, already, several distinguished writers of Rum (Rumelia, Turkey of Europe) have deplored, in Turkish and Persian lamentations, the defunct Sultan, the beneficient martyr, and the poet Miri-Liwa Osman bey cries about him in this Arab elegy, with painful cries and abundant tears.

Here starts the elegy.

The defunct Sultan, having defeated by His armies, the *Kral* (King) of the Poles and returned at last victorious and fortified, He wished then the pilgrimage to the Ka'aba, beautiful in the sacred enclosure of the Mecca, and to visit the Elected Mahomet, guide of humanity. The Sultan's plea was wrongly interpreted, his standard was trampled under the feet. In their revolt the troops suddenly attacked the Sultan, in the Residence of Felicity, lodged with nobility, in the greater Constantinople, the Capital; and from his elevated throne, people with reckless enterprise made the Sultan descend into the abyss. They have violated the pact of fidelity towards the dynasty of the pious Osman. They have vilely assassinated their king homonymous of Gazi Osman, like in the murder of the Caliph Othman, master of the two lights and the right path.

The perseverant Sultan found himself tied up in their castle. He himself alone, he fought his troops. In their injustice, they fixed on the head of their Master, the King of kings, a blade of sharpened iron. They cruelly dipped the nails of their pointed irons in the bleeding wound of his skin. And without any regard for the respect due to the Master, those surrounding the victim grabbed Him, in such a way that, despite His vigor he was overcome. They were hostile to Him like Jews. and by their tyranny they threw a rope around His neck to strangle Him. They have strangled the Caliph: we belong to God and we shall return to the Master of the honor."

To-morrow God will accuse them of their hatred. Alas! for Him! the Sultan dragged to the floor the face soiled by dust, struck after the ruin. And for the defunct Osman, there is a preceding model in his homonym the Caliph Othman and Ali and Hüseyin and the courageous martyrs among the companions of Mahomet.

It was a misfortune the like of which had never been suffered in the family of the Monarch, homonymus to the Caliph of judgement, Othman, since the time that these noble Sultans sat on the royal throne and spread over the earth and the sea, to the east and west, and ran in the plains and in the universe, and the kings of the earth tried to obey their order.

**

*

Version 4 is a Hebrew *qasidah* (eulogy) of 84 couplets in the possssion of Danon. The first verses form the acrostic "Elie Afeda Beghi", a Karaite writer. While the Karaite writers like him remained enclosed in their ghetto and absorbed in their religious compostions, they employed their leisure time to register the external events. Beghi's elegy remained truncated in its last part.

It starts by a summary of Ahmed I's reign:

"I wish to exalt the value, more precious than gold, of Sultan Ahmed and his reign; God has elected as king of his people, this monarch of such beautiful phsionomy. This sacred cherub has ascended the throne, in the place of his father, while still a child. He was generous, and by His prodigalities he made all His people participate in His joy. In all his military enterprises the warrior's genious has been revealed. By the gravity of his face he resembled a lion. He was caring for public good. Still very young He fell gravely ill with a very serious infirmity (small-pox) and his time came. His children were minor, that is why His elder son Osman could not succeed Him in the throne. His brother Mustafa whom He loved replaced Him. Mustafa went to Eyub (place where it was traditional for the new Sultan to assume authority) with munificence. He was an untractable misogynist who did not let any woman approach his bed. In all his actions he acted like Jehu (King of Israel, exterminator of the Omride dynasty), whose tapid style of walking gave the image of a madman, which he was not."

Writing in a language unknown to the Turks, from the safety and seclusion of the ghetto, Beghi can afford to be candid about the imbecility of Mustafa I: "When his Muftis and his Eunuchs saw a king of such mentality, they concerted themselves to destitute Him and to give Him Shah Osman as a successor. The Mufti and all the Ministers of the Empire told Him: 'Get up, Our Lord! You are not fit to sit on this royal throne, surrounded of munificence!' They took away his gold crown and turban. They relegated Him to a room and told Him: 'Here is Thy place of rest!' The days of his reign had been 94 well counted."

Then reigned Sultan Osman, a beautiful king only fourteen years old. He was circumcized and went to Eyub Sultan pompously escorted with all his troops. He gave the usual gratifications of advancement (money distributed to the troops upon the advent of a new Sultan).

Sultan Osman arranged peace with Shah Abbas of Persia through the intermediary of his delegate Grand Vizier Halil Pasha. As soon as Halil returned to Constantinople Halil was destituted. The new Grand Vizier Okuz-Mohammed lasted only a few days. Osman elevated Ali Pasha to the Grand-Vizierate. The honest *Kizlar-Agasi* (Guardian of the Harem) was exiled to Egypt to be replaced by an evil man, the perversity of whom was known to all. The Grand Vizier Ali Pasha gave immense sums to his Sultan at the expense of the Treasury and created concern among the Grandees of the Empire. Sick of an incurable disease, at his death he was replaced by Hüseyin.

Sultan Osman put to death his brother Sultan Muhammed, distinguished by his nobility, based on the Ottoman practice of fratricide by *raison d'état* (to prevent attempts to take over of the throne). He took the road to combat with a great army and cavalry to make war on Poland. On campaign the Grand Vizier was once more replaced and the dignity went to Dilaver Pasha. The Polish princes prostrated themselves before Osman, recognizing His glory, His heroism, His victory. Osman triumphantly returned to Constantinople.

Osman knew no rest in his actions and wanted to go to Mecca. He concerted with his counselors who gave him pernicious advice. One was Osman's childhood tutor Khodja Ömer Efendi. The second was the *Kizlar-Agasi* "a nigger like tar", who caused Osman's ruin. The third was the Grand-Vizier Cemal Dilaver. They all counseled the pilgrimage to Mecca. The imperial decision caused turmoil among the ministers and the nation. The scholars (doctors of *Sheriat*, Moslem Law) were

216

asked if this imperial travel (absence of the Sultan from his capital for reason of pilgrimage) was in conformity with religious law. After deliberation, the judges and the Mufti said that there was no case for the Sultan to go to Mecca, and that it would be preferable for Him to stay in His Palace in order not to darken the country and His fatherland.

The scholars wrote to Osman a letter which they sent to Him by the intermediary of His Reader. Osman became angry and tore up the letter. There was gossip about Osman, His chamberlain and His expedition. But the Sultan remained firm on His voyage to Mecca. He started preparations.

His *Kuls* (Soldiery) said: "we shall go nowhere by His order!" Osman decided to replace them and to enroll others in their place. He gave the order to a man by the name of Aski (Eski, Old) Yussuf for his undertaking of a mission undoubtedly to Syria.

The truncated elegy ends here, but the above enterprise was ill-fated, it led to the Janissary-Spahi (*Kuls)* rebellion and the ultimate regicide.

The elegy continues with Osman II's preparations for travel to Mecca.

Version 5 is by the interpreter of the Christian convert Abaza Pasha, governer of Erzurum, who decided to be the avenger of Osman II. He ended up struck by the dagger of Murad IV, Osman II's brother. Version 5 is a Turkish text rhymed and vocalized composed of four quatrains.

Abaza Pasha said to Hüsrev Pasha (could be Khosrev pasha, Aga of the Janisssaries or his homonym, the Grand Vizier:
"Who is the Padishah? Let me go! If my demand is heard by the Law, I will crush their great and small. What they have done to their sovereign, they are infidels to do it to their **Kral** (King). Is it just that it remains like this, their crime unpunished. Till my death I will not let them escape. They wounded Him and made His soul fly to heaven. It is the blood of Gazi Sultan Osman Khan. Till death I shall strive to avenge Him. My intent is to go to Istanbul to arrange the throne of the Ottoman dynasty and to make myself vizier of Sultan Murad Khan. If after that Idie, I do not care. From God's side a sign has come to me; the Janissaries must be exterminated. I know who has been the cause of thuis affair: neither the Aga allowed it, nor the Vizier-Pasha. They defaced (the Janissaries) the Harem reserved to their sovereign. They placed in the Tower (*Yedi-Kule*) this superior of the religion. They assassinated the Caliph of the surface of the earth. The Janissaries are infidels returned to the evil religion. Myself, I shall bring them to the true faith, or else, by this zeal, I die."

INDEX

123; Osman conducted to the
dreaded prison of *Yedi Kule*
124; Osman awakened in his
cell by Grand Vizier Daud and
henchmen 124; Osman
overpowered after putting up
good fight; struck on the head
with an axe and strangled 124;
forty Jewish doctors employed
in the service of the Palace
124; Sephardi luminary
Abraham Danon's booklet
offering five versions of the
tragedy of Osman II 205-214
Osmanlis 12
Ottoman(s) 3, 4
army 8
court 25; syncretistic
atmosphere 147
culture 1
Divan 72
dominion(s) 23, 36
dynasty 3
Empire 16, 23
(the) first 3
fleet 65; destroyed by
Venetians 73
histories by Hammer,
Hayrullah Efendi,
Mehmet Ârif Bey 147
Jewry, ransom of slaves 36
Judaism, stagnation during
Ibrahim and Mehmed IV
(Spinoza vs. Sabbatai Sevi)
142-43
life of 177
multinational state 23
possessions in Rumelia 5
punitive expedition 8
regime 11
ruler 4
state 11
Sultanate 7
Palamas, Gregory,

Archbishop of Thessalonika
4, 147, 148; Epistle to
Thessalonians 177
Paleologues 15
Palermo leaders 19
Panturkism 2
Papal States 55
Pardes (Orchard) method
of explanation 64
Pardes Rimonim (the
Orchard of Pomegranates)
Moses Cordovero's *magnum
opus*, clearest and most
rational exposé of the
Kabbala in existence
192
parere (opinion) 32
Paris 1
Parnas (Notable of the
community) 66
Parnas of Rhodian
community, R. Abraham
Mir demands *herem* of tax-
farmers breaking into the
house of R. Juda Apomado
56
Pasha 17
Pashalik 17
Passi, David, second Duke
of Naxos 106; some hand
in sultanic finances 106;
severely wounded when
rebellious Janissaries
clamoring for the heads of
those responsible for the
debasing of the coinage
invaded the *Divan* 106-107;
figure of the Jew in an
Elisabethean drama 107
Passover 38, 177
Patriarch Philotheos
Kokkinos 148
Patrik 15
Paul III, Pope 56
Paul IV, Caraffa 51;